The AENEID

THE LIBRARY OF LIBERAL ARTS

Oskar Piest, *Founder*

The AENEID

VERGIL

SECOND EDITION

A VERSE TRANSLATION BY

FRANK O. COPLEY

Professor of Latin
The University of Michigan

•

WITH AN INTRODUCTION BY

BROOKS OTIS

Paddison Professor of Latin
The University of
North Carolina at
Chapel Hill

THE LIBRARY OF LIBERAL ARTS

published by

Bobbs-Merrill Educational Publishing
Indianapolis

Publius Vergilius Maro: 70–19 B.C.

The Bobbs-Merrill Company, Inc.
4300 West 62nd Street
Indianapolis, Indiana 46268

Second Edition
Sixth Printing—1981
Cover design by R. Masheris Associates
Designed by Joseph P. Ascherl

Library of Congress Cataloging in Publication Data

Vergilius Maro, Publius.
  The Aeneid.

  (The Library of liberal arts; 212)
  Bibliography: p. xxvii
  I. Copley, Frank Olin, tr.   II. Title.
PA6807.A5C65 1975   873'.01   74-28088
ISBN 0-672-61370-0 (pbk.)

CONTENTS

The AENEID

PREFACE TO THE SECOND EDITION

One of the most disturbing, and at the same time, the most comforting dogmas of the literary world, is the assertion that poetry can never be translated. And it is certainly true that the translator, no matter how carefully he may have tried to do his job, is bound to be the object of criticism and even of scorn. Most translations are immediately discovered to be inferior to the original, to be full of mistakes and prejudiced interpretations, to have been either too literal or not literal enough, to have been unscholarly, to have failed to capture this, that, or the other aspect of the original, and so on. If, as does rarely happen—notably in the case of Ezra Pound—the English version turns out to be even greater than the original, the translator is accused of having distorted and romanticized it, of having indulged in a meretricious attempt to trap the interest and tickle the fancy of his readers. Always over the head of the translator hangs the ghostly figure of Richard Bentley and his comment on Alexander Pope's translation of Homer's *Iliad:* "It is a pretty poem, Mr. Pope, but you must not call it Homer."

Bentley, of course, was both right and wrong. No translation of any poem, not even the most expertly and conscientiously executed poem, will be what the original was. But, while Pope's version of the *Iliad* could never be Homer to a classical scholar like Bentley, it was indeed Homer to many other readers, who either did not know the Greek original, or simply took delight in Pope's version of the poem in its own right, skillfully written, and for its day, a joy to read.

The same, no doubt, could be said of Dryden's translation of Vergil's: *The Aeneid.* Its versification is superb, its rhymed couplets graceful and euphonious, and its dignity and poetic music quite in harmony with the original. For the modern reader, however, Dryden's version has two manifest faults: in the first place, we are no longer patient with an endless series of rhymed couplets, however euphonious and graceful; in the second place, Dryden, by failing to keep to a line-for-line translation, created a poem *almost half again as long* as the *Aeneid,* and one that thereby loses all sense of the architecture, the balance and proportion, of Vergil's poem.

But Dryden's translation is undeniably poetry, and thus stands in sharp contrast to the work of a much later translator, J. W. Mackail, who contented himself with translating the *Aeneid* into prose. In his version, such matters as proportion, balance, architecture, music, etc., are even more completely lost to view than they are in Dryden's couplets. But Mackail was a conscientious worker and scholar. His English words reflect with a kind of deadly accuracy the lexicographical meanings of Vergil's—that is to say, if we were to look up Vergil's words in the Latin dictionary—we would find that in scarcely any case did Mackail deviate from the meanings designated as correct and well-attested. If we were looking for something of the majesty and dignity of the *Aeneid,* we might still turn to Dryden; if what we wanted was the simple substance of the poem, and help in following the Latin text, Mackail would be right to hand.

The same sort of thing, *mutatis mutandis,* would have to be said of every other translation of the *Aeneid* with which we might become acquainted. Some are too graceful and too polished, and remind one of Ovid, rather than of Vergil. Others are over-elaborate and even sensationalistic in their prettying-up and modernizing of Vergil's text. No one ever has produced, and no one ever will produce, an *Aeneid* that *is* the *Aeneid* in English; it remains, as it will always remain, a great monument of *Latin* poetry, to be truly comprehended only by those who are able to read the original—and unfortunately, not even by all of them.

This does not mean, however, that attempts to translate the *Aeneid* should have never been made, and should not now be made. In the first place, to utter a rather worn truism, there are entirely too many people in the world who do not know Latin, and, who are never going to learn Latin. If they are to have any contact with this monument of Western European poetry, they must do so through the medium of translations. This gives the hopeful translator a practical reason for attempting his English version; if he cannot bring Vergil's readers all the way back to Augustan Rome, then at least he can bring them part way along the path. In the second place, and perhaps more importantly for anyone who loves the ancient classics, the temptation to try to put them into English is nearly irresistible, and as a sheer task, infinitely tantalizing and fascinating. Even among classicists, who would never care to translate an entire poem such as the *Aeneid*, there will be those who vastly enjoy taking bits and scraps of ancient poetry, and for the benefit of some un-Greeked or un-Latined audience, turning them into what they hope will be representative English. Classicists, in general, have this in common with poets; they are fascinated by words, as a painter is by pigments or a sculptor is by a block of marble. And like them, he can scarcely resist the impulse to make something of his own out of the material he sees in front of him.

It was in this spirit that, nearly twenty years ago, I first attempted to translate Vergil's: *The Aeneid*. My first version of a book or two was quite rightly rejected by the referees as totally inadequate. It found its way into the wastebasket, and I began all over again. Some seven years of work finally produced the first version of the *Aeneid* that seemed to me, and this time, happily to the referees, worthy of being put into print. Like every other translation ever made by anyone, my version was only a partial representation of Vergil's poem. In the attempt to keep the English within the limits of the Latin original, bits and pieces here and there were lost, since the available space simply would not permit the inclusion of enough English words to say everything the Latin said. In other places, the attempt to reproduce in English a version of the word-patterns and stylistic devices of the original—keeping run-on lines as run-on lines, keeping key-words in roughly the same position in the English line that they had held in the Latin, creating something that in some way would reflect the sound-patterns of the original —the English version occasionally became stilted, unnatural, and self-consciously stylized.

Fortunately for all modern translators, the "he hath's" and "thou wert's" of an earlier day had long since been tossed into limbo, but some of the older devices still persisted in making themselves seen and heard. Such words as "woe," "ire," "the foe," and "the deep," kept re-appearing, partly, of course, because they were simply handy, shorter than "sorrow," "anger," "the enemy," and "the ocean." These words are convenient, but convenience is the enemy of both the translator and the poet, for his task must be not to find what will fit, but what is right.

Then there are the inversions. The poets of earlier generations delighted in them, in such upside-down patterns as "meadows green" or "pastures new." And who would have thought of objecting to such lines as "From thee have I been absent in the spring" and

"Ere half my days in this dark world and wide." The literary taste of those times accepted and employed inversions of this kind with a regularity that nearly amounted to a rule.

But this is no longer true. The modern poet scrupulously avoids words like "woe," "foe," and the like, unless he intends to use them for some special effect, and the same might well be said of inversions. In the attempt at once to avoid what had become hackneyed and tired, our modern poets not only brushed aside the old rhetorical conventions, but largely because of the work of writers like Pound, Eliot, Stein, and Cummings, produced versions of English that were free as the language had never been since the days of Shakespeare. They turned away from the old poetic style, which doubtless served its purpose well enough in its day, to an English style that more nearly represents the language as it is, in fact, spoken and written now.

This second version of my translation of the *Aeneid* has tried, rather more systematically than did the first, to follow these changes in English poetic usage. Thus, for example, at 2.328, "tall stands the horse" becomes "the horse stands tall;" at 3.191, "to course in hollow bark the boundless sea" becomes "to course wide ocean in our hollow ships." And two lines farther on, a self-conscious attempt to reproduce Vergil's word-order—"sky only, and only sea"— has become "just sky and water alone." Similarly, at 10.40–41, "to the world dispatched Allecto riots" has become "loosed on the upper world Allecto riots." "The main" has become "the sea" or "the ocean," "lads" have become "boys," Aeneas' "train" has become his "men," "the steel" has become "the sword," and so on. The changes, wherever they occur, have been the result of a re-study of the Latin original and of my earlier English version, and have been made in the attempt not only to create an *Aeneid* in an idiom that is more congenial to the modern ear and eye, but hopefully, more nearly true, in the sense that in some degree at least, this is how Vergil might have written the *Aeneid* if he were alive today and a native speaker of the English language. That is probably too bold a statement; I can only hope that it does accurately represent my philosophy of translation and that this new version may bring the un-Latined reader of the *Aeneid* a little closer than did the first to the spirit, vocabulary, verse, and general form of Vergil's poem.

Frank O. Copley

INTRODUCTION

Vergil was born on October 15, 70 B.C., and died on September 21, 19 B.C.[1] These dates are significant, for they embrace the final period of the Civil War and the definitive establishment of the Empire under Augustus. Nor is their importance only political: they also marked the full efflorescence of Roman literature and culture. Before Vergil, Latin verse had not reached sufficient perfection to enable anyone to write a great epic; after his death, the possibilities of great epic were definitely exhausted. Neither the political nor the aesthetic climate would have permitted another *Aeneid*. Vergil, in other words, represented the maturity of a culture in crisis.

It is in this sense that T. S. Eliot has correctly defined the *Aeneid* as *the classic* of Western society.[2] The *Aeneid* is mature and civilized as no comparable work of the Western world can be said to be. Homer, Dante, and Shakespeare came too early in their respective cultures to be called fully mature, while the so-called classical period of Western society—the French seventeenth or English eighteenth centuries—produced no such genius of its own. One can argue with very great cogency that Vergil as a poet is inferior to Aeschylus or Sophocles, Dante or Milton, Shakespeare or Goethe. But Vergil commanded the peak of a world civilization as none of these did. Vergil is universal where Sophocles is Greek, Goethe German, and Dante medieval. He had the luck to be born at the right time—a time when Rome had overcome the

1 Julius Caesar had reformed the calendar in 46 B.C.; Vergil was actually in his fifty-second year at the time of his death.

2 See T. S. Eliot, *What Is a Classic?* (London: Faber & Faber, 1944). I am indebted to this excellent essay, as will be seen, although I do not agree with all of it. It remains one of the great statements of the *Aeneid*'s claim to *classical* status.

provincialism of Greece and of itself, and had not yet entered upon its long decline. Never since has one city stood on such a summit: this is why the *Aeneid* remains unique, of all the classics that which is most classical.

To understand the *Aeneid*, therefore, one must try to understand its timeliness, its capture of the center of a vast era. Vergil's genius, in fact, was largely in his ability to seize his opportunity. A single city had conquered the known world—the unconquered regions were swamps, forests, and deserts, or fabulous blanks on the map—and had then consolidated its own strength under a single government and ruler. For the first time it was possible to talk realistically of imposing peace upon the world. History in this sense had turned a corner. But the turn was prepared for by the whole experience of the Roman rise to power and also by the entire course of Hellenic culture. Rome now could make effective the arts of Greece as Greece herself had never done and could never do. In ending the Civil War Augustus had finally permitted Rome to exert its full ecumenical force.

Yet one cannot at all understand the *Aeneid* in simply political terms. The uniqueness of the poem is not just that it is the voice of a supreme moment of civilization. That moment, of and in itself, had no voice, no aesthetic form, no language in which its message could be conveyed. The Romans were latecomers in the cultural sphere and, like their Greek contemporaries, could only contemplate the faraway Greek classics as we today contemplate Shakespeare or Dante. Homer was seven hundred years dead: epic was an impossible anachronism despite all the would-be imitators of the epic form and style. Yet epic alone was big enough and serious enough to be the right voice for Vergil's moment. Nothing in his own culture—that is, no strictly contemporary form or genre—could possibly serve his purpose. Only one form could serve, that of the very source and masterpiece of all ancient literature, that of Homer. The difficulty was that Homer belonged to an utterly different age, an age of heroes, an age of easy contact with the gods, an age of religion and poetry and not of politics and prose. It was as if a modern writer were to turn from the novel or the play to Beowulf and the Eddas, or perhaps to Chaucer and Dante. Many have tried: none has succeeded.

One must, therefore, try to see just why Vergil had to turn to Homer and how, despite the anachronism involved in using that model, he could succeed.[3] To a man who stands on what may be called the height of the times (I am thinking of Ortega y Gasset's great phrase, *la altura de los tiempos*)—on the point from which the greatness of an immense span of history can be not so much understood as felt and poetically expressed—only the greatest and most comprehensive of literary forms can suffice. This is epic and, for Vergil, Homer's *Odyssey* and *Iliad*. But why is this so? Because, briefly, the epic and, most of all, Homer's epics give us the heroic man and mood in their most adequate or, in the full sense of the word, *classical* representation. A great writer at such a great moment needs a great hero and must, at whatever cost, capture the heroic spirit.

But the hero is not a creature of the great metropolis—whether ancient Rome or modern New York—or even of a provincial capital, such as seventeenth-century Paris or eighteenth-century London, but of a simpler society in which gods can meet men with some naturalness and ease, and in which both heaven and earth can be involved in one tremendous combat between two individuals. Judged by a sophisticated or modern standard, Odysseus and Achilles, Hector and Ajax are simple souls with obvious motives and undeveloped characters. Odysseus was a "man of many wiles," but the wiles are all on the surface. Nor are the gods and goddesses that display such interest in the heroes the sort of divinities who would suffice for a "high religion" such

[3] I have written a book on this subject—especially on its technical or stylistic aspects—but I shall here only refer the reader to it, and try to state the problem in other and, I hope, simpler and better words. (See Brooks Otis, *Virgil: A Study in Civilised Poetry* [Oxford: Oxford University Press, 1963].)

as Christianity, Buddhism, or Islam. They are indeed all too human: awe may be engendered when Zeus's nod shakes Olympus but hardly when he yields to the sexual seductiveness of Hera. In short, Homer's heroes and gods are of their age: to the later Socrates or Plato, or, for that matter, to Cicero or Vergil, they were almost as grotesquely devoid of awe as they are to us. Nonetheless, just these and no others were the heroes and gods available to all post-Homeric antiquity. They persisted in lyric and tragedy until Euripides and the Sophists began to satirize them, whereupon literature became realistic or, to put the same thing in other words, lost its heroes altogether. In effect, the age of prose—of philosophy and history and political speeches—had replaced the age of poetry.

Yet why did heroes die with Homer and with the poets (lyricists and tragedians) who for a while continued to use Homer's heroes and gods? It is enough to say here that Homer's vision of the hero had a power that resisted imitation and could not really be transferred to another age and society. Yet his heroes had also—and this is the more important point—an appeal to all the later and very un-Homeric generations. No later men consorted with the gods; none touched the divine in their deeds; none seemed instinctively made for poetry. It seemed that heroism could exist only in a simple age but that no sophisticated age could wholly do without it.

Homer's epics had also, of course, a purely literary quality. Much has recently been written about his oral technique and style and of its basic similarities to such "oral epics" as those sung by Yugoslavian guslars and other more or less contemporary poets of cultural backwaters. In order to realize the limitations of such parallels, one need only read some of the Yugoslavian epics that Professor Albert B. Lord has now made available. The greatness of Homer is surely much more than that which comes from a nonliterate environment and an oral technique. He too was in some sense a man at the height of the times, who gave nostalgic poignancy to a past ideal at the very moment when that ideal and its epic recorders were passing away.

The problem thus confronting Vergil was that of investing the Roman of his own great historic "moment" with the heroic significance of a Homeric character—or, in other words, of restoring heroism to a modern society which in one sense had it, but in another sense had lost it, and seemingly beyond hope of recovery. There were perhaps a number of ways in which Vergil could have done this. The way he chose was to reproduce Homer in a fairly literal manner, so that the imitation was obvious and palpable to his contemporaries, and then to show, at one and the same time, both the basic difference and the basic identity of the two conceptions of heroism, the Homeric and his own. Had he merely copied the Homeric style and plot, he would have written only one more anachronism. Had he transposed modern events into a Homeric style and setting, he would have failed even more badly, for the antiqued modernity would have been only grotesque. Instead he made a hero who was, *at one and the same time,* Homeric and Roman, ancient and modern, at once a contemporary and comrade of the well-known Homeric characters and a true Roman and Augustan. But he could do this successfully only because he put back, so to speak, the "moment" or "height of the times" from his own Rome of 29–19 B.C. to the actual "moment" of which Homer wrote. He redefined the Homeric hero as a man who can decide a whole civilization, who can unite past, present, and future in himself, and whose heroism therefore consists precisely in the fact that he does and can do this while others cannot.

This approach to epic can be explained in great technical detail, but the main point to grasp is not a technical one at all. Vergil's inversion of times—his transference of an essentially Augustan to an ostensibly Homeric "moment"— was made possible in the first instance by his own appreciation of his own moment. In seeing that it transcended history, was, as it were, the culmination of ages and the foundation of ages to come, he was released from his own temporal and social limitations. His view transcended his own present, and he really perceived the true relevance of present, past, and future to each other.

In order to illustrate these generalities, I shall take out of the plenitude of the *Aeneid* a few examples which I think will enable the reader to see what I mean, and to see much more for himself.

In the second book of the poem Aeneas relates to Dido (who is already hopelessly in love with him) the story of the fall of Troy. The story is at once Homeric and un-Homeric. Homer is almost always on the side of the victors. Although he writes sympathetically of Hector, Andromache, Priam, and other Trojans, he is clearly describing the triumph of the side he approves. Hector may be noble, but Achilles is the great hero. The *Odyssey*, too, is the story of a man who wins, who both returns to his home and rids it of his enemies. But the second book of the *Aeneid* is the story of defeat. Aeneas the hero is unable to do anything but withdraw from his ruined city. We know, of course, that this is fated, that Aeneas is meant to be not a Trojan but a Roman hero, that the triumph of the future is founded on the death of the past and the tragedy of the present. But at once the problem of the meaning of victory and defeat is posed, the long historical view is introduced, the old Homeric hero is confronted with the necessity of becoming a new sort of hero altogether. One by one the old associations and supports are stripped away from Aeneas: he sees his comrades die, his city ruined and in flames, and he must, with terrible reluctance, accept his inability to do more than save his immediate family—his aged father, his wife, his little boy. Yet even this is not enough: in the withdrawal, he also loses his wife, Creusa. When she re-encounters him, she is a ghost who tells him that his new destiny is to marry another woman far overseas. Thus, with none of the hopes of Odysseus, for whom son, wife, and father and his own kingdom are still waiting, Aeneas must undertake an equally wearisome journey to an unknown world and destiny. Without describing how well or ill Vergil narrates these events, I wish to point out how he transposes the "moments," gives heroism a historical sense. To reject the near and dear for the far and terrible is indeed a heroic task. We see it in a Homeric setting, with Homeric gods and an originally Homeric cast, but we see also that it is not Homeric at all. Yet in the process of transference Rome has gained Homeric resonance and Homer has gained a civilized, sophisticated meaning. Here is no simple fighting, victory, or defeat—no naked participation of the gods—but a beginning whose very ambiguity is the test of the hero.

In Books One and Four Aeneas encounters Dido, the queen of Carthage and a passionate woman. Homer had already created or inherited the figure of the obstructing woman— the goddess or nymph or princess who tries to detain the hero and keep him from his home. She is but one of the detaining elements of the *Odyssey*—the angry sea god Poseidon, the storm, the terrible Cyclopes, Scylla and Charybdis, and so forth. But the goddess Calypso does not move Odysseus in the least: his detention is only physical (he is on an island and has no means of leaving it), for his affections are not engaged. It is Penelope and his home, above all, that still control him. Nostalgia is his overwhelming feeling and motive. How different are the relations of Dido and Aeneas! Although some commentators have suggested that Aeneas was as un- moved by Dido as Odysseus was by Calypso, Vergil himself provides no support for their notion. Aeneas, he tells us, was deeply shaken by his love for Dido. And the whole story bears it out. Aeneas, unlike Odysseus, had no home to which he might return. Furthermore, his wife Creusa's death had been followed by that of his father, Anchises; only the child Ascanius and his fellow Trojans (who, it would seem, were not themselves very insistent on going to Italy) were left to urge him on. How could he have resisted passion at such a moment of desertion? But such passion is precisely what stands in the way of his destiny, of Rome, the future, and everything for which he is now called to be a hero. Here we may debate how Aeneas should have acted, how he was at

fault, how "priggish" or otherwise his behavior actually was—
it is always easy to champion love and romantic engagement
—but we cannot overlook the choice before him. There are
times when the hero must resist love, especially when love
is incompatible with his heroic destiny. For again it is clear
that neither Dido nor Aeneas can choose for themselves: on
each the fate of two empires—Carthage and Rome—depends
and thus, in a sense, the entire course of history. We may
not like this preference of duty or *pietas* to passion or
conjugal fidelity; or we may wish that Aeneas had rejected Dido
in the first place or piously sat apart from her in the cave.
We may criticize his trepidation at the intervention of the
gods. Nevertheless, for Vergil himself, Dido was clearly the
test of his hero. Aeneas' heroism was based on a historical
idea: his present could not be a moment of passion because
it was instead a moment of destiny. Again the reader must
decide how well or ill Vergil treated this dilemma or problem.
What we cannot deny is its existence and, once more, the
inversion of Homeric time that it implies.

I need hardly dwell on the pivotal sixth book in which
Aeneas finally and fully encounters the future—the Romans
to be—and accedes, once and for all, to his Roman destiny.
Here the juxtaposition of Homeric and Roman "moments"
is perhaps almost too overt and obvious, although I think
that Vergil's plan really required such disclosure. Yet, in a
sense, Aeneas' encounter with the future Romans is much
less interesting than his prior encounter with the ghost of
Dido. And I single out this encounter for its illumination of
another significant difference between Homer and Vergil. We
may, as I have indicated, accept the necessity of Aeneas'
rejecting Dido in Book Four even though the conception of
such an "unromantic hero," or such a "priggish" one, may
still bother us. Yet we cannot, I think, accuse Vergil of
representing Aeneas as possessed of an "easy conscience" in
the matter. That Dido will not forgive—indeed, that she is
re-introduced at all—is a most significant clue to Vergil's
conception of Aeneas' heroism. The Homeric hero was not

particularly bothered by the suffering of his enemies or victims; such brutality was perfectly compatible with his heroism. But Aeneas' feeling for Dido, his hope for some sort of reconciliation, his very unwillingness to leave her in the mood in which he found her, indicate a peculiar sensitivity, an awareness of other people's feelings and a conscience that seem oddly un-Homeric. The Roman hero must walk over others on the road to his destiny—otherwise he could not have gone on or become a hero at all; but this process is also a torment to him. At every turn he must deny both past and present (for example, Troy, Creusa, Dido), for he has chosen to live for the future, for things quite beyond his ken or desire, but the choice is decidedly unpleasant, perhaps even tragic, and the hero knows it in his bones. He is sorry for Dido and for the self he can never be. If only he could have stayed with her or in Troy! This mood does much to mitigate the repugnance that success so often excites. As Vergil saw it, Roman defeat of Carthage was by no means a simple and unambiguous event. Dido dead was after all allowed her silence and, in this sense, her proper revenge.

The combination of an uneasy conscience with heroism and heroic resolve is peculiarly Vergilian. It is in just this respect that Aeneas is most Augustan or modern. Though the inversion of times—the transference of the Augustan moment to the Homeric moment—gave Vergil a great deal of trouble and led, in fact, to some of his least successful scenes, still it also produced perhaps the most poignant effects in the whole poem. The last six books are the least finished (as a good deal of evidence indicates) and, in many respects, the least satisfactory parts of the *Aeneid*. On the one hand, Aeneas must, for obvious reasons, fight like an Achilles, with the result that even the few passages describing his battle prowess seem altogether too Homeric to be in character. On the other hand, Aeneas' very acceptance of his Augustan destiny—the fact that in Book Six and thereafter he has personally acknowledged the "inversion" of Homeric time— makes him a somewhat unsympathetic character; we now sympathize with the poor, ignorant victims of Roman fate. And although Vergil makes plain the wickedness of Mezentius, the violence of Turnus, the rage of Amata, and so forth, he yet leaves us with the impression that their final fates are bitter and harsh, even in some sense undeserved. Yet it seems evident that this happens despite Vergil's real intention—he probably knew that the last six books needed much done to them—and he did after all show his true feeling in a few episodes even if these are not, as the poem now stands, completely in harmony with the others.

The Trojans represent, in one sense, a higher civilization than the Latins. But this distinction is not very important: if we omit the key figures (Turnus, Mezentius, Aeneas), the difference between the Trojans and the Latins is not very great. What is important is the difference between Aeneas and all the others, Trojan or Latin. He alone stands in a time that is not his own time, or acts in the present with an eye on the future. In Book Eight (the voyage to Rome) he encounters both a past exemplar—the god-man Hercules, into whose ritual celebration he opportunely arrives—and a future one—the god-man Augustus, who adorns the very center of the shield given him by his mother, Venus. Aeneas' mission is, like theirs, the pacification of the violent and destructive. But unlike Hercules he is no figure of remote mythology, and unlike Augustus he is some thousand years ahead of his time. To a certain extent, therefore, he resembles the hero of *Berkeley Square* (or James's *Sense of the Past*)—a modern, civilized man put back into a relatively uncivilized world of the past. Furthermore, his mission is not to destroy or simply to defeat his Latin and Italian enemies: they are instead his potential allies and fellow citizens, future Romans in effect. He must, of course, fight like the Homeric hero that he in one sense is, or for that matter like any good Roman. But he is also a civilized man, an Augustan and Vergilian man who abhors war and sees it as the nasty necessity that it is. To make matters worse, he is fated to win; he knows and is the future. How can a man in such a position appear anything but intolerable and repugnant?

Vergil deals with this situation, which he fully appreciates even to its smallest detail, by emphasizing first of all the tragic plight of Aeneas' Latin and Italian opponents. They are at once noble and primitive, blinded by their own violence and lack of civilization but endowed also with the courage and virility that made Rome what it was. Some of them—Mezentius, Turnus, Lausus, Camilla—must die, die for their own excesses and their own involvement in the fate of others; but their deaths are glorified, or at least invested with tragical pathos. The oppressiveness of Roman success is mitigated by Aeneas' and Vergil's sense of its sadness. The opponents of Roman destiny die as they must (Aeneas is too involved in other obligations to spare even Turnus), but their death is represented as the tragic price of civilization, of the final Roman peace that is to come. Two great moments reveal the tragically historical consciousness of Aeneas. The ostensible plot of Books Seven through Twelve has a Homeric basis: as Achilles killed Hector to avenge Hector's killing of Patroclus, so Aeneas kills Turnus to avenge the latter's killing of the young Pallas. But the difference between Turnus and Aeneas, so unlike that between Hector and Achilles, is shown in their attitudes toward their young enemies. Turnus' killing and despoiling of Pallas is Homeric and brutal and is dramatically contrasted with Aeneas' killing of the young Lausus.[4] Aeneas sees that Lausus is not his equal and warns him off; he admires Lausus' devotion to his wounded father; he kills him, for he has no alternative, but he recognizes his nobility after his death and pointedly returns his body, untouched, to his comrades. Lausus, he declares, is an image of filial devotion, *pietatis imago*. But Aeneas feels most the futility of such a tribute. What can he do but honor the dead? His unspoken premise is the tragedy of the whole situation, of war and of the hard necessity which makes him

[4] Both episodes occur in Book Ten.

a Homeric hero when he is really a civilized man. We see this perhaps most effectively in his farewell to the dead body of Pallas ((Book Eleven): he can only pause for a moment, for the horrid fates of war call him once more to further tragedies; all he can do is utter an empty farewell.

As I have said, Vergil did not quite bring off the blend of Homeric and non-Homeric feeling in the Aeneas of the last six books. The Augustan statesman must be as it were galvanized into Homeric warfare, and the discrepancy of the two occasionally becomes obtrusive and disturbing. But the problem is more than Homeric. Vergil knew that war is also part of civilization, that the Roman peace was based largely on the subduing and killing of those who resisted. Unlike Tacitus he did not particularly favor the primitive as such, but he certainly saw the tragedy of the civilizing process. The hater of war must make war and even summon the occasional rage that the making of war requires. The problem was to stop in time, to resist the delight in killing, or the lust for plunder, or any of the things that convert war from a means into an end. One cannot say that either Vergil or Aeneas quite solved the problem. Yet if Vergil was humane and civilized, he was also a Roman and therefore nothing at all of a pacifist.

It is in the first six books, rather than the last, that the Homeric and the non-Homeric elements achieve a peculiarly Vergilian harmony. Here Aeneas is actually developing from a Homeric into an Augustan man, and the very difficulty of the development excites our interest and exactly fits the melancholy ethos of Vergilian verse. A Homeric hero did obvious, intelligible things. He rejoiced in food and battle and sex. He endured hardship only for a clear reason. But Aeneas' destiny is always opposed to his desires or passions. How can a man of the future live happily in the past? Here the tension between the Homeric and the Roman in Aeneas, which is also the tension between the human and the superhuman (the burden of destiny imposed on a mere man), is given a deep psychological basis in the very roots of his familial and erotic life. His father Anchises is a dual figure, at once a real father, a true object of filial piety, and a peculiar kind of deity, the mouthpiece of the gods, the prophet of Rome, who in his short life after Troy's fall and in death is the supreme superego or conscience. Aeneas' struggle with passion—the Dido episode—is thus also a struggle with his father, who now comes to him in dreams and immediately precedes the even more awful warning of Mercury.[5] Yet it is finally clear that Aeneas cannot continue to depend on his father: such dependence is, as in any man's psychology, a weakness that must be overcome. The necessity of the descent to the Underworld is thus explained: Aeneas must return to his past (Dido, and Deiphobus, who is the representative of Troy) and receive the future from his father's hands before he can be either free of the past or truly self-reliant. It is a terrible struggle, an immense ordeal, quite literally the overcoming of death itself and a consequent rebirth or new birth. All this is a thrilling experience beside which the battles of the later *Aeneid* look pale and wooden.

Seen in this light the classic maturity of the *Aeneid* begins to emerge. Aeneas is the hero of our whole civilization; his roots are in Homer and the heroic age, but his civilized and tormented psyche is quite modern. He is heroic precisely because he conquers himself—his human passions and anxieties—and renounces present happiness for a universal destiny. Only such behavior, Vergil insists, can guarantee the sort of empire that can give peace to the world. Only so is civilization possible. To be sure, there is here evident a very simple identification of Rome and civilization that obviously conceals a large element of nationalistic pride. But the *Aeneid* is no nationalistic epic. The Roman hero is credible and honorable because he accepts the necessity of sacrifice, because he does not live for himself, and also, of course, because he feels so deeply the painful price of empire. Aeneas too went down in defeat when he lost his native city. The *Aeneid* ends with the noble death of Aeneas' enemy, not with a fanfare

5 See IV. 351–359.

of victory. Dido is so pathetic that many readers of Vergil have preferred her to Aeneas, as some also have preferred Turnus. This is not the defect but the triumph of Vergil's art. The attainment of civilization is hard because so much that is admirable—the passionate, romantic, reckless, and vehement side of life—must be piously put down or, to state the matter baldly, piously killed. Yet only the civilized hero can do this with the humanity by which, after all, the fighting and killing are justified, for unfortunately the Didos or Turnuses, if left to prevail or even merely to live, would quickly put a stop to any civilization, humanity, or peace.

In saying this, I attempt to reproduce Vergil's view, not my own. I believe that there are grave difficulties, to say the least, with his epic justification of *Romanitas*. A nation cannot play God in quite the way that Vergil thought. A very good corrective to the *Aeneid* is, I think, the Second Inaugural Address of Abraham Lincoln. But we must bear in mind that Vergil could not refer, as Lincoln did, to a transcendent, wholly universal deity. His age, origin, and position almost necessitated his identifying Jupiter with the Stoic *Reason* and the Stoic *Reason* with Roman government and Octavian Augustus. And the necessity was quite fatal. Yet Christianity has not, I think, put the *Aeneid* out of date or, indeed, lessened its position as the mature classic of Western society. On a human, political, and even poetical level, we still face the problem of civilization in terms very like those of Vergil himself. And we shall do well indeed if we can keep as much humanity in our heroism and as much heroism in our humanity.

Much indeed remains to be said about the *Aeneid*. General observations, such as the fragmentary ones made here, never touch the concrete substance of a literary work, especially a poem. Furthermore, even translations such as this—and Professor Copley, I believe, has done by far his best work in this translation and has allowed Vergil himself the most prominent place in it—do not fully render the Latin original. Vergil is notoriously resistent to translation, more so than

Homer or most of the Greeks. My best advice to the reader who wants to get at Vergil himself is that he try a few lines in the Latin (using the translation), even if only a very few. The great merit of poetry is that a very small amount of it is often very rewarding, and that the drudgery of coping with a foreign language is so quickly repaid. And Vergil comes through in a small sample, for almost every line conveys his characteristic ethos—the melancholy grandeur, the pathos in heroism, and the heroism in pathos.

I do not think that Vergil requires a great deal of historical explanation or introduction. A brief account of the final phase of the Roman Civil War and the coming to power of Octavian (Augustus) can give one some idea of the poem in its most directly political aspect.[6] It is enough, really, to know that Vergil looked on Augustus as the savior of the ruined Roman state and the creator of a new order of things, an endless regime of ecumenical Roman peace. Reading or knowing something of Homer's *Odyssey* and *Iliad* is also helpful. But the poem is after all the thing, and it is, as always, far better to read it than to read about it.

BROOKS OTIS

Stanford, California
July 1965

6 See, for example, Ronald Syme, *The Roman Revolution* (Oxford: Oxford University Press, 1960). This is the most exciting single book about the Civil War and Augustus' coming to power. Syme does not view Augustus with Vergilian eyes, but his book is sharp and interesting.

VERGIL—A BIOGRAPHICAL NOTE

Publius Vergilius Maro was born October 15, 70 B.C., at Andes, near Mantua, in the Po Valley. His family were people of some substance, if not of wealth or distinction; they sent the young Vergil to school in Verona and Milan, and ultimately in Rome. No doubt he began composing poems very early in life; the earliest work now attributed with certainty to him is the collection called the *Eclogues* or *Bucolics,* written between 43 and 37 B.C.; these ten pastoral poems show a skillful artistry that can only have been the result of years of practice.

While Vergil was engaged on the *Eclogues,* his family property near Mantua was confiscated. After the battle of Philippi, in 41 B.C., it became necessary for Octavian and Antony to find lands on which to settle their discharged veterans. Somehow, the territory around Mantua was chosen. One of the officials in charge of the confiscation was Asinius Pollio, a close associate of Octavian and a man of culture; he urged Vergil to petition the emporor for return of his land. The petition was granted, but Vergil seems not to have gone back to his old home. For the rest of his life, he lived mostly at Naples.

During the negotiations with Pollio and Octavian, Vergil became acquainted with Maecenas, the closest and most trusted of Octavian's advisors. He became the patron and friend of Vergil, who from then on was able to live comfortably and in the peaceful retirement which his shy and gentle nature required. For seven years, from 37 to 30 B.C., he was engaged on the *Georgics,* four long poems on agriculture. Ostensibly modeled on Hesiod's *Works and Days,* the *Georgics* are in fact highly original, and are a most remarkable combination of sound agricultural principle, peasant lore, Italian landscape, and consummate poetry. Dryden is said to have called them "the best poems of the best poet." Few would care to dispute him.

From 29 until his death in 19 B.C., Vergil was absorbed in the composition of the *Aeneid*. According to tradition, he at first planned to write an epic on the Roman kings, then changed to the exploits of Augustus, but finally settled on the story of the wanderings of Aeneas from Troy to Italy. This story, part history, part legend, was well enough known and accepted to have the authority of strong national tradition; at the same time, its purely legendary aspects gave the poet ample room for invention and for adapting the whole tale to his immediate and specific purpose: the composition of an epic poem that would incorporate, illustrate, and—as Milton was later to say of God's ways— "justify" the "way" of the Roman Empire to man.

At the time of his death (September 21, 19 B.C.) Vergil is said to have felt that the *Aeneid* was too far from finished to be published; in his will, he directed that the manuscript be destroyed. Fortunately, the emperor intervened; the manuscript was saved and given to two of Vergil's friends, Varius and Tucca, to be edited and published. The two men, according to all accounts, scrupulously refrained from adding anything of their own to the text; they contented themselves with removing duplications and obviously misplaced lines, in other respects leaving the poem as close to the manuscript version as was possible.

Tradition has it that Vergil was a man of delicate physique, and one whose natural reticence and shyness made him avoid society. He spent his life in study and writing, and was deeply loved by the few men—mostly other poets, such as Horace, or philosophers, such as Siro the Epicurean—with whom he associated on terms of close friendship. He died at Naples, where he was buried; his tomb—or what was reputed to be his tomb—was for many years an object of veneration.

F.O.C.

SELECTED BIBLIOGRAPHY

BAILEY, CYRIL. *Religion in Virgil*. Oxford: Clarendon Press, 1935.

CONINGTON-NETTLESHIP. *The Works of Virgil*. Photographic reproduction. Olms: Hildesheim, 1963. Volume II, pages ix–lxiii.

CRUTTWELL, R. W. *Vergil's Mind at Work*. Oxford: Oxford University Press, 1946.

ELIOT, T. S. *What Is a Classic?* London: Faber & Faber, 1944.

HEINZE, RICHARD. *Vergils Epische Technik*. Leipzig, 1903.

KNIGHT, W. P. JACKSON. *Roman Vergil*. London: Hillary, 1944.

LEWIS, C. S. *A Preface to Paradise Lost*. Oxford: Oxford University Press, 1942.

OTIS, BROOKS. *Virgil, a Study in Civilised Poetry*. Oxford: Oxford University Press, 1964.

PÖSCHL, VIKTOR. *Die Dichtkunst Virgils*. Wiesbaden, 1950. Translated into English as *The Art of Virgil: Image and Symbol in the Aeneid*, by GERDA SELIGSON. Ann Arbor: University of Michigan Press, 1962.

PRESCOTT, H. W. *The Development of Virgil's Art*. Chicago: University of Chicago Press, 1927.

PUTNAM, M. C. J. *The Poetry of the Aeneid*. Cambridge, Mass: Harvard University Press, 1965.

QUINN, KENNETH. *Vergil's Aeneid, A Critical Description*. Ann Arbor: University of Michigan Press, 1968.

SYME, RONALD. *The Roman Revolution*. Oxford: Oxford University Press, 1960. Paperback.

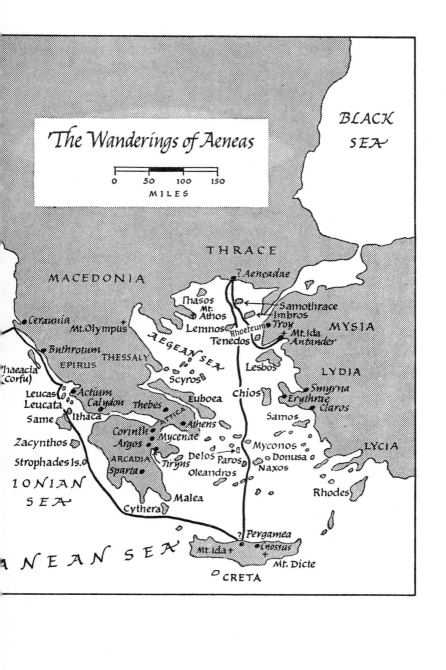

The Wanderings of Aeneas

0   50   100   150
MILES

BLACK SEA

THRACE

MACEDONIA

? Aeneadae

Thasos
Mt. Athos
Lemnos

Samothrace
Imbros
Rhoeteum Troy
Tenedos

MYSIA

Ceraunia
Mt. Olympus

AEGEAN SEA

Mt. Ida
Antander

Buthrotum
THESSALY

EPIRUS

Lesbos

LYDIA

Phaeacia (Corfu)

Scyros

Chios

Smyrna
Erythrae
Claros

Leucas
Leucata

Same

Actium
Calydon
Ithaca

Thebes

ATTICA

Euboea

Samos

Zacynthos

Corinth
Mycenae

Athens

Myconos
Donusa

LYCIA

Strophades Is.

ARCADIA
Sparta

Argos
Tiryns

Delos Paros
Oleandros

Naxos

Rhodes

IONIAN SEA

Malea

Cythera

...NEAN SEA

? Pergamea

Mt. Ida
CRETA

Cnossus
Mt. Dicte

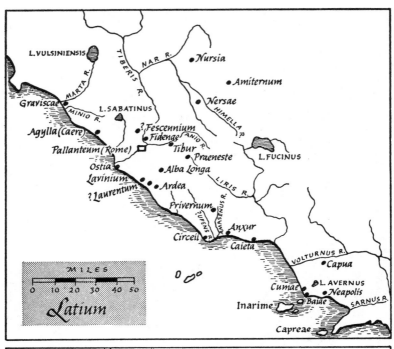

L. VULSINIENSIS
Nursia
TIBERIS R.
NAR R.
Amiternum
MARTA R.
Nersae
Graviscae
L. SABATINUS
HIMELLA R.
MINIO R.
Agylla (Caere)
? *Fescennium*
Fidenae
ANIO R.
L. FUCINUS
Pallanteum (Rome)
Tibur
Praeneste
Ostia
Alba Longa
LIRIS R.
Lavinium
Ardea
? Laurentum
Privernum
UFENS R.
AMASENUS R.
Anxur
Circeii
Caieta
VOLTURNUS R.
Capua
MILES
0 10 20 30 40 50
Cumae
L. AVERNUS
Neapolis
Inarime
Baiae
SARNUS R.
Latium
Capreae

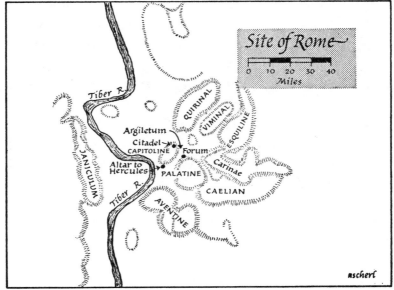

Tiber R.
QUIRINAL
VIMINAL
Argiletum
Citadel
CAPITOLINE
ESQUILINE
Forum
Altar to
Hercules
Carinae
JANICULUM
PALATINE
Tiber R.
CAELIAN
AVENTINE

Site of Rome
0 10 20 30 40
Miles

ascherl

The AENEID

BOOK ONE

My song is arms and a man, the first of Troy
to come to Italy and Lavinian shores,
a fated fugitive, harried on land and sea
by heaven's huge might and Juno's endless hate,
5 harried by war, till he could found the City
and bring his gods to Latium, whence the race
of Latins, our Alban sires, and towering Rome.

Muse, tell me the causes: how was godhead wronged,
how injured the queen of heaven that she must force
10 through many a fall of fate and many a toil
that great, good man: can heaven hold such ill will?

A city once stood, a colony of Tyre,
Carthage, across from Italy and far
from Tiber's mouth, rich and ready for war,
15 a spot that Juno loved more than all lands,
more even than Samos: here stood her arms and here
her chariot; throne of the world it was to be
if Fate allowed; this was her cherished aim.
But men would spring of Trojan blood, she'd heard,
20 and some day lay her Carthage in the dust—
a race of world-wide kings, whose pride meant war
and death for Libya: so ran the thread of Fate.

This she feared, and remembered too, that war
when she first fought for her dear Greece at Troy.

3

25 She still recalled the anger and the pain
that sent her there: deep in her heart lay stored
the judgment of Paris, the insult to her beauty,
a hated people, a Ganymede raped and honored.
Her anger flared; she scattered all over the waves
30 the Trojans Achilles and Greece had cast aside,
and kept them far from Latium; year on year
they wandered, dogged by Fate, across the seas.
Such matter it was to found our Roman race.

Scarce out of sight of Sicily they sailed on
35 lighthearted, while the bow cut brine to foam,
when Juno, ever nursing her wounded heart,
thought thus: "What? Drop my design? Am I defeated,
and can't keep a Trojan king from Italy?
Fate forbids it? Pallas could burn the ships
40 of Argos and drown their crewmen in the sea
for Ajax' lone offense—that lawless fool!
She threw Jove's shaft of lightning from the clouds,
shattered the fleet, and blew calm waters wild.
Through Ajax' heart she drove a hissing flame,
45 whirled him away, and nailed him to a cliff.
But I, who stand here queen of heaven, to Jove
both wife and sister, year after year have fought
one single people. Who'll worship Juno now,
honor my altars, or come to me in prayer?"

50 Turning these thoughts within her flaming heart
she came to Aeolia, home of clouds, a land
big with wild winds. Here Aeolus is king,
and keeps prisoned and locked in his vast cave
the battling storms and roaring hurricanes.
55 They curse and howl behind their granite bars
and moan at the bolts; he sits on his high throne,
scepter in hand, and holds them in constraint:
if he did not, they'd sweep the world away,
and whip sea, earth, and heaven through the air.

60   But Jove the almighty locked them in lightless caves
     for fear of this, and piled a mountain range
     upon them, and gave them a king with stern command
     when to release and when to bolt and bar.
     Juno then made her humble plea to him:

65   "Aeolus, you have power from father Jove
     to calm the waves or whistle up the storm:
     a people I hate are sailing the Tuscan sea,
     bringing to Italy Troy and her conquered gods.
     Make your winds wild! Capsize and sink their ships!
70   Or scatter them, crews and corpses, over the waves!
     I have twice seven Nymphs of splendid form;
     of these Deiopea, the loveliest,
     I'll give you for your wife; she shall be yours
     and, for the help you give, shall spend her years
75   with you, and make you father of fine, strong sons."

     Aeolus then: "My lady, you need only
     work out your wish and speak: I must obey.
     My throne, my scepter, all my power, my place
     at the feasts of gods, you've won from Jove for me;
80   you've made me ruler over cloud and storm."

     With that he turned his spear and struck the mountain
     full on the flank. The winds, formed in a column,
     rushed through the gap and roared across the world.
     Down on the sea to stir it from its depths
85   fell East and South Winds, and with stormy squalls
     the Sou'wester; on toward shore the combers rolled;
     men shouted orders, while shrouds and tackle screamed.
     Clouds ripped across the sky to steal the light
     from Trojan eyes; black night fell over the sea.
     The heavens thundered; lightning crackled and flashed;
90   wherever men looked they saw the face of death.
     A chill swept over Aeneas; his limbs went weak;
     he moaned in terror and stretched his hands toward heaven,

calling aloud: "Oh, three times, four times blessed,
95 those men who died beneath the walls of Troy,
watched by their fathers! O Diomede, you bravest
of Greeks, why could you not have spilled my life
on Trojan soil? Why could I not have fallen
where Achilles laid Hector low, where tall Sarpedon
100 lies; where Simois rolls beneath his waves
the helmets, the shields of heroes, and those brave dead!"

Amid his cries a screaming Northerly squall
set sails aback; the waves rose toward the stars.
The oars were broken; the vessel yawed and swung
105 broad-on; a craglike comber rose astern.
Some hung on the crests; some in the gaping troughs
saw bottom between the waves; the sand boiled up.
A Southerly drove three ships on hidden reefs
(Italians call them "The Altars"; far offshore
110 they lie, their great backs just awash) ; three more
an Easterly swept to a shallow (tragic sight!) .
They grounded hard; the sand piled up around them.
One, with Orontes and his Lycian crew,
was swamped: Aeneas saw the huge sea rise
115 and crash on her quarterdeck; overboard went her helmsman
headfirst in the water; a moment she stood stock-still,
then spinning three times round sank in a flurry.
A few men bobbed up swimming in the swirl;
a spear, a plank, the flotsam wealth of Troy.
120 Ilioneus' stout ship and brave Achates',
the one that Abas rode, and old Aletes,
fell to the storm. Through weakened, gaping seams
they took in deadly water; their frames gave way.

Now Neptune heard the roaring, raving seas,
125 the wild wail of the winds, and felt the waters
come rolling from the deeps; in vast concern
he lifted his head serene above the flood.
He saw Aeneas' fleet strewn far and wide,

and Trojans battered and beaten by wind and wave.
130 Juno was angry—he knew his sister's work!
He called to the East and West Winds and addressed them:

"So sure of yourselves? Of rank and privilege?
Without my leave how dare you winds confound
heaven and earth and raise the waves so high?
135 You, whom—! But first I'd better calm the sea.
Next time you'll not pay penalty so light.
Go quickly now, and tell this to your king:
The sea's not his domain, not his the trident;
they're mine by lot. He has his pile of rocks,
140 a home for all you winds. Let Aeolus
play monarch there—and keep his winds locked up."

He spoke, and at once he calmed the swollen seas,
swept off the cloud-rack, and brought back the sun.
Cymothoë then, and Triton, heaved the ships
145 off the sharp reef, while Neptune with his trident
cleared the great sandspit and broke up the waves;
his chariot wheels rolled lightly over the water.
As when in some great nation the masses rise
in riot, and savage, ignoble hearts run wild;
150 now fire and stones, the weapons of madness, fly—
then, if some patriot stern and honor-laden
stands forth, the shouting ends, the people stop
to hear; his words bring back the public peace;
so ceased the roar of waters when their lord
155 looked out and rode beneath the open sky,
with skillful hand reining his car and team.

Bone-weary, the sons of Aeneas ran for land—
the nearest shore; they raised the Libyan coast.
In a byway lies a bay; an island blocks
160 its entrance and behind it makes a lee
where every wave breaks to a gentle roll.
On either shore a rocky headland lifts

a rampart toward the sky; beneath those peaks
wide waters are silent; a sylvan backdrop hangs
165 rustling above a gloomy, lightless grove.
Ahead, a beetling cliff, at its base a cave
with a bubbling spring and seats of living rock,
home of the Nymphs. Here weary craft may rest
unheld by hawsers or the anchor's bite.
170 In sailed Aeneas with the seven ships
saved from his fleet; the Trojans leaped to land,
kissed the dear earth, and made the beach their own,
there to lay down their tired and salt-sick limbs.
Achates took his flint and struck a spark,
175 caught up the fire on leaves, and put dry tow
and tinder about it, then nursed it to a flame.
The men unloaded implements and supplies
all soaked in brine; dog-tired, they sorted out
the best, built up the fires, and cooked their meal.

180 Meanwhile Aeneas climbed the cliff and searched
the sea to the far horizon: could he find
the ships of Antheus riding out the storm?
Caicus on his quarterdeck? or Capys?
Not one ship was in sight, but on the shore
185 he saw three wandering stags; stretched out behind,
a whole herd followed browsing on the hills.
He stopped, and from Achates snatched the bow
and arrows that his faithful friend had brought.
First he shot down the leaders, who carried high
190 their antlered heads, then at the rest let fly
and sent them all stampeding through the woods,
nor stopped his archery till his shafts had laid
seven aground—for each ship one fat deer.
Then back to the harbor to divide the spoils!
195 This called for wine, the casks that kind Acestes
gave them the day they sailed from Sicily.
Aeneas shared them out and spoke good cheer:
"This isn't the first time, men, that we've known trouble!

We've suffered worse, and God will end this, too!
200 You sailed close by those cliffs where Scylla raged
and roared; you saw the Cyclops and his home
on Aetna. Take courage, now! No fears nor sorrow!
Some day these memories, too, will bring a smile.
Whatever may happen, whatever perils we face,
205 it's on to Italy! Once there, we'll rest.
So God reveals; there Troy must rise again.
Hold hard and save yourselves for better days!"

These were his words, though he was sick with care.
He forced a smile and kept his sorrows hidden.
210 The men made ready to cook their venison.
They stripped flesh from the bones and bared the entrails.
Some cut and spitted the pieces of fresh meat;
others set up the pots and tended fires.
Food restored strength. They lay back on the grass
215 and had their fill of wine and good fat meat.
With hunger appeased and dinner cleared away
they talked for hours, hung between hope and fear,
about the friends they'd lost: were they alive,
or were they gone and passed beyond recall?
220 Aeneas the good thought sadly of Orontes,
of Amycus and his fate, of Lycus' death
so cruel, of Gyas the brave, and brave Cloanthus.

Silence had fallen when Jove from heaven's height
looked out on sea and sail and level plain,
225 searching the coasts and nations; then on high
he stopped, and fixed his gaze on Libya's realm.
And as he pondered deeply, much concerned,
Venus, her eyes all bright with welling tears,
sadly addressed him: "Dear my lord, who rule
230 god and man forever, who hurl the thunder,
how could my son, Aeneas, offend you so?
How could the Trojans? They've seen so many die;
and yet, for Italy's sake, all doors are locked.

In days to come, they were to give us Rome—
235 leaders, recalled to life from blood of Troy,
who'd hold and govern every land and sea:
you promised sure! What, sir, has turned your heart?
This helped me bear the fall and tearful wreck
of Troy: I balanced one fate by the other.
240 But there's no change! The same hard lot pursues them!
Dear lord and father, when will you grant them rest?
Antenor could slip through the Argive lines,
sail up the Adriatic, and find safety
far in Liburnia, past Timavus' wells,
245 where through nine mouths a roaring mountain torrent
floods over fields and plunges toward the sea.
Yes, he could build a town and make a home
for Trojans, name his nation, and set up
a Trojan standard. Now he rests in peace.
250 But we, your children, to whom you grant high heaven,
have lost our ships for one lone person's hate!
We are betrayed and barred from Italy's shores!
Thus are the righteous honored and thrones restored?"

The universal father turned on her
255 the smile of peace that brings a clear, calm day.
He bent and kissed his daughter; then he spoke:
"No fear, Cytherea! Your people's fate remains
unchanged. You'll see the city and promised walls
of Lavinium; you shall carry to heaven's high stars
260 Aeneas the great and good: my heart's not turned.
But now (since care consumes you, I shall speak
more fully and reveal Fate's hidden page)
he'll wage hard war in Italy; savage tribes
he must defeat, and give them homes and laws.
265 But once the Rutulans are pacified
the Latins shall know him king for three full seasons.
Then young Ascanius, whom we name 'Iulus'
('Ilus' he was, in Ilium's royal days),
shall hold the throne while the long months roll round

270 through thirty years. He'll leave Lavinium
and build his seat of power at Alba Longa.
Here kings of Hector's lineage shall rule
three hundred years, till Ilia, priestess-queen,
shall lie with Mars and bear twin sons to him.
275 Then, glad of a nursing she-wolf's sheltering hide,
King Romulus shall found the walls of Mars,
and name his people 'Romans,' for himself.
For them I set no bounds of place or time;
rule without end I grant them. Juno, too,
280 whose cruelty now scares earth and sky and sea,
shall come to better mind, and with me bless
the Romans, lords of the world, the toga'd race.
This is decreed. In time the day will come
when Phthia and proud Mycenae shall be slaves
285 to the sons of Priam, and Argos wear their yoke.
A Caesar shall spring of noble Trojan line
(Ocean shall bound his power, the stars his fame)—
Julius, a name come down from great Iulus.
Laden one day with spoil of the East, he'll have
290 your welcome to heaven, and men will pray to him.
Hard hearts will soften then, and wars will cease;
old Faith and Vesta, Remus and his twin
will rule the world; tight bands of steel will close
the terrible temple of War, where Blood-Lust caged
295 will crouch on barbarous spears, bound hundredfold
with chains of bronze, screaming and slavering blood."

So speaking, Jove sent Maia's son from heaven
to spread the lands and keeps of Carthage wide
in welcome to Trojans: Dido, untaught of fate,
300 must not repulse them. Through large air he flew
and with quick wing-beats came to Libyan shores,
then did as ordered; the Tyrians, by God's will,
put off their savage ways; their leader and queen
conceived peace and good will for men of Troy.
305 Faithful Aeneas lay thinking all night long,

determined, soon as daylight came, to search
this unfamiliar land: Where had the wind
brought him? Who lived here? man? (he saw no homes)
or beast? He must find out and tell his men!
310   In a wooded cave beneath an overhang
he hid his ships where they were screened by trees
above and ahaft. Then with one friend, Achates,
he went forth, clasping a spear in either hand.
Out in the woods his mother came to meet him.
315   She seemed a girl; her face and garb were those
of a Spartan maid or Thracian Harpalyce
whipping her horses to outrun Hebrus' current.
Over her shoulder a bow hung ready to hand;
her hair lay loose and scattered by the wind,
320   her flowing gown belted to bare her knee.
She hailed the men: "Tell me, sirs, have you seen
one of my sisters wandering down this way?
She'd have a quiver and spotted lynx-hide cape;
perhaps she was hot on the trail of a foam-flecked boar."

325   So Venus; and Venus' son replied to her:
"None of your sisters have I seen or heard,
O—what shall I call you? That's no mortal face,
that voice no girl's. You are a goddess, sure!
Sister of Phoebus? One of the Nymphs' descent?
330   Blessed be your name, whatever it is! But help us!
What land is this? On what coasts of the world
have we been tossed? Tell us, for we are lost.
High waves and winds have left us helpless here.
We'll offer prayer and rich blood-sacrifice!"

335   Then Venus: "I am not worthy of such honor.
We girls of Tyre by custom bear the bow
and lace the scarlet boot high on the leg.
This land is Punic; our city and name of Tyre,
around us are Libyans, people untamed by war.
340   Our queen is Dido; she left the city of Tyre

to escape her brother—a long and tortured tale
of cruel deception. Hear while I tell it briefly.
Her husband, Sychaeus, held the richest lands
in all Phoenicia; he was the man she loved,
345   her first, to whom her father gave her, a bride,
a virgin. But her brother, the king of Tyre,
Pygmalion, had no peer in monstrous crime.
The two men quarreled; blind for love of wealth
Pygmalion murdered Sychaeus at the altar,
350   catching him off his guard; his sister's love
left him unmoved. He kept the crime long hidden
and cheated the heartsick girl with empty hopes.
But as she slept, her husband's unlaid ghost
came to her, showing a face all strange and pale.
355   He told of the murder, bared his wounded breast,
and brought the whole foul story to the light.
'Hurry! Run! Leave our fatherland!' he urged,
'and for your help, look, here a treasure buried—
silver and gold, more than you ever knew!'
360   His words led Dido to prepare for flight.
She brought together those who loathed the tyrant
or feared him. Ships, it happened, stood complete;
they seized them, put the treasure aboard. To sea
went greedy Pygmalion's gold. A woman led them!
365   They came to the place where you shall see the walls
huge rising and the towers of Carthage-town.
Here they bought land—'as much as one bull's hide
enclosed'—for this the place is called 'The Purse.'
But who are you? From what coasts have you come?
370   Where are you going?" Aeneas at these words
heaved a deep sigh and drew speech from his heart:
"My lady, if I began with first-beginnings,
and you were free to hear our tale of toil,
day would lie locked in heaven before the end!
375   We are from ancient Troy—if you have heard
the name of Troy?—We'd traveled many a sea
when storms by chance drove us to Libyan shores.

I am Aeneas the good; the gods I saved
ride in my ships. My name is known in heaven.
380   My goal is Italy, land of my fathers' line.
With twice ten ships I put to sea from Troy
to follow the path my goddess-mother showed me;
just seven, battered by wind and wave, remain.
I walk these Libyan wastes a helpless stranger
385   exiled by East and West." Venus could bear
no more, but spoke to end his sad account:

"Whoever you are, no hostile heaven brought you
breathing and living to our Tyrian land.
Go now, and make your way to Dido's court.
390   Your men are safe, and changing winds have blown
your ships to safety. This I can tell you now,
unless I was taught to read the birds all wrong.
See there: twelve swans flying in joyful ranks;
Jove's eagle, swooping down from open sky
395   frightened and scattered them; now with lines new-formed
they're settling to earth or hovering over the land.
As safely returned they beat their whistling wings
or soared in a flock to wreathe the sky with song,
just so your ships and men have come to port
400   or under full sail have reached the harbor's mouth.
Go now, and let this pathway guide your steps."

She turned to leave; a glow of light shone out
behind her head; her hair sent forth ambrosial
perfume; she let her train fall down full-length,
405   and walked in god-like majesty! He knew
his mother, and as she hastened off he cried,
"What? Your son? Heartless again you trick him—
you, too—with empty shows? Why was your hand
not laid in mine? Why could we not speak truth?"
410   With this reproach he turned toward Dido's town.
But Venus walled the two in lightless air
and clothed them all about in heavy mist

so none could see them and no man had power
to hold them back or question why they came.
415 Then she flew off to Paphos, and with smiles
came home again, where incense wreathes her shrine
and hundred altars sweet with fresh-plucked blooms.

The two men meanwhile hurried down the path
and soon were climbing the highest hill that hangs
420 over the town and looks down on its walls.
Aeneas was awed: so vast, where once was camp-ground!
The wonder of gates, and avenues paved, and crowds!
Working like mad, those Tyrians; some at walls,
some toiled at forts, surveying, or hauling stone;
425 some marked out homesites and drew boundary lines.
They had their laws, their courts, their councilmen.
Here they were dredging a harbor; there they laid
a theater's undercroft, and cut tall columns
out of a quarried cliff to adorn the stage.
430 Like bees in June out in the blooming fields
busy beneath the sun, some teasing out
the new young workers, others pressing down
clear honey or making nectar burst the cells,
still others taking the loads brought in, while others
435 police the hive and drive off lazy drones:
the work hums on; the combs are sweet with thyme.
"O blessed by Fate! Your walls are building now!"
Aeneas said, as he watched the ramparts rise.
Walled in the cloud (a miracle!), he walked
440 among the workmen, and no one saw him there.

In mid-town was a pleasant, shady park,
marking the spot where Tyrians, tempest-tossed,
as Juno had foretold, had dug to find,
a horse's head—a sign that they should be
445 great soldiers and good farmers down the years.
Here Dido of Sidon built a temple to Juno,
a huge vault filled with wealth and holiness.

Above its steps the doorway was of bronze,
the beams bronze-nailed, the doors and hinges brazen.
450   Here in the park Aeneas saw a sight
that eased his fears and made him first dare hope
for safety, and take heart for all his troubles.
As he surveyed the temple, stone by stone,
awaiting the queen, and wondering how this town
455   had come to be, amazed at the workmen's zeal
and skill, he saw, scene after scene, the war
at Troy, battles now famed through all the world:
the Atrides, Priam, and, savage to both, Achilles.
His tears welled up. "What place, Achates, now,"
460   he said, "what land does not know all we suffered?
See: Priam! Here too the brave have their reward!
The world has tears; man's lot does touch the heart.
Put off your fears: our story will save us yet!"
Aeneas spoke, and let this empty show
465   nourish his grief and flood his face with tears.
He saw how men had fought the fight for Troy:
here Greeks retreating, here Trojans pressing hard,
here their allies, here plumed Achilles' car.
Nearby were Rhesus' snowy-canvassed tents—
470   (he knew them and wept!) his men, just fallen to sleep,
betrayed and butchered by bloody Diomede;
gone, too, his fiery team before they knew
the taste of Trojan feed or Xanthus' waters.
And here was Troilus, running, his weapons lost
475   (poor boy! he was no man to meet Achilles!),
his horses pulled him clinging to his car,
still gripping the reins; his head and shoulders dragged
over the ground; his spear wrote in the dust.
And here the women of Troy in sad parade
480   were bringing the robe to cruel Athena's temple
with humble prayer, beating their breasts in grief:
with stony eyes the goddess stared them down.
And there Achilles peddled the lifeless corpse
of Hector, dragged three times around Troy-walls.

485 Aeneas could not hold back a cry of pain
to see the car, the ransom, his dead friend,
and Priam stretching out defenseless hands.
He saw himself, surrounded by great Greeks,
and Memnon the Moor, with his Arabian troops.
490 And leading her crescent-shielded Amazons
Penthesilea fought madly amid the ranks.
One breast lay bare above the sword-belt clasp—
a warrior-maiden who dared to fight with men.

As Aeneas of Troy stood marveling at these sights,
495 unable to speak or turn his eyes away,
into the temple came Dido the beautiful,
the queen, with all her bodyguard around her.
As by Eurotas or on the height of Cynthus
Diana leads her dancing mountain-maids,
500 a thousand ringed about her; there she goes
quiver on back, head-high above them all
(no word betrays her mother's heartfelt joy) —
just so was Dido, and just so her joy
to see her people working, building, planning.
505 She entered the temple; under its central dome
she took her place enthroned, walled by armed men.
There she sat judging, framing laws, assigning
work to her men by fair shares or by lot,
when all at once a crowd came rushing in.
510 Aeneas saw they had Sergestus, Antheus,
Cloanthus, and others whom the storm at sea
had scattered and carried away to distant shores.
Aeneas was speechless; Achates was struck hard
by joy and fear at once: they were afire
515 to greet their friends—but still, what did this mean?
Pretending calm, clothed in their cloud, they watched.
What had these men endured? Where were their ships?
Why were they here? Each ship had sent her man
to beg for mercy. Pleading, the group moved on.

520 Once they had entered and gained the right to speak,
Ilioneus, the oldest, spoke words of peace:
"My lady, Jove has let you found your city
and bring both right and rule to savage tribes.
We're Trojans, helpless, driven by wind and wave.

525 We beg you: do us no wrong, nor burn our ships.
Spare a good people! Be merciful! Hear our plea!
We have not come in arms to scorch the earth
of Libya, to plunder your homes and load our ships.
The vanquished have no heart for such presumption.

530 There is a place called 'Westland' by the Greeks,
an ancient country, powerful, warlike, rich;
the Oenotri settled it; now, we hear, their sons
are calling it 'Italy' for their founder's name.
This was our goal.*

535 But all of a sudden waves and rain and wind
drove us on unseen banks; squalls from the south
scattered our ships. Some sank; some hung on reefs
uncharted. We few swam here to your shores.
What kind of people are you? Civilized?

540 What laws are these? We have been kept from shore,
forbidden to land, and met with shows of force.
If men and mortal arms arouse your scorn,
be sure the gods take note of right and wrong.
Aeneas was our chief; he had no peer

545 in justice, goodness, and the arts of war.
If fate has saved him, if he lives and breathes,
and has not fallen to rest in heartless dark,
we have no fears. However great your kindness,
you'll not regret it. In Sicily, we have towns

550 and arms, for Acestes boasts his Trojan blood.
We're badly damaged: let us beach our craft,
shape timbers in your woods, and strip out oars;
then if we find our friends and chief, we'll sail
for Italy, Latium—Italy with a will!

* This is the first of many verses left incomplete by Vergil.

555 But if it's finished, if our well-loved lord
is lost at sea, and hope of Iulus gone,
then let us cross to Sicily, whence we came.
Acestes will take us; he shall be our king."
Thus spoke Ilioneus; with one great shout
560 the sons of Troy assented.

Then with a gracious nod, Queen Dido answered:
"Put fear from your hearts, Trojans; dismiss your cares.
Our lot is hard, our kingdom new; for this
our laws are stern, our whole land under guard.
565 Who doesn't know Troy, Aeneas, and his people,
those brave fighters, and that great holocaust?
We Punic folk are not so dull of heart;
the sun starts not his course so far from Tyre.
You're bound for the Westland, Saturn's wide domain?
570 or Sicily, and Acestes for your king?
I'll help you, keep you safe, and send you on.
Or will you settle here and share my lands?
The city I build is yours: pull up your ships.
Trojan, Tyrian, all shall be one to me.
575 If only that same storm had forced your chief,
Aeneas, here too! I'll send out men to search
the shores and all the ends of Libyan land:
he may be safe, but in some backwood lost."

Her words set hearts to beating in Achates
580 the brave and Lord Aeneas; they longed to burst
their cloud. Achates first was moved to speak:
"My lord, what thought arises in your heart?
Here we are safe; our ships and men are found.
One only is missing, but far at sea we saw
585 him drowned. The rest is as your mother told us."
Scarce had he spoken when their veiling cloud
burst all at once and turned to clearest air.
There stood Aeneas, splendid in bright light,

grand as a god, for Venus breathed on him
590 to give him strength and vigor, the glow of youth,
and made his eyes shine out with power and joy—
like ivory carved to beauty, like some work
of silver or Parian marble chased with gold.
His presence and his words burst on the queen
595 and all her men: "You want me? Here I am,
Aeneas the Trojan, saved from Libyan seas.
You pitied, you only, the terrible toil of Troy.
We few that Greece had left on land and sea
have suffered every blow, lost everything,
600 yet you would share your city, your home, with us!
My lady, how can we thank you, we and all
the sons of Troy, now scattered across the earth?
Oh, if the gods note goodness, if there are
such things as justice and hearts that know the right,
605 you shall be richly blessed. What happy year
bore you? What noble parents got you so?
While rivers run to sea, while shadows cross
the curving hills and fires feed the stars,
your name will live in honor and in praise
610 wherever the world may call me." With these words
he turned to greet Ilioneus, Serestus,
and the others, Gyas the brave, and brave Cloanthus.

Dido of Tyre, struck speechless at the sight
and at the man's misfortune, spoke at last:
615 "What happened, my lord? What ill luck dogged you here?
What dangers forced you onto rock and reef?
Are you Aeneas of Troy, Anchises' son?
Whom Venus in Phrygia bore by Simois' waters?
Yes! I remember! Teucer came to Tyre
620 driven from Salamis, searching for new lands:
'Would Belus help?' (Belus—my father—was then
reducing fertile Cyprus to his power.)
And since that time I've known the tale of Troy,
the city, your name, and all the Argive kings.

625 Teucer, who fought the Teucri,* praised them high,
and loved to claim descent from Teucrian stock.
Enter my home! My welcome to you all!
My fate, like yours, has harried me through great toil
and trouble, to place me in this land at last.
630 By evil schooled, I know what mercy means."

With that she led Aeneas to her palace
and called for prayers of thanks to all the gods.
Nor did she forget his men: down to the beach
she sent off twenty steers, a hundred hogs
635 (fat tuskers all), a hundred lambs and ewes,
and wine, god's gift of joy.
In the great hall splendor to ease a king
was set out, and a banquet was prepared;
the cloths were royal red, embroidered fine;
640 on tables massive plate, and golden cups
chased with historic scenes, the long, long line
of deeds heroic since the race began.

Aeneas, whose father-heart could not rest easy,
dispatched Achates to the ships, to tell
645 Ascanius the news and bring him back;
his every thought was for the son he loved.
"We need gifts, too," he said. "Bring what we saved
when Ilium fell—that coat all worked in gold,
the scarf bordered with yellow acanthus leaves
650 that Argive Helen wore, brought from Mycenae
when she set sail for Troy and wedded bliss
unlawful—they were her mother Leda's gifts;
yes, and the staff Ilione used to bear—
oldest of Priam's daughters—and her chain
655 of beads, her golden coronet, thick with gems."
Achates ran to the ships to speed compliance.

* One of the eponymous heroes of Troy was also named "Teucer";
hence, the Trojans are sometimes called "Teucri" or "Teucrians" ("sons
of Teucer").

But Venus had new schemes at heart, new plans
devised: Cupid should change his face and form
and take Ascanius' place, to set the queen
660 afire with love and wrap her heart in flames.
(Who could have faith in Tyre, the double-tongued?
Who could sleep sound with Juno on the rage?)
And so to winged Love she turned and spoke:
"Son, my strength, my power and might, dear son,
665 who only scorn our father's giant bolt,
help me, I beg you; grant me your godly aid.
Your brother, Aeneas—how on every sea
and strand he has been harried by Juno's hate,
you know, and you have often shared my grief.
670 Now Punic Dido holds him by her charms
entranced. I fear where Juno's gentleness
may end. Fate hinges here: she'll not be idle.
I shall prevent her schemes and ring the queen
with flames of passion, past all power to change;
675 love for Aeneas shall bind her to my side.
How may you help? Hear now what I have planned.
The little prince, my darling, soon will go
to Tyrian town at his dear father's call,
with gifts saved from the sea and flaming Troy.
680 He'll sleep; I'll hide him sleeping in my shrine
on Mount Cythera or holy Idalium:
he must not know our plan, nor intervene.
You change yourself—for just one night, no more—
to look like him, take his young face for yours:
685 when Dido smiles and holds you in her arms
(while princes feast and drink their royal wines)
and clasps you close to give a perfumed kiss,
breathe soft on her the poisoned flame of love."
Cupid obeyed his mother's word, stripped off
690 his wings, and gayly mocked Iulus' stride.
But Venus on Ascanius poured the peace
of sleep and took him cradled in her arms

to Mount Idalium, where soft marjoram
with blossoms breathing nectar wrapped him round.

695 Obeying his mother, Cupid carried gifts
to the Tyrians, happy to walk with good Achates.
When he arrived, Dido had found her place,
her golden couch, all hung with royal red;
then Lord Aeneas, and then the men of Troy
700 came in and took their seats on purpled thrones.
Slaves brought water for washing, put out bread
in baskets, and offered soft and fleecy napkins.
In kitchen fifty maids prepared the food,
each dish in order, and kept the hearth-fires bright;
705 a hundred others, paired with men to match,
waited on table and set the wine cups out.
The Tyrians came, too, crowding through the doors
to take their places and make holiday.
They admired Aeneas' gifts, admired Iulus
710 (his glow was a god's, his charming speech a sham)
and the coat and scarf with yellow acanthus leaves.
Above all, the Punic queen, already doomed
to suffer much, looked and could not be filled;
both gifts and lad alike stirred up the flames.
715 The boy, his arms around Aeneas' neck,
kissed him and filled him with false-fathered love,
then ran to the queen; she looked and loved, and loved
again, and held him to her, unaware
what power to hurt lay there. He, with a mind
720 to Venus' orders, gently began to drive
Sychaeus out, and fill with a living love
a heart long unaroused and half forgetful.

As soon as the feasting lulled, they cleared the board,
set out the mixing bowls, and crowned the wine.
725 The noise of voices rose and filled the hall
to the gilded ceiling where the lamps hung down

alight, and flaming wicks drove out the dark.
Then Dido took her golden jeweled cup
and filled it full—the one that Belus used
730 and all his children. Silence fell. She prayed:
"Jove, whom we name the god of guest and host,
hallow this day for Tyre and Troy alike,
and bid our children keep its memory fresh!
Bless us, good Juno! Bacchus, give us joy!
735 Come, Tyrians, join us in our holiday!"
She spoke and poured libation on the table,
then—only then—just wet her lip with wine,
and passed to Bitias: "Drink!" He drained the cup,
wine, froth, and all, down to its golden base,
740 and handed it on. Iopas struck his lyre
a golden note, as Atlas the great had taught.
He sang the wandering moon, the toiling sun;
whence came mankind and beast, whence rain and fire,
Arcturus, the rain-stars, and the twin Triones,
745 why the sun hurries to dip below the seas
in winter, and why the nights must limp and lag.
The Tyrians cheered aloud; the Trojans joined them.
And Dido, too, prolonged the night with talk
and to her sorrow drank long draughts of love:
750 "Tell me of Priam, tell me! And Hector, too!
The son of Dawn—how blazoned was his shield?
Diomede's team—what breed? How tall Achilles?—
No, no, my lord! From the beginning tell
how the Greeks tricked you, how your city fell,
755 and how you lost your way—full seven years
have seen you wandering over land and sea."

BOOK TWO

All talking stopped; all faces turned to watch.
Aeneas looked out on the hall and then began:
"What? Know that sorrow again, my lady? What words
can tell how royal Troy, the throne of tears,
5 fell to the Greeks? I saw that tragedy
and in it played great part. Who'd tell that tale—
Myrmidon, Thracian, or cruel Ulysses' man—
and keep from tears? Now dewy night is fading
from heaven; the setting stars warn men to sleep.
10 But if you want so much to learn our fate,
to hear in a word how Troy travailed and died,
though memory makes me shrink and shudder with grief,
I'll try.
          "Broken by war, forced back by fate,
the Argive kings watched year on year slip by,
15 then built with help of Pallas' holy hand
a horse tall as a mountain, ribbed with pine—
'For a safe trip home,' they said. (The lie spread fast.)
They threw dice for a crew and slipped them in,
locking them deep inside that lightless cave
20 to fill the monster's womb with men-at-arms.

"Offshore lies Tenedos, famed and storied island,
rich and a power while Priam's throne held firm,
now only a bay where keels ride rough to anchor;
thus far they sailed, to hide by moldering piers.
25 We thought them gone with the wind and homeward bound.
All Troy shook off her shackled years of pain,

threw open the gates, ran out in joy to see
the empty Dorian camp, the vacant shore:
here tented the Thracians, here the cruel Achilles;
30   here lay the fleet, here ranged the ranks of war.
Some stopped to stare at Pallas' deadly gift,
amazed at a horse so huge. Up spoke Thymoetes:
'Inside the walls with it! Station it in our fort!'
(Treason? Or just the turn of fate for Troy?)
35   But Capys and all our wiser heads bade throw
this Grecian trick and generosity suspect
into the sea, or bring up fire and burn it,
or pierce it and see what hollow wombs might hide.
Divided, bewildered, the people turned here, turned there.

40   "Laocoon strode to the front. (With a crowd of priests
he'd run in fury and haste from Castle Hill.)
He shouted, 'You fools! You wretched, raving fools!
You think the enemy gone? Who left this 'gift'?
Greeks? And you trust it? This is our 'friend,' Ulysses?
45   That wooden thing holds Argives locked inside,
or else it's an engine built to attack our walls,
to spy on our homes and fall from above on us all.
There's treachery here. A horse? Don't trust it, Trojans!
Whatever it is, I fear Greeks even with gifts.'

50   "So speaking he heaved and hurled his heavy spear
against the creature's flank and vaulted paunch;
the shaft stood trembling; from that wounded womb
came sounds of cavernous and hollow moaning.
And had Fate and our hearts not been perverse,
55   we would have bloodied that Argive hiding-hole,
and Troy and Priam's towers would still be standing.

"Up came a man, hands bound behind his back,
dragged on by shepherds shouting, 'Where's the king?
We're Trojan; this stranger met us and surrendered!'
60   (He'd plotted and planned it so, to open Troy

to the Greeks—sure of himself—prepared both ways:
to turn his trick, or keep his day with death.)
From all sides, eager to see, our Trojan men
came rushing to ring the captive round with taunts.
65 Now hear how Greeks can lie; from this one crime
learn of them all!
We watched him. There he stood, unarmed and frightened,
looking from face to hostile Phrygian face:
'O gods!' he cried, 'what land will take me in?
70 What sea? What's left for one like me? What's left?
I have no place among the Greeks, and now
the Trojans call for my blood to slake their hate.'
His pitiful cry softened our hearts and dulled
our every impulse. What was his name? we asked.
75 What did he want? How dared he trust to capture?
At last he laid his fear aside and spoke:

" 'I'll tell it all, my lord, yes, all, and tell
it true,' he said. 'I'm Greek. Be that confessed
first off. If Fortune molded Sinon luckless,
80 she shall not mold him foul and a liar, too.
Has anyone told you—has word reached your ears
of Belus' son, Palamedes? Fame has called him
"the great." He hated war; for this, the Greeks
slandered, harried, and hounded the saintly man
85 down to his death. Now that he's gone, they mourn him.
I was his cousin. My father, a humble man,
sent me, no more than a boy, to be his aide.
While he stood king among the kings, full-fledged,
full-powered, I held my small lieutenancy
90 with honor; but Ulysses' craft and hate
(you know them!) sent him from this world of men.
That crushed me. I lived in darkness and in sorrow,
privately cursing my cousin's unjust fate.
Then like a fool I talked and swore revenge
95 if ever my luck should bring me home to Argos.
My silly boasting won me harsh ill will.

That was my downfall; from that hour Ulysses
brought charge after frightening charge, and spread dark hints
among the people, determined to see me dead.
100 He knew no rest until with Calchas' help—
but this is waste! Why tell unwelcome tales?
Why wait? If "Greek" means just one thing to you,
and the name is enough, exact the penalty now!
Ulysses would cheer, Agamemnon pay you well!'

105 "Then how we burned to question and inquire,
unschooled in crime so vile and Argive craft.
He trembled but spoke on, with feigned concern:

" 'Many times the Greeks had longed to abandon Troy
and run away home from the weary years of war;
110 and oh, that they had! Many times an angry sea
blocked them, and storms deterred them from departure.
Worst: when the wooden fabric stood complete—
that horse—all heaven flashed and roared and rained.
Worried, we sent Eurypylus off to seek
115 Apollo's will; the word he brought was grim:
"With blood of a virgin slain you won the winds
when you set sail, you Greeks, for Trojan shores;
with blood you'll buy return: an Argive soul's
the price to pay." When this word reached the ranks
120 men's hearts went numb; an icy tremor ran
down through their bones: whom had Apollo claimed?
Riot was near when the Ithacan drew Calchas
into our midst. "Speak, priest," he said, "and tell
God's will." (Men prophesied that murder plot
125 was aimed at me. They watched but said no word.)
Ten days he held his tongue, guarding against
one word that might send some man to his death.
At last Ulysses' bluster brought him round
to speak, as planned, and mark me for the altar.
130 No one protested; indignation died,
now that one wretch was scape for all their fears.

The dreadful day drew near; the rites were readied—
salt meal and sacred ribbons for my head.
I ran from death—yes, ran. I broke my bonds
135   by dark of night; in muddy marsh and reeds
I lay and waited, praying that they would sail.
Now I've no hope to see the hills of home,
my little sons, the father that I love—
the Greeks may well assess on them the price
140   of my escape—their deaths acquit my sin.
And so, sir, by God's name and power and truth,
by all the honor that still lives unstained
in mortal man, have mercy on my pain;
have mercy on a heart unjustly used!"

145   "His tears won him a pardon and our pity.
Priam at once commanded him relieved
of shackle and chain, then spoke as to a friend:
'Whoever you are, you've lost your Greeks: forget them!
Be one of us! Now speak out, tell the truth:
150   Why the huge horse? Who moved to place it here?
What is it? An act of worship? A siege machine?'
Sinon had learned his part; with Argive craft
he sloughed his irons and raised his hands to heaven:
'O fires eternal, O power beyond blaspheme,
155   be witness,' he cried; 'O altar and unblessed blade
that I escaped, O ribbons I wore to die:
I solemnly renounce my Argive oaths
and curse the Greeks. No law, no loyalty
bids me beware of telling all I know.
160   And if I keep Troy free, then keep your word
and promise—if I speak truth and give full measure.
The Greeks went off to war with hope and trust
based full and forever on Pallas' help; then crime
and crime's inventor—Diomede and Ulysses—
165   sinfully wrested from her hallowed shrine
Pallas the Less. They killed the temple guards,
pulled down her idol, and with hands all blood

dared touch the virgin goddess' holy bands.
Thereafter nothing was certain. Argive hopes
170 faltered, their strength was gone, their goddess angry.
No room for doubt! Tritonia gave clear sign:
scarce was her image based in camp, when fire
flashed from her staring eyes and salty sweat
ran over her limbs, and thrice (wonder to tell!)
175 she leaped up, shield in hand, and shook her spear.
"Run!" Calchas warned them. "Take to the seas at once!"—
Never could Argive power cut Troy down
till they went home to learn God's will, and brought
his blessing anew in curved keels over the sea.
180 And home they've gone, riding the wind to Greece.
They'll win God's favor again, recross the water,
and land here unforeseen—so spoke the prophet.
This horse is payment for their heinous crime:
for godhead wronged, for Pallas the Less defiled.
185 And Calchas bid them build it massive, tall,
beam upon beam, to tower toward the sky—
too wide for the gates, too huge to pass the walls
and by some ancient covenant save your people.
For if your hand should harm Minerva's gift
190 then death (on Calchas' head may that doom fall!)
would come to Priam's Trojans and his power.
But if by your hand it climbed within your city
then Asia would some day march on Grecian walls,
and in that war our grandsons groan and die.'

195 "Strategy, perjury vile! Sinon by craft
won our belief; tricks and counterfeit tears
took captive men whom Diomede, Achilles,
ten years, and a thousand ships had never tamed!

"Here something worse and far more frightful rose
200 to meet us and trouble our unsuspecting hearts.
Laocoon, chosen by lot as Neptune's priest,
was killing a great bull at his sacred shrine,

when out from Tenedos, over the quiet floods
(I shudder to tell it) two snakes, coil on huge coil
205 breasting the sea, came slithering toward the shore.
Their necks rose high in the troughs, their blood-red manes
crested the waves; their other parts behind
slid through the water, twin bodies winding vast.
The salt sea roared and foamed. Now they reached land.
210 Their eyes were hot, bloodshot and flecked with flame;
through hissing lips their tongues flicked in, flicked out.
Bloodless we fled the sight; they never wavered
but went for Laocoon; first his two young sons—
poor little boys!—they hugged in their twin coils
215 wrapping them round and tearing at leg and arm.
Laocoon leaped to the rescue, sword in hand;
the great snakes seized him, wrapped him round and round,
two scaly coils at his waist, two at his throat.
Above his head, their heads and necks rose high.
220 With his hands he tried to pry the loops apart,
while blood and venom soaked his sacred bands.
He screamed to make high heaven shudder—screamed
like a bloodied bull run roaring from the altar
to shake free of his neck an ill-aimed ax.
225 But those twin snakes slipped off toward Castle Hill
and escaped. They made for cruel Tritonia's shrine
and hid at her feet behind her circled shield.

"We stood and shook while into every heart
fresh terror crept. 'He sinned and paid fair price,'
230 we said. 'Laocoon stabbed a sacred thing;
sin rode the spear he hurled against that flank.
Bring the horse home,' we cried, 'and let us pray,
pray to our lady of might.'
We cut through walls and flung our ramparts down.
235 All stripped for the work; under the horse's feet
we slipped rollers, and from its neck we rove
hempen halyards. Up rode the death machine,
big with armed men, while boys and virgin girls

sang hymns and joyed to lay hand to the lines.
240 Into mid-city the menacing mass rolled on.
O homeland, god-land, Troy! O Dardan walls
famed for your soldier sons! Four times it balked
at the sill, four times its belly rang with arms,
but we pushed on, forgetful, blind, and mad,
245 to set the luckless monster in our fort.
Even then Cassandra cried, 'Death! Men will die!'
but Apollo had bid the Trojans never heed her.
In festive mood (poor souls! this day would be
our last!), we banked our hallowed shrines with flowers.

250 "The vault of heaven turned; night rushed from Ocean
enfolding in vast darkness earth and sky
and Myrmidon guile; on the walls our sentries lay
scattered, wordless, weary, sound asleep.
Now came the Argive ships in battle line
255 from Tenedos under a silent, friendly moon,
heading for well-known shores. A torch flamed out
from the royal ship. Sinon, by unkind fates
preserved, softly slipped back the bolts of pine
and freed the Greeks from the womb. The opened horse
260 released them; glad from that wooden cave they poured.
Thessander, Sthenelus—lords—and dire Ulysses
let down a rope and slid, then Acamas, Thoas,
Machaon, next Neoptolemus, son of Achilles,
Menelaus, and he who laid the plot, Epeus.
265 They fell on a city buried in sleep and wine,
murdered the watch, threw open the gates, let in
their friends—a column of schemers, hand in hand.

"It was the hour when gentle sleep first comes,
welcome, by God's grace, welcome to weary men.
270 I dreamed, and there before my eyes stood Hector,
sorrowed and sad, his face a flood of tears.
He seemed as when the chariot dragged him: bruised,
bloody, dusty, thongs through his swollen feet.

O God! How he looked! How changed from that great man,
275 the Hector who wore Achilles' armor home,
who hurled into Argive ships our Trojan fire.
His beard all dirt, his hair was stiff with blood;
he wore each wound he'd earned before our walls—
our fathers' walls. I dreamed that I wept, too,
280 and hailed the man and let my grief pour out:
'O light of Troy! Dardania's hope unfailing!
What held you, Hector? Where have you been? How long
we waited! Your people—so many of them are dead;
our men, our city have borne so many trials!
285 We are weary! We see you—but what is wrong? Your face
is clouded dark: Why? Why do I see these wounds?'
He said no word, nor heeded my vain questions,
but with a groan drawn deep from a burdened heart,
'Run, goddess-born,' he cried; 'run from these flames!
290 Greece owns our walls; the towers of Troy are tumbling!
To country and king all debts are paid; my hand
had saved them, if any hand had power to save.
Her holy things, her gods, Troy trusts to you.
Take them to share your fate; find walls for them:
295 wander the wide sea over, then build them great.'
He spoke, and in my hands laid mighty Vesta,
her ribbons, and—from her inmost shrine—her fire.

"And now from the walls came screams and cries and groans.
Louder and louder, although my father's house
300 was set far off, apart, well screened by trees,
came the noise of battle, the terrible clash of arms.
I shook off sleep, and climbed to the highest peak
of the roof, and there I stopped and strained to hear:
as when a flame by wild winds driven falls
305 on a grain field, or a mountain stream in flood
sweeps farms, sweeps crops away and plowman's toil,
and topples trees; the shepherd high on his cliff,
hearing the thunderous noise, sits blank with fear.
Then all—the word of honor, the Argive lie—

310 came clear. Deiphobus' palace crashed and fell
in a roof-high holocaust; Ucalegon's next
caught fire; the straits reflected back the flames.
I heard men shouting, heard the trumpet-call.
Like a fool I seized my sword—what sense had swords?
315 But I was ablaze to round up men for war   favor ?
and with them rush to the fort; a senseless rage
propelled me: 'Glory!' I thought. 'To die in battle!'

"But here came Panthus running from Greek spears—
Panthus, priest of Apollo on Castle Hill—
320 arms full of holy things and conquered gods,
trailed by his grandson, panicking toward the gates.
'Panthus, how do we stand? What have we gained?'
He cut me off and answered with a groan:
'Dardania's end, her scapeless hour has come.
325 Trojan and Troy, we've had our day, our power,
our glory. A heartless Jove has handed all
to the Greeks. Our city is ashes! Greece is lord!
The horse stands tall inside our fort, and births
her soldiers. Sinon, prancing his glory-dance,
330 sets fire on fire. Through gates flung wide, they come,
those myriads—all who marched from great Mycenae.
Posts have been set, spear locked with spear, to block
our streets; they stand, a line of shining steel,
blades ready for blood. Our first-line watch can scarce
335 form battle rank; they fight without command.'

"The words of Panthus and God's holy will
sent me toward flames and fighting, where Mars roared
his challenge, and battle cries rose up to heaven.
Friends joined me: Rhipeus and that champion,
340 Epytus, guided by moonlight; Hypanis, Dymas
fell in at my side, and young Coroebus, too,
the son of Mygdon, just now come to Troy,
fired with foolish passion for Cassandra
(accepted, he fought for Priam and his people—

345 unlucky youth, who would not heed the word
of his prophetic princess!) .
I watched them boldly form a battle group,
then spoke to them: 'Good men, brave hearts—but brave
for nothing! If you feel you must fight on
350 and dare to the end, you see how fortune stands.
They've gone from every temple, every shrine,
the gods who blessed our power. You seek to save
a city in flames. But on to war! We'll die!
Sole hope of the vanquished is their hopelessness!'
355 This fired their mad young hearts afresh. Like wolves
hot for a kill at murky midnight, blind,
driven by horrid belly-lust—their cubs
are waiting with blood-parched throats—through hostile arms
we rushed to certain death, and held our way
360 through mid-town; night swung sable wings around us.
That night of ruin, night of death—who'd tell
its story or match our sorrows with his tears?
An ancient city, queen of the ages, fell;
the dead men lay by thousands in her streets,
365 in home and palace, at the hallowed gates
of gods. Nor only Trojans paid their lives;
sometimes courage returned to conquered hearts,
and Danaan victors died. Here grief heartrending,
terror, and death over all in countless forms.

370 "Androgeos first approached us, at the head
of a column of Greeks; mistakenly he thought
us comrades in arms and spoke to us as friends:
'Hurry, men! You are late! What held you back
so long? The rest have ripped and stripped and fired
375 Troy. Have you just now left the tall-sparred ships?'
He broke off then (our answers seemed not made
for trust) and sensed he'd fallen midst enemies.
He stopped, clapped hand to mouth, and stumbled back.
As one who, feeling his way through brambles, steps
380 on a sudden snake, jumps and shudders and runs
from head held high to strike, and hood spread wide—

just so Androgeos saw and jumped and fled.
Shield lapped to shield, we charged and hemmed them in.
On unknown ground, they panicked; one by one
385 we killed them. Fortune blessed our first assault.
Our luck now made Coroebus' heart beat high;
'Look! Fortune,' he said, 'has shown us how to win!
Success lies where she points the way: let's follow!
Let's take their shields and wear the Greek device
390 ourselves. Deceit or daring, in war, who cares?
Arms are here for the taking.' He spoke, and seized
Androgeos' plumed helmet and his shield
with its proud device, and buckled on his sword.
Rhipeus, Dymas and all their company
395 laughed as they took the spoil to arm themselves.
Under false signs we mingled with the Greeks
and mounted many a battle while night was blind,
and sent to Orcus many a man of Greece.
Still others scattered and ran for trusted ship
400 and shore, while others in shame and terror climbed
the horse again, to cower in its great belly.

"'Man, trust not the gods except with their consent!'
Here, dragged by her long, long hair, came Priam's daughter,
holy and virgin, torn from Minerva's shrine;
405 in vain toward heaven she turned her burning eyes—
eyes, for her soft, young hands were bound with chains.
This sight Coroebus could not bear; his heart
went wild; he rushed against their ranks to die.
Behind him we charged in a body, sword by sword.
410 And now—disaster! Down from the temple's top
came Trojan spears to spill our wretched blood:
our arms and plumes had wrongly marked us Greeks.
Then—for we'd seized the girl—the Argives roared
with fury, formed ranks and charged: Ajax the chief,
415 the twin Atridae, the whole Thessalian host;
as when sometimes the winds whirl till they burst
then crash head-on: Westerly, South, and East

rich with his Orient steeds; the woodlands wail
and Nereus stirs his deeps to foam and fury.
420 And those whom darkness and our stratagem
had put to flight pell-mell down every street
now showed themselves; they first detected shields
and swords not ours, and caught our foreign speech.
Sheer numbers crushed us; first Coroebus fell
425 by hand of Peneleus at Minerva's altar;
and Rhipeus died, the justest man that lived
in Troy, unwavering servant of the right
(yet heaven forsook him) ; Hypanis died, and Dymas
transfixed by friends; not all your piety,
430 Panthus, could save you, nor Apollo's bands.
Ashes of Troy! Last flame of all I loved!
Bear witness that at your death I never shrank
from sword or sorrow, and had Fate so decreed
I had earned a death at Grecian hands! We ran,
435 Iphitus, Pelias, and I—one old and tired,
the other limping from Ulysses' wound—
straight toward the sound of war by Priam's palace.

"Here was huge battle to make all other strife
and death through all the city seem like nothing.
440 Here Mars ran wild, and Argives rushed the walls;
we saw them march the 'tortoise' toward the gates.
Up went the ladders next to the very doors;
men climbed the rungs; their left hands held their shields,
bulwark to blows; their right hands seized the roof.
445 Our Trojans on their side ripped loose and flung
whole towers and rooftrees; seeing the end had come,
as death approached they made these weapons serve.
Gilt beams, the glory that roofed their sires of old,
they tumbled down, while others bared their blades
450 and stood to the doors, a barricade of men.
Our strength came back; we ran toward Priam's walls
to help our friends and give the vanquished courage.

"There was a secret hall and door, a passage
between the royal mansions—a gate that none
455 would notice; often, while our throne held firm,
Andromache—poor thing!—had walked this way
taking her son to grandsire or to uncle.
Here I slipped in and climbed to the roof; there stood
our Trojans, hurling spear on useless spear.
460 On a steep gable stood a tower, the peak
of the palace, where we were wont to keep the watch
over Troy and Grecian fleet and Argive camp.
We hacked at this where tower and rooftop joined—
the fabric's weakest spot—and tore it loose
465 from its base and pushed it over; down it went
to crack and shatter and scatter its fragments far
over Argive troops. But more marched up, though stones
and weapons of every kind rained down.

"At the very door of the palace Pyrrhus pranced
470 with a flourish and brazen flash of spear and blade—
like a snake fed on foul herbs, come from his hole
swollen from long, cold months beneath the soil.
Stripping his skin he turns out sleek and young
and ripples his liquid coils; he lofts his head
475 up toward the sun and flicks his three-forked tongue.
Periphas and Achilles' charioteer,
the squire Automedon, all the Scyrians, too,
charged the palace and tossed fire toward the roof.
Pyrrhus was leader; he seized a double ax,
480 chopped through the threshold and ripped out post and hinge,
fittings and all, then hacked at oaken beam
and panel to make a huge hole gaping wide.
There stood the house revealed, there stood its halls,
the home of Priam, of a long line of kings;
485 there at his doorway stood his bodyguard.
Inside the house rose cries and screams of terror
commingled, while the caverned inmost vaults

shrieked with the women; the outcry struck the stars.
Mothers in fright ran madly round the halls,
490 threw arms about the columns and kissed them close.
On pressed Pyrrhus, strong as his father; nor bolts
nor guards could hold him back. Crash! came the ram;
down fell the door; down tumbled post and hinge.
Force paved a way; in burst the Greeks to slaughter
495 the guard and fill the palace, wall to wall.
Not so from a broken dam a stream bursts forth
that foams and swirls and sweeps the dikes away;
its crest runs raging over field and plain
to bear off beast and barn. I saw blood drive
500 men mad: Achilles' son, the twin Atridae;
I saw Hecuba, her hundred daughters: Priam
fouling with blood the altar flame he'd blessed.
His fifty rooms, rich hope of a line of sons—
pillars of Orient gold, girt proud with spoils—
505 all fell. Where fire failed, the Argive ruled.

"Perhaps you wish to know how Priam died.
There lay his city—lost, there lay the ruin
that was his palace, there at his hearth, a foe.
The old king threw his armor, long unused,
510 on his shaking shoulders—useless gesture!—bound
his sword at his waist, and rushed to fight and die.
Within the close, beneath heaven's naked pole,
stood a high altar; nearby an old bay tree
leaned toward it and wrapped the household gods in shade.
515 Here Hecuba and her daughters vainly fled
headlong (like doves before the black rain cloud)
and tight in a ring sat suppliant round the gods.
Then she saw Priam dressed in his young man's arms
and said, 'What dreadful madness, my poor lord,
520 led you to wear those weapons? Where will you charge?
This is no hour for help like yours, no time
for such defense—no, even were Hector here.

Come, stand by me; this altar shall shield us all,
or you will die with us.' So saying, she placed
525   the old man at her side on holy ground.

"Here now, escaped from Pyrrhus' blade, Polites,
a son of Priam, dashed through enemy lines,
ran down the cloisters and round the empty halls,
wounded. Enraged at having missed his aim,
530   Pyrrhus pursued him, caught him, and stabbed him down.
He crawled on, till before his parents' eyes
he fell, and with his blood coughed out his life.
Then Priam, though death already gripped him round,
could not hold back or check his angry words:
535   'You murderer!' he cried. 'You foul blasphemer!
If heaven has righteous gods to mark such acts,
oh, may they thank you well and pay the price
you've earned, who made me watch my own son die,
and with his death befouled a father's eyes.
540   Achilles—you lie, to say you are his son!—
never treated me so! I came a suppliant,
an enemy, yet he honored me and gave me
Hector's corpse to bury and sent me home.'
With that, the old king hurled his harmless spear
545   to touch and clang against the shield; it stopped
and dangled useless from the brazen boss.
Then Pyrrhus: 'Be my enemy! Tell your tale
to my father! Remember: call me barbarous
and name me "Neoptolemus, unworthy son!"
550   Now die!' He dragged him to the altar, faint
and slipping in the blood his son had shed.
His left hand gripped the old man's hair; his right
drew out a sword and sank it in his side.
So Priam died. His final, fated glance
555   fell on a Troy in ashes, on the ruins
of Pergama—sometime proud imperial power,

'of Asia, king.' On the strand his vast frame lies,
head torn from shoulders, a corpse without a name.

"Then for the first time, savage fear closed round me.
560 I froze. My own dear father's form rose up
as I watched the old king through that horrid wound
gasp out his life. Creusa—alone!—rose up:
my house—in ruins! My son, Iulus—where?
I turned about: What forces still remained?
565 Not a man! Heartsick and beaten, they had leaped
to the street or thrown themselves into the flames.

"I alone survived—but no! By Vesta's shrine,
lurking wordless, hiding in a dark corner—
Helen! I saw her lighted by the flames
570 as I searched the ruins, looking everywhere.
She feared the fury of a vanquished Troy,
Greek vengeance, a deserted husband's anger.
A fiendish curse to friend and foe alike,
hated, she'd sought asylum at the altar.
575 Flame burst in my heart as anger cried, 'Revenge,
for a country lost! Penalty, for her crimes!
Shall she, unscathed, see Sparta? Shall she march
in royal triumph through Mycenae's streets?
She, see her husband, her father's house, her children,
580 trailed by the women of Troy, her Orient slaves?
Yet death by the sword for Priam? Troy in flames?
A shore so often drenched in Trojan blood?
Never! Although men win no fame or glory
for punishing women (such victory earns no praise),
585 still to have stamped out sin, and made it pay
due price, is good; good, too, to fill the heart
with vengeful flame and vindicate the dead.'
Such the wild thoughts that swept my heart along
when—never before so clear for eye to see—
590 a vision shone through darkness, pure and bright:

my loving mother, goddess confessed, her form
and stature as in heaven. She seized my hand
and held me hard; her sweet lips spoke to me:
'My son, what pain has roused such unchecked wrath?
595 Are you mad, or have you lost all thought of me?
What? Not look first where your old father waits,
Anchises? See if yet Creusa lives,
your wife? Your son, Ascanius? All around them
Greeks walk their lines at will; but for my care,
600 flames or an enemy blade had borne them off.
No blame to Helen of Sparta's hated face;
no, nor to Paris: gods, the pitiless gods,
threw down the might and golden towers of Troy.
Look, for I'll rip it all away—the cloud
605 that blocks and blunts your mortal sight, hung dank
and dark around you; you must never fear
a mother's word or disregard her wish.
Here where you see the masonry all tumbled,
stone upon stone, where dust and smoke boil up,
610 Neptune is rocking our walls, and with his trident
knocking their base-blocks loose; our homes and halls
he'll pull to the ground. There, at the Scaean gates,
Juno in blood-lust waves her columns on
from the ships with her drawn sword.
615 Look back! On Castle Hill Tritonia sits
in a cloud of flame, flashing her Gorgon head.
Our father himself gives comfort, power, and strength
to the Greeks—yes, hurls the gods against our arms.
Hurry, my son! Take flight! Call this work done!
620 I am always with you, to guide you safely home!'
She spoke, and hid herself in night's black shades.
There rose up faces full of death and hate
for Troy—a ghastly glory of gods.

"Then came collapse; I saw all Ilium fall
625 in flames—saw Neptune's Troy come crashing down.
As when on mountain top an ancient ash

is hacked by the steel; blow after blow falls
as farmers vie at the felling. The old tree leans,
her foliage shakes, she bows her stricken crown,
630   till bit by bit her wounds win out. She groans
her last and falls and strews the ridge with wreckage.

"Divine grace led me down through flame and foe
with ease; swords made a way and flames fell back.

"Soon as I stepped inside my father's house
635   and ancient home, I sought him out and begged
he'd let me carry him off to the high hills.
He answered, No: his Troy was lost, and life
in exile not for him. 'You young in years
and blood,' said he, 'who yet own strength and sinew,
640   do you take thought for flight.
If heaven had wished me further years of life
they'd saved my home for me. Enough that once
I lived to see my city fall and die.
Just let me lie here; say farewell and leave me.
645   I'll find death by myself. The Greeks will say
"Too bad!" and strip my corpse. A grave's well lost.
I've lived unloved of heaven, useless, old,
for years, since Jove, the father of gods and men,
touched and scorched me with lightning's fiery breath.'

650   "He spoke and stood his ground, unmoved, unmoving.
But we burst out in tears—my wife Creusa,
Ascanius, our whole house—'He must not ruin
us all, or hasten the death that threatens us.'
He would not change, or leave his chosen spot.
655   I turned to my arms with bitter prayer to die.
What plans could be; what fortune granted now?
'You think, sir, I could take one step and leave
you here? Monstrous! This, from a father's lips?
If by God's law our city must be destroyed,
660   and you are resolved to cap the death of Troy

with death of you and yours, that door stands wide:
Pyrrhus is coming bathed in Priam's blood—
son before father, father by altar slain.
For this you haled me, mother, through steel and flame,
665   that I might see the enemy in my house,
and you, Ascanius, and Creusa too,
heaped in one bloody sacrificial pile?
Arms, men! To arms! We're lost! Our last day calls us!
Back to the Greeks! I'll see the fight renewed
670   once more. We shall not all die unavenged!'

"I buckled my sword again and strapped my shield
to my left arm with care, then moved outside.
But there at the door my wife fell at my feet
and kissed them, and held Iulus out to me:
675   'You go to die? Take us, too—anywhere!
But if experience gives you faith in arms,
guard first your home. Abandon us? Your son,
your father, me—once called your wife? To whom?'

"While thus she pleaded, filling the house with sobs—
680   wonder to tell!—a miracle occurred.
There in our arms, before his parents' eyes,
Iulus' little cap, right at its peak,
seemed to shed light. A harmless flame licked down
to touch his hair and play about his brow.
685   In panic terror we slapped at his burning hair
and tried to quench the holy flame with water.
But father Anchises smiled, and raising eyes
toward heaven, spread out his hands, and spoke in prayer:
'Almighty Jove, if any prayer can move you,
690   look down and for our merit grant just this:
a sign, father! Confirm this omen for us!'

"Scarce had he spoken when with sudden crash
came thunder on the left; down the dark sky

a meteor fell in a burst of sparks and flame.
695 We watched it glide high over roof and hall
—so bright!—then bury itself in Ida's woods,
its path marked clear. Behind it, furrow and line
shed light and left a smoking reek of sulphur.
My father now was certain; he turned toward heaven,
700 hailed godhead, and adored the holy star:
'No hesitation now! Lead on! I'll follow,
gods of my fathers! Oh, save my house and line!
Yours was that sign; your will embraces Troy.
I yield, my son; I'll gladly share your way.'

705 "Just then through our walls we heard a louder noise
of fire and closer rolled the holocaust.
'Come then, dear father, and climb upon my back.
Ride on my shoulders; the load will not be heavy.
Whatever may happen, we'll share a single risk,
710 a single rescue. Iulus, little son,
walk by me! Wife, stay back, but trace my steps!
And all you others, listen to my words!
Outside the city is a hill and shrine
of Ceres, long unused; nearby, a cypress,
715 gnarled, and for years held sacred by our fathers.
Each go your way; we'll meet at that one spot.
You, father, carry our holies and household gods.
Fresh come from all the fighting, blood, and death,
I dare not touch them till I wash my hands
720 in running water.'
With that I spread across my neck and shoulders
a cloak, and over that a lion's skin,
and lifted my burden; little Iulus seized
my right hand, following two steps to my one;
725 behind us, my wife. We moved through pitch-black plazas,
and I was afraid, though minutes before no spear
nor prowling Greek patrol had worried me.
I started at every breeze; at every sound

I stiffened, fearful alike for father and son.
730 And now I was near the gate, and clear, I thought,
of the streets, when all at once I caught the sound
of many marching feet. My father peered
through the night, and cried out, 'Hurry, son; they're coming.
I see their shields alight and the flash of blades.'
735 I panicked then, as some strange, unkind power
left me confused and mindless. Hurrying down
byways, I'd left familiar streets behind,
when Creusa—she was gone! Did cruel death take her?
Or had she lost her way? Or stopped to rest?
740 We've never known, nor ever seen her since.
I had not turned around nor marked her lost
until we reached the hill and ancient shrine
of Ceres. Here as we called the roll we found
her missing. Son nor husband—none had seen her.
745 Half mad, I railed at everyone, god and man:
What had I seen in captured town more cruel?
My son, my father, the household gods of Troy,
I left to my men, deep hidden in the hills.
I turned back to the city, armed again,
750 determined to take my chances, to go back
through all of Troy, and risk my life once more.
First to the walls and that half-hidden gate
where I'd gone out, I turned, and traced my steps
back through the night, my eyes' own light my guide;
755 no sound relieved the prickling sense of fear.
Then on to my house: Had she—had she perhaps
gone there? All doors were down, Greeks everywhere.
My house was wrapped in flames; wind-whipped they licked
at the roof, then raced in triumph toward the sky.
760 I ran to Priam's palace and the fort:
there on the empty porch of Juno's temple
a squad of sentries with Phoenix and Ulysses
were guarding the spoils. Here all the wealth of Troy,
ripped from her burning temples—holy tables,
765 wine bowls of solid gold, and captured vestments—

were heaped. Mothers and children, a long, long line,
terrified, stood nearby.
I even dared to shout. I filled the night
and dark streets with my sobbing cries: 'Creusa!'
770 No answer! 'Creusa!' I called, again, again.
I was pressing my search from house to endless house
when a luckless ghost, Creusa's very shade,
rose to my sight—her likeness, taller than life.
My hair stood up in terror; my voice stuck fast.
775 But then she spoke and banished all my fears:
'Why such indulgence of a pointless pain,
dear husband? Nothing but by the will of God
has happened. You were not meant to take Creusa
with you; so rules the lord of tall Olympus.
780 Go into exile; furrow the empty sea
to a western land of men and fertile fields,
where Tiber pours his gentle Tuscan stream.
There is your birthright: wealth, a throne, a queen.
You loved Creusa; but brush away your tears.
785 I'll catch no sight of Thessaly's haughty halls—
not I!—nor humbly serve the dames of Greece,
I, child of Dardanus, wife of Venus' son.
No; the mother of gods detains me here.
Farewell, and always love the son we share.'
790 With that, for all my tears, for all I hoped
to say, she turned to emptiness and air.
Three times I tried to fold her in my arms,
three times for nothing! The ghost-thing fled my grasp,
light as a breeze, most like the wings of sleep.
795 The night was gone when I rejoined my friends.

"And here I stood in wonder at the crowd
of people newly come—mothers and men,
children, huddled for exile—poor, lost souls.
They'd brought what they could save; they'd brought their
  courage;

800 they'd follow the course I set, no matter where.
And now the dawn star rose from Ida's heights
to bring the day. Greek guards were everywhere,
at every gate. We knew no help could come.
Bearing my father, I started toward the hills."

BOOK THREE

"With Asian power and Priam's tribe uprooted,
though blameless, by heaven's decree; with Ilium's pride
fallen, and Neptune's Troy all smoke and ash,
God's oracles drove us on to exile, on
5   to distant, lonely lands. We built a fleet
down by Antander and Ida's Phrygian peaks,
uncertain which way Fate led or where to stop.
We marshaled our men. When summer first came on
Anchises bade us trust our sails to fate.
10 With tears I left the shores and ports of home,
the land that once was Troy, and sailed away
with friends and son, with gods both small and great.

"Miles off, the land of Mars lay wide and flat
(Thracians farm it; Lycurgus was once its king),
15 friend and ally of Troy from ancient times
in our good days. I sailed there. Near the shore
I laid out a town (Fate frowned on my attempt)
and coined the name 'Aeneadae' from my name.

"I offered prayer to Venus and to all gods
20 who bless new ventures, and for heaven's high king
I thought to slaughter a white bull by the shore.
Nearby was a mound, so happened; a dogwood tree
grew on its top, and myrtle thick with thorns.
As I stepped over to pull the greening shrubs
25 from the soil, to deck my altar with leafy boughs,
I saw a fearsome portent, strange to tell:

49

The first bush that I broke loose from its root
and pulled from the ground oozed blood in dead black drops
and spotted the earth with gore. My hair stood up
30 in a chill; I shivered; my blood congealed with fear.
Trying again, I tugged the pliant stalk
next on, seeking the cause I could not see:
from its bark, too, the dark black blood ran down.
Puzzled, I muttered prayers to the rural Nymphs
35 and to Mars the father, who rules the Getic plains:
'Oh, bless this sign; may it rest light upon us!'
I attacked a third stalk then. Down on my knees
I pulled and worked and battled with the sand,
when—dare I tell it?—deep in the mound, I heard
40 a moan of sorrow, and words came to my ears:
'Aeneas, why tear at the tortured? Spare my tomb;
spare to pollute clean hands. I am of Troy,
no stranger to you. No plant has shed that blood.
Run from this heartless land, this greedy shore.
45 I'm Polydorus. Transfixed by steel, I grow
a crop of spears and a cover of pointed shafts.'
What should I do? Fear pressed upon my heart,
my hair stood up in terror, my voice stuck fast.

"This Polydorus had once been sent by Priam,
50 with sacks of gold, covertly, to the king
of Thrace for safety—trust in Trojan arms
was waning and our city ringed with steel.
When Ilium's power collapsed and Fortune left her,
this king joined Agamemnon's conquering arms;
55 defying the right, he killed Polydorus and seized
his gold. (To what do you not drive men's hearts,
damned money-lust!) When trembling left my limbs,
I summoned our chosen leaders—my father first—
told of the sign, and asked their views and votes.
60 They all agreed: to leave this land of crime,
where guest law was blasphemed, and put to sea.
We gave Polydorus new burial and piled high

his mound with earth; an altar to his ghost
stood dark with ribbons of grief and cypress wreaths;
65 round it the women of Troy let down their hair.
We brought up pitchers foaming with warm milk,
and plates of hallowed blood. His soul we laid
in the tomb and called his name that loud last time.

"Soon as we trusted the ocean, and winds brought peace
70 to the waters, and Auster called us soft to sea,
my men hauled down the ships and filled the shore.
We sailed from port; the lands and towns receded.
In mid-sea lies an isle * much-loved and sacred
to the Nereids' mother and Neptune the Aegean.
75 It floated free until the archer-god
bound it to Gyaros and Myconos' cliffs,
to be a base for homes and mock the winds.
Here we found peace for the weary and safe haven;
on Apollo's ground we stepped out reverently.
80 Up ran King Anius—king at once and priest
of Apollo (he wore his bands and sacred crown
of laurel) . He knew Anchises, an old, old friend.
He made us welcome and led us to his home.

"I prayed the god in a temple of moldered stone:
85 'Apollo, grant us a home, grant walls to the weary,
a city to last, a bloodline; save this second
Troy, these few that Achilles and Greece have left.
Who will guide us, and where? Where shall we settle?
Grant, father, a sign; come and possess our hearts.'

90 "Scarce had I spoken when suddenly all things shook,
the temple, the sacred laurel; the whole hill moved
around us. The shrine sprang open; the tripod clanged.
As we fell prostrate, a voice came to our ears:
'Oh, Dardans! Hardy men! The land that first
95 gave you and your fathers birth, with wealth and joy

* Delos (see Glossary).

will take you back. Look for your ancient mother.
Here shall Aeneas' line rule all the world—
his sons, their sons, the sons to be born of them.'
So Phoebus. My men raised shouts and cheers of joy
100 commingled. They asked in a body what walls these were,
where they must wander, where Phoebus bade return.
Then father, recalling the records of men long gone,
said, 'Hear me, you captains, and learn what we may hope.
Crete, island of Jove the king, lies in mid-sea;
105 there stands Mount Ida, and there our tribe was cradled.
Men live in a hundred cities there, rich realms.
Thence, if I read memory right, our sire,
Teucer the great, first sailed to Cape Rhoeteum
and chose that spot to rule. (No Troy yet stood,
110 nor walls of Pergama. Men lived in the hollows.)
Hence came great Cybele and her priests, their songs
and Idaean groves, their rite of silent prayer;
here lions learned to draw our lady's car.
Come, let us follow where the gods command;
115 pray to the winds, and make for Cnossus' throne.
It's no far course; if only Jove be with us,
three days will set our fleet on Cretan sands.'
With that, he made due offering at the altar:
for Neptune, a bull; a bull for the lord Apollo,
120 and lambs—black for Tempest; for Zephyr, white.

"Report ran that Idomeneus had been driven
from his father's throne, that Cretan shores were desert,
no enemy there, and empty, waiting homes.
We left Ortygia's port and sped downwind,
125 past Naxos' Mount of Bacchus, green Donusa,
the Isle of Olives, white Paros, and the Sea
of the Circling Isles—waters thick-flecked with lands.
Sometimes we raced; loud rose the coxswain's cry:
'On, men, to Crete! To our ancestral home!'
130 As we sailed on, the wind rose brisk astern;
at last we raised the Curetes' ancient shore.

City we prayed for! I hurried to build its walls
and name it 'New Pergama,' to our people's joy;
I bade them love their homes and fortify them.
135   And now our hauled-out ships were nearly dry;
young couples married and worked their new-found farms.
I was granting titles and lands, when heaven turned foul
and dropped upon us a sudden, wretched rot;
trees wilted, too, and crops: the year brought death.
140   Men left sweet life or dragged themselves about
plague-stricken; Sirius scorched the sterile fields,
while pastures withered and blight denied us food.
'Back to Ortygia's oracle, back to Apollo!'
my father urged. 'Go pray for his good will!
145   What end to suffering? Whence does he bid us seek
help for our troubles? Where must we lay our course?'

"It was night, sleep held all creatures here on earth,
when—holy vision!—the Phrygian household gods
I'd brought with me from Troy, and from her flames
150   had rescued, seemed to rise before my eyes
as I lay sleeping. A bright light showed them clear
where through the window frames a full moon shone.
They spoke and with their words washed care away:
'What you would sail to Ortygia to learn,
155   Apollo will tell you here. Unasked, he sent us!
We followed you and your sword from flaming Troy,
and under you sailed over the swollen sea;
Some day we'll place your sons among the stars,
and bring your city power. For greatness, build
160   great walls! Your way is long, but don't grow weary!
Move on! Apollo of Delos never meant
these shores, nor bade you make your home in Crete.
There is a place called "Westland" by the Greeks,
an ancient country, powerful, warlike, rich;
165   the Oenotri settled it; now, we hear, their sons
are calling it "Italy" for their founder's name.
Here is our rightful home; hence Dardanus sprang

and father Iasius, hero, first of our line.
Arise! Rejoice! Go tell your aged sire
170 our words! Have faith! Seek Corythus and the land
Ausonia! Jove forbids you Dicte's plain.'
Amazed at the sight and at this holy voice
(it was no dream; those gods were *there;* I saw
their features, ribbons, hair, their moving lips;
175 and icy sweat ran over all my body),
I tore myself from bed and stretched my hands,
with a cry toward heaven, and sprinkled on the hearth
pure offerings. My office done, in joy
I told Anchises the story, straight and true.
180 He saw his error: two lines, two ancestors
confused, and two old place-names interchanged.
He spoke then: 'Son, beset by Ilium's fate,
Cassandra alone told me such things would be.
She said (I recall) this was ordained for us,
185 and often cried, "The Westland!" "Italy's throne!"
But who'd have thought that Teucrians would leave
for lands in the West? Who'd heed Cassandra then?
Phoebus has warned us; obey him and be wise.'
We heard his word and shouted our assent.
190 This home we abandoned, too (some stayed behind),
to course wide ocean in our hollow ships.

"Once we had got to sea, and no more lands
were to be seen—just sky and water alone—
a slatey rain cloud rose above my head
195 to bring us night and storm and shadowed squall.
The wind set waters rolling; waves rose up
huge, to scatter and toss us over the swirl.
Clouds covered the sky; a dripping night stole heaven
away; redoubled lightning split the murk.
200 Driven off course, we wandered unknown waters.
Palinurus himself could not tell night from day,
nor call his course to mind, there in mid-sea.
Three days the sun was dimmed by blinding fog

as we blandered about; three nights there were no stars.
205 The fourth day brought us in sight of land at last
with mountains visible far, and coils of smoke.
We dropped the sails and leaped to oars; our men
heaved, swept, and churned blue water into foam.
I first from the waves found safety on those shores,
210 the Strophades (Greek for 'the Spinners'); the islands lie
in the broad Ionian, home of dread Celaeno
and all Harpies, since Phineus' house was locked
and they fled in terror from their former feast.
No monster grimmer than they, no plague more savage,
215 no wrath of God, has fled the shores of Styx.
They are women, but winged; the refuse of their bellies
is foul; their hands are taloned, and they wear
an endless pallor of hunger.
As we bore in and entered port, we saw
220 herds of fat cattle wandering the fields,
and a flock of goats, unguarded, in the grass.
We hurried to slaughter and called on Jove himself
and the gods to share our booty; on the beach
we spread our couches and set out the rich, fat feast.
225 But here, from the hills, with a shriek and sudden swoop
the Harpies came; loudly they rattled their wings.
They tore at our meats and left their filthy prints
over all; they croaked, and stank like carrion death.
Once more in a pocket beneath a rocky ledge,
230 locked in by trees and awe-inspiring shade,
we set the tables and built fresh altar fires;
once more, from a different place, from unseen dens,
the noisy flock flew round and clawed their spoil;
their spittle fouled our feast. 'Men, fetch your arms,'
235 I shouted. 'We'll drive the fiendish creatures off!'
As ordered, they hid their swords in handy spots
under grass, and laid their shields in hiding-holes.
Then, when the birds came shrieking down the shore,
Misenus from a hilltop gave a signal
240 on hollow brass. My men attacked—strange war!—

they strove to bloody those filthy birds with steel.
But nothing pierced their plumage; never a wound
they got, but fled off flapping toward the stars,
leaving half-eaten meats fouled by their claws.

245 Alone on a spire of rock Celaeno settled
(that voice of doom) and from her throat broke speech:
'What, war? Slaughter our cows, stampede our steers,
and then make war, you sons of Laomedon,
and drive us guiltless from our native land?

250 Well then, hear this, and nail it to your heart—
the Almighty told it to Phoebus, Phoebus to me;
now I, chief of the Furies, declare it to you.
You sail for Italy and pray for winds:
you'll go to Italy, pass into her harbors,

255 but never wall your promised city round
till hunger, and guilt for what you murdered here,
shall make you gnaw your tables halfway through.'
She spoke, spread wing, and fled into the woods.
My men shuddered. An icy fear congealed

260 their blood; their spirits fell. They'd fight no more,
but beg for peace, they said, with prayer and vow,
if those were goddesses or gruesome birds.
Anchises on the shore spread wide his hands,
called on the powers, and bade obeisance due:

265 'O gods, these threats forfend! Avert this fate!
Be kind! Preserve the faithful!' Then, 'Cut loose
the moorings!' he cried. 'Free lines, and let them run!'
The South Wind filled our sails; on foaming waves
we sped where wind and pilot laid our course.

270 Now in mid-sea we raised tree-clad Zacynthus,
Dulichium, Samë, Neritos steep and rocky;
we raced by Ithaca's cliffs, Laertes' realm,
and cursed the land that suckled cruel Ulysses.
Soon, too, Leucata's clouded mountain peaks

275 and Apollo, terror of sailors, came to view.
Here we sought rest, close by a little town.
The anchors went out; the fleet lay stern to shore.

"Thus, unexpectedly, we came to land;
we purged our stain and payed our vows to Jove,
280 then, there at Actium, staged the Trojan games.
Stripped and anointed, my men took part in sports
ancestral. (Joy! We'd slipped past all those towns
of Greeks! We'd escaped, though enemies hemmed us in!)
Meanwhile the sun rolled his great circle round,
285 and a wintry North Wind roughened the icy waves.
On an entryway I nailed the curved bronze shield
huge Abas carried, and marked it with a verse:
This shield Aeneas, from the conquering Greeks,
then ordered, 'Man the thwarts and put to sea!'
290 My men vied at the stroke and swept the waters.
Phaeacia's airy towers soon dropped behind;
we skirted Epirus' shores and made the port
of Chaonia, near Buthrotum in the hills.

"Here came report, incredible to our ears,
295 that Helenus, Priam's son, was king in Greece,
possessing the throne of Pyrrhus and his wife—
Andromache gone to a man of Troy once more!
Speechless, my heart aflame with strange desire
to address the king and hear so great a tale,
300 I walked from the harbor, leaving ship and shore.
At the city gates I chanced on funeral foods
and gifts in a grove by a counterfeit Simois;
Andromache there made offering to the dead
and called the ghosts to Hector's grass-grown mound—
305 empty, with twin altars—cause of her tears.
She saw me coming, saw my Trojan arms,
and thought me a phantom of madness and of fear.
She looked and stiffened; the warmth fled from her limbs,
she tottered, but at long last she came to speech:
310 'Is this your face? Is this your voice I hear,
Aeneas? Are you alive? Or if you've lost
the light of life, where is Hector?' She burst out
in a flood of tears and frenzied sobs; I scarce

could put in a stumbling word, now here, now there:
315 'Living, yes—and a life of endless peril.
Never doubt: you see reality.
What fate caught you and cast you from so regal
estate? What fitting fortune came to you,
Hector's Andromache? Still the wife of Pyrrhus?'
320 She bowed her head and spoke as if in shame:
'Of Priam's daughters, call her only blessed
who died beneath the lofty walls of Troy
on hostile tomb. No lots were cast for her;
she was no war prize for some victor's bed.
325 From a home in flames I sailed through many a sea
and bore, the merest slave, the proud contempt
of Achilles' half-grown son. Then he pursued
Hermione, Spartan princess, child of Leda,
and passed me on to Helenus—slave to slave.
330 Orestes, for his stolen bride enflamed
with love, and fury-driven for his crimes,
caught Pyrrhus and killed him at his father's shrine.
At Pyrrhus' death, a share in power passed
to Helenus; he has called this land "Chaonia"
335 for Chaon of Troy, these plains "Chaonian,"
and built in the hills a fort called "Ilium."
But say what winds, what fates have shaped your course?
You could not know the way: what guided you?
Your son—does he still draw the breath of life?
340 In Troy you kept him by you.
And does the boy still miss his poor lost mother?
Does he feel drawn toward old-time strength and courage
by Aeneas, his father, and by his uncle, Hector?'
She spoke in a flood of tears, and as she sobbed
345 long and in vain, down from the walls he came—
King Helenus, Priam's son, with all his guard.
He knew his kin and joyed to lead them home
with a word—then tears—then a word—then floods of tears.
As I walked, I saw it: a little Troy, a fort
350 just like the great one, and a dried-up stream

called 'Xanthus,' a Scaean Gate—I kissed that gate!
My people, too, all shared the city's welcome.
The king received them in his ample halls,
then in mid-court they drank a toast of wine,
355 and ate from golden plates, and raised their cups.

"One day and then a second passed; then breezes
called to our canvas; a Southerly swelled our sails.
I went to our prophet and prince and thus inquired:
'Scion of Troy, God's prophet, who sense the will
360 of Phoebus in tripod and laurel, who know the stars
and the speech of birds, and the meaning of their flight,
tell me (for all sound prophecy foretells
travel, and heaven's universal will
bids me seek Italy and her far-off lands;
365 only the Harpy sang of sacrilege
and strange forebodings, telling a carrion tale
of wrath and hunger), where lie my greatest dangers?
What course will carry me past all obstacles?'
Then Helenus, killing first the ritual calves,
370 prayed for God's peace, and from his hallowed head
untied the ribbons. He took me by the hand
and led me, filled with awe, to Phoebus' temple,
then spoke—a priest and voice of God—these words:

" 'Aeneas, we dare not doubt some greater power
375 sends you across the sea: so Jove allots
men's fate and turns the wheel of history.
I'll tell you a little, to help you cross strange waters
more safely to Ausonia, and come there
to harbor; all the rest the Fates forbid
380 me to know, or Juno says I may not tell.
To begin: This Italy, which you think so close,
whose nearby ports you may invade at will,
lies land past distant land, down trackless ways.
First you must bend oar in Sicilian wave
385 and sail the circuit of Ausonian seas,

the pools of hell, and Circe's Aeaean isle,
before you'll see your city safely founded.
I'll tell you the signs; you lay them to your heart:
In an hour of trouble, beside a far-off stream
390 where oaks grow on the shore, you'll find a sow,
huge lying, having borne her thirty young—
white she will be, white babies at her teats.
Here build your city, find peace and labor's end.
For fated "gnawing of tables," have no fears:
395 Apollo will hearken, and fate will find a way.
But all these lands, these coasts of Italy
nearby, washed by this ocean and this tide:
Shun them! Vile Greeks infest their every town.
Here Locrians of Naryx laid their walls,
400 and here Idomeneus sat his army down
on plains Salentine; here on ramparts rises
Petelia, Philoctetes' modest home.
No—cross the water, and when you come to land,
build altars on the shore and pay your vows;
405 but with a purple shawl veil head and hair,
that while the fires of holy office burn
no view of hostile face confuse the signs.
(Preserve this way of prayer, you and your people;
so may your sons in purity keep the rite.*)
410 Then sail away; the wind will bring you close
to Sicily. Where Pelorus opens out,
bear off to port and follow coast and sea
the long way round. Shun starboard waves and shore.
These lands were once by earthquake ripped and riven
415 (long, long ago; such changes time has wrought!).
They leaped apart, men say, though they had been
one mass before; in rushed a roaring sea
to cut Hesperian from Sicilian shores.

* Vergil here allows himself to imagine how certain features of Roman prayer ritual might have begun. While praying, the priest must not see anything ill-omened or unlucky, for this would vitiate his act of worship; hence, he covers his head.

Now narrow waters ebb and flow between them.
420 The right shore Scylla guards; the left, insatiate
Charybdis. Thrice, in her maelstrom pit, she gulps
the floods deep down, then belches them again
up to the air, to splash the very stars.
But Scylla hides in lightless, caverned lair;
425 her lips reach out to suck ships to the reefs.
Human her face, her lovely breast a girl's—
so to her waist. Below, a shapeless fish,
a womb of wolves, tapered to dolphin's tail.
Better to pass the pillars of Pachynus,
430 taking the time to make the long course round,
than catch one glimpse of that vast-vaulted monster,
Scylla, and of the reefs where blue dogs bark.
Further, if Helenus has prophetic powers
worthy of trust, if God's truth fills his heart,
435 one thing, Aeneas, one thing before all else
I'll tell and advise you, again and again the same:
To Juno the queen make your first adorations;
to Juno, lady of power, chant willing prayers
and win her with humble gifts. So shall you gain
440 passage to Italy from Sicilian shores.
Once set down there, move on to Cumae's town,
her hallowed pools, Avernus' rustling groves.
There you'll find a prophetess: under a cliff
she sings of fate and writes her runes on leaves.
445 The leaves, with their recorded songs, she lays
in order and stores them deep within her cave;
they stay in place and never change their sequence.
But when some door is opened and a breeze,
the merest whisper, stirs the fragile leaves,
450 they flutter all over the cave. She never tries
to catch them, sort them out, or match the lines.
Men leave no wiser, and curse the Sibyl's see.
Count not too high the cost of tarrying here.
Though men complain, though breezes call you brisk
455 to sea and you could fill your canvas full,

still go to the lady, humbly beg her speak
and sing her runes, and let her words flow free.
The peoples of Italy, wars that are to be,
how best to shun or bear each single trial,
460   she'll tell, and map your course to victory.
Thus far my voice may guide you. Go your way
and by your works exalt great Troy to heaven.'

"Thus spoke the prophet with the voice of love,
then ordered gifts heavy with gold and carved
465   ivory, sent to the ships, and crammed the holds
with silver ingots, cauldrons from Dodona,
a suit of mail, hook-linked and twilled with gold,
a shining helmet, peaked with horsehair plumes—
Neoptolemus' arms. Gifts for my father, too,
470   and horses he gave, and guides;
new oars for the ships, new armor for my men.

"Meanwhile Anchises bade the fleet make sail
to catch each minute of a favoring breeze.
With deep respect, Apollo's priest addressed him:
475   'Anchises, whom proud Venus deigned to wed,
heaven-blessed, twice rescued from a ruined Troy,
there lies your land, Ausonia! Sail there now!
But slip on down that coastline, as you must:
the shores Apollo names lie far beyond.
480   Blessed in the goodness of your son, sail on!
I'll say no more, nor block the rising winds.'
Andromache, too, sad at this last farewell,
brought garments pictured with a weft of gold;
for Ascanius, Trojan coats (he too was honored)
485   and piles of gifts of her weaving. Thus she spoke:
'These are for you, to call my hand to mind,
dear child, and witness to the lasting love
of Hector's wife. Take them, our parting gifts,
O image of Astyanax, all that's left me:
490   the eyes, the hands, the face—he bore them so,

and he'd be your age now, a boy like you.'
I turned to go, and tears flowed as I spoke:
'Be happy! Your trials are over, and you know
your fortune. We're hurried on from fate to fate.
495 You have found peace; you need not plow the sea
nor seek Ausonia, land that ever drops
below the horizon. You see Troy and Xanthus—
their likeness—built by your hands, and blessed, I pray,
more richly, and less in the path of Greeks.
500 If ever I enter Tiber and the lands
by Tiber, and see my people's promised walls,
that day shall see our towns, our nations, kin:
Hesperia to Epirus—one in blood
and one in fate; our hearts will build them both
505 one Troy. Be that our mandate to our sons!' *

"We took to the seas close by Ceraunia
whence lies the shortest course to Italy.
The sun went down; black shadows hid the hills.
We found our posts, then stretched out by the waves
510 on earth's dear breast, there where the sand was dry,
and rested. Sleep flowed over our weary limbs.
The Hours had not yet borne Night to mid-course
when Palinurus, never the sluggard, rose
to listen for the breeze and test the winds.
515 He marked each star that crossed the silent night—
Arcturus, the rain stars, and the twin Triones,
and searched all round Orion, armed with gold.
Soon as he saw that heaven was at peace,
he sounded a clear signal. We broke our camp,
520 made way on course, and spread our winging sails.
The stars had fled, when, with the blush of Dawn,
we raised the misty hills and low shore line

* It is not certain what Vergil means here. He may be referring only
to the fact that both settlements were of Trojan origin and hence were
"one." Some have seen a reference to Augustus' founding of Nicopolis in
Epirus.

of Italy. 'Italy, ho!' first cried Achates.
'Ho, Italy!' came my people's shout of joy.
525 Then Father Anchises crowned a mighty bowl
with flowers, filled it with wine, and standing high
on his quarterdeck, called the gods:
'O gods, who govern sea and land and storm,
grant us fair weather and a following wind!'
530 As he prayed, the gusts came faster; now we saw
a harbor, and on a hill Minerva's temple.
My men struck sail and turned our bows toward shore.
The harbor was bent to an arc by eastern waves;
athwart it, reefs in a mist of salty spray
535 hid it. Twin arms, like walls, came sweeping down
from a turreted cliff. The temple stood well back.
I saw first sign: Four horses in a field,
cropping the grass, each by itself, snow-white.
My father spoke: 'Host land, you bring us war.
540 The horse is accoutred for war; these beasts mean war.
Yet sometime, too, they learn to draw the cart,
these four-foot creatures, and wear the reins and yoke:
there's hope of peace.' We prayed to Pallas the holy,
clasher of arms, who first received our thanks
545 (at her altar we veiled our heads with Trojan shawls);
then heeding Helenus' earnest plea, we made
to Juno of Argos our due adorations.

"The minute our prayers and litanies were done,
we braced our yards and sheeted the canvas home,
550 then left these Greekish halls and suspect lands.
Tarentum next (called 'Home of Hercules'),
was seen facing Lacinia's sacred hill,
Fort Caulon, and Point Scylax, grave of ships.
Then far across the strait we saw Mount Aetna
555 and heard a distant roar of reefs and breakers
crashing, strange voicelike sounds along the shore.
The long waves leaped; the tide was roiled with sand.
Then said Anchises: 'See! This is Charybdis,

the rocks that Helenus sang, the dreadful reefs.
560 Put about, men! Stand to the oars, now, all together!'
They obeyed commands. Palinurus took the lead
with a 'Hard a-port!' athwart the howling waves;
with oar and sail the whole fleet swung to port.
Up one vast swirling slope we rode to heaven,
565 then dropped to hell as the wave slipped out from under.
Thrice reefs and hollow caverns gave a roar,
thrice we saw spume and spray that flecked the stars.
The wind, failing at sunset, left us tired;
not knowing our way, we put in to Cyclops land.

570 "The harbor itself is windless, glassy, wide,
but near it Aetna's hideous ruin roars.
Sometimes toward heaven it hurls a dead-black cloud,
a pitchy swirl of smoke and glowing sparks,
and shoots out balls of flame that lick the stars;
575 sometimes it tears its own guts out and heaves
a vomit of boulders; up roll molten rocks
with groans and bubbles and seething, deep, deep down.
Men say Enceladus, scorched half dead by lightning,
lies underneath that mass, with Aetna huge
580 atop him breathing bursts of chimneyed flame;
whenever, wearied, he stirs, all Sicily
grumbles and shakes and veils her sky with smoke.
That night beneath the trees we saw and heard
things eerie, weird, and could assign no cause.
585 There were no fiery comets, no bright bands
of light at the pole; the sky was dark with clouds
and gloomy night enveloped the moon in mist.

"The next day's early light of dawn was rising
and Aurora had cleared the sky of dew and dark
590 when suddenly from the bush a strange, wild shape—
a man in hunger's final hour, all rags—
came running toward the beach, his hands outstretched.
We looked around: filth, stench, a ragged beard,

clothes pinned with thorns, but in all else a Greek,
595 sent once with his father's sword to fight at Troy.
Soon as he saw our Dardan dress, the arms
of Troy, he stumbled, terrified at the sight,
and checked his pace, then rushed on toward the shore
sobbing, gasping, praying: 'In heaven's name
600 and the gods', by light of day and breath of life,
save me, Trojans! Take me to any land!
That's all I ask. I know: I am a Greek;
my sword attacked the homes of Ilium.
For that, if I have done such hurt and wrong,
605 strew me over the waves, or sink me deep.
I'll die—die gladly by the hand of man!'
With that he fell to his knees and seized my knees
and clung there. Who he was, sprung of what line,
we bade him tell, and what the fate that felled him.
610 With little ado Anchises gave his hand
to the fellow, and by that pledge brought courage back.
At last he laid aside his fear and spoke:
'I'm called Achaemenides, Ithacan, of the crew
of cursed Ulysses. My sire, Adamastus, sent me
615 to Troy (a poor man—would he had so remained!).
My shipmates, running in fear from savagery,
forgot me, left me behind, deep in the cave
of the Cyclops—house of clotted bloody feasts,
black, enormous—and he's so tall he knocks
620 the stars awry (God save earth from such horror!).
No man could stand to see him or hear him speak;
he lives on the guts and blood of luckless men.
I saw him! I saw him seize two of our muster
in his huge hand; then halfway up the cave
625 he smashed them against a rock; the place fair swam
with gore! I saw him gnaw their bleeding flesh—
muscles still warm and twitching between his teeth!
But not unavenged: Ulysses stood no such thing,
nor lost his Ithacan wit, for all the danger.
630 The Cyclops, stuffed with food and drowned in wine,

soon bowed his head and fell to the floor, a bulk
elephantine, vomiting clots and bloody wine
and bits of flesh as he slept. We said our prayers,
threw dice for places, then all as one together
635 rushed him. With sharpened stake, we stabbed his eye
—just one, half hidden in his scowling brow,
huge as an Argive shield or Phoebus' lamp—
rejoicing to avenge our shipmates' ghosts.
But go, for pity, go, and cut your lines
640 from shore.
Now in his cave Polyphemus folds his sheep
and milks them; and like him, as huge as he,
a hundred others live along this shore,
each a foul Cyclops, wandering these high hills.
645 Three times the moon has filled her horns with light
while in the lonely woods where wild beasts lurk
I've dragged out a life, climbing up cliffs to watch
Cyclopes, trembling to hear them tramp and shout.
My food—poor stuff!—was berries and stony fruits
650 from trees, and a root or two ripped from the sod.
I've watched and watched; your fleet is the first I've seen
heading this way. To you, whatever may be,
I've turned. Enough, to escape these fiendish creatures!
Far better you took my life, however you will!'

655 "He scarce had spoken when high in the hills we saw
Polyphemus the shepherd, vast and lumpish, moving
among his sheep, and heading for shores he knew,
a horror, misshapen, huge, his eye put out.
A pine trunk guided his hand and steadied his step;
660 his woolly sheep came with him—they alone
were joy and solace in his pain.
Soon as he came to the sea where waves ran high
he washed from the pit of his eye the gouts of blood,
howling and grinding his teeth, then to mid-channel
665 strode out, and the wave had still not wet his flank.
Quickly we took our suppliant Greek (poor man!)

on board, and then in silence cut our lines,
put about, leaned on our oars, and raced away.
He heard our voices and whirled to track us down.
670   But when he found us past his power to reach,
and Ionian waves too deep for him to breast,
he raised a savage yell that set the sea
to shaking, frightened Italy's inmost heart,
and made the vaulted caves of Aetna roar.
675   The tribe of Cyclops heard, and from the woods
and hills rushed to the shore and filled the beach.
We saw the brethren of Aetna halt and scowl
in vain, despite their heads that reached to heaven,
a council of fright. They stood there towering high
680   like lofty oaks or cone-clad cypresses—
some forest of Jove or woodland of Diana.
Sharp panic drove us to rush, to let the sheets
run free, and set the sails to catch the wind.
But Helenus had warned us not to course
685   'twixt Scylla and Charybdis—there the route
lay pinched between two deaths: We must put back!
Just then a Norther, blowing from Pelorus,
came down; I sailed past ports of living rock—
Pantagia, Megara, Thapsus flat and low.
690   These spots Achaemenides named, retracing now
his errant course, the crewman of cursed Ulysses.

"Athwart a Sicilian bay an island lies,
Plemyrium of the waves, its earlier name
Ortygia. Here, men say, the stream Alpheus,
695   comes up from hidden channels under the sea
to be 'Arethusa' and join Sicilian waves.*
As bidden, we worshiped the local gods, and then
pushed past the fat, wet soil of Swamp Helorus.
Thence we skirted the cliffs and jettied reefs

---

   * Tradition had it that the river Alpheus, in Elis, passed through a
underground channel to come up on the shore of Sicily as a larg
spring, separated from the sea only by a reef.

700 of Pachynus, then Camerina, by the Fates
decreed forever fixed; next, on to Gela
the monstrous, lying flat by laughing streams.
Thereafter Akragas on the hill displayed
her ramparts—breeder once of splendid horses.

705 Past palmy Selinus we drove with freshening breeze,
and sounded our way through Lilybaeum's reefs.
Then Drepanum's harbor and its joyless shore
received us. Here after all those storms at sea
I lost my father, solace of every care

710 and blow, Anchises. Father, you left me wearied;
was it for this I'd saved you from those perils?
Not Helenus, for all his tales of terror,
nor foul Celaeno prophesied such grief.
This was my final trial, my journey's end.

715 From there I sailed; God brought me to your coasts."

Thus Lord Aeneas held them all intent,
telling his tale of travel, of God and fate.
At last he stopped, sank back, and made an end.

BOOK FOUR

Now Dido had felt the heavy slash of care,
the wound that grows in the vein, the lightless flame.
Aeneas' great courage, the glory of his people,
coursed through her mind; fast in her heart lay fixed
5 his face, his words. She knew no rest or peace.
The next day's lamp of sun was lighting earth,
and Dawn had cleared the sky of dew and dark,
when she, sick soul, spoke to her loving sister:
"Anna! My dreams! They leave me tense with fear!
10 What strange outsider has come here to our home?
How proud his bearing! How brave his heart and hand!
I believe—not lightly—he is a child of gods.
Fear proves the soul debased; but he, though battered
by Fate, tells how he fought war after war.
15 Had I not fixed it firm within my heart
never to yield myself to marriage bond
since that first love left me cheated by death,
did I not sicken at thought of bed and torch,
to this one sin, this once, I might succumb.
20 No, Anna, I'll speak: Since poor Sychaeus died,
since brother drenched my house with husband's blood,
Aeneas alone has moved my heart and shaken
resolve. I mark the trace of long-dead flame.
But, oh, may the earth gape wide and deep for me,
25 or the father almighty blast me down to death,
to the paling ghosts of hell and the pit of night,
before I play honor false or break her laws.
The man who first knew union with me stole

70

my heart; let him keep and guard it in the tomb."
30 She spoke; the well of her tears filled and ran over.

Then Anna: "Your sister loves you more than life:
why squander youth on endless, lonely grief,
with no sweet sons, without the gifts of love?
You think mere ashes, ghosts in the grave, will care?
35 So be it! You've mourned; you've turned all suitors down
in Libya, and Tyre before. You've scorned Iarbas
and all the chiefs that Africa, proud and rich,
parades: why battle a love that you've found good?
Have you forgotten whose lands you've settled here?
40 This side, Gaetulians (race untamed by war),
savage Numidians, and a barrier sea;
that side, the desert, thirst, the wild nomads
of Barca. Why tell of wars that rise in Tyre
or how your brother threatens?
45 I'm sure the gods have blessed the Trojans' course,
and Juno favored the wind that blew their ships.
Oh, what a city you'll see, what kingdoms rise,
with such a man! Allied with Trojan arms
Carthage will raise her glory to the sky.
50 Pray for the gods' forgiveness; give them gifts.
Be kind to our guest; weave tissues of delay:
'Winter—the sea is wild—the rains have come—
your ships are damaged—you cannot read the skies.'"

Such talk inflamed her heart with uncurbed passion,
55 gave hope to doubt, and let restraint go free.
First they went to altar and shrine to beg
God's peace; they made due rite of sacrifice:
sheep to Ceres, to Phoebus, to Father Bacchus,
and most to Juno, lady of marriage bonds.
60 Dido the beautiful lifted a cup of wine
and poured it between the horns of a pure white cow,
or danced where the gods watch over blood-rich altars.
Each day began with victims; she slit their throats,

and hung over living vitals to read the signs.
65 But priests are fools! What help from shrine and prayer
for her madness? Flames devoured her soft heart's-flesh;
the wound in her breast was wordless, but alive.
Fevered and ill-starred, Dido wandered wild
through all the town, like a doe trailing an arrow
70 that, heedless in Cretan forest, she had caught
from a shepherd who shot but never knew his bolt
had flown to the mark; she ranges field and grove
of Dicte; the shaft of death clings to her flank.
Now Dido escorted Aeneas from wall to wall,
75 showed him her Tyrian wealth, her city all built—
she'd start to speak, but in mid-word fall mute.
Again, at wane of day, she'd fill her hall
and ask to hear once more of Troy's travail,
and hang once more, madly, upon each word.
80 Then when they'd parted and the shadowed moon
had paled, and fading stars warned men to sleep,
in the empty hall she'd lie where he had lain,
hearing him, seeing him—gone, and she alone;
or hold Ascanius close, caught by his father's
85 likeness, in hope of eluding a sinful love.
Her towers grew no taller; her army ceased
maneuvers and worked no more to strengthen port
and bastion for war: work hung half-done, walls stood
huge but unsteady; bare scaffolds met the sky.

90 As soon as Jove's dear wife knew Dido gripped
by the plague and grown too mad to heed report,
she, daughter of Saturn, spoke harsh words to Venus:
"What glorious praise, what rich return you've gained,
you and your son; such might, such fabled power!
95 One woman, tricked and beaten by two gods!
I'm not deceived: you feared my city, and me,
and hence held Carthage and her halls suspect.
Is there no limit? Why this vast rivalry?
Why not make peace for good, and carry through

100   the match you planned? You've gained your heart's desire:
       Dido has drawn love's flame deep as her bones.
       Why not join hands, join peoples, share the rule
       between us? Let Dido serve her Trojan prince
       and lay her dower—her Tyrians—in your hand."

105   Venus knew Juno spoke with veiled intent
       to turn Italian power aside to Carthage.
       Thus she replied: "To that, who but the mad
       could object? Who'd choose to go to war with you?
       If only success may crown our stratagem!
110   But I'm not sure of fate: would Jove allow
       a single city for people of Tyre and Troy?
       Approve such mingled blood, such conjoint rule?
       You are his wife: seek out his will. You may.
       You lead, I'll follow." Then Juno spoke to her:
115   "That shall be my concern. How best to meet
       the need of the moment, hear, while I briefly tell.
       A hunt is planned. Aeneas, and Dido with him,
       are off to the woods soon as tomorrow's sun
       rises and with his ray reveals the world.
120   They'll see the clouds turn black with hail and rain;
       then as their beaters rush to encircle a dell,
       I'll pour down floods and shake all heaven with thunder.
       Their men will scatter in darkness and disappear.
       Your prince of Troy and Dido both will come
125   to a cave. I'll be there, too. With your consent,
       I'll join them in marriage and name her 'lawful wife.'
       This shall be their wedding." Venus opposed
       no word, but nodded. Such tactics made her smile.

       Meanwhile the Dawn rose up and left the sea.
130   Out from the gates at sunrise young men ran
       with nets and snares and broad-tipped hunting spears;
       out galloped Moors with packs of keen-nosed hounds.
       The queen was late; beside her hall the lords
       of Carthage waited; there stood her horse, in gold

135   and purple caparison, nervous, champing the bit.
       Surrounded by bodyguards, she came at last,
       wrapped in a scarlet cloak broidered with lace.
       Gold was her quiver; gold held her plaited hair;
       a brooch of gold fastened her purple gown.
140   In marched a Trojan group, Iulus too,
       smiling and eager. Then, towering over all,
       Aeneas joined them and brought their ranks together.
       Like Apollo, leaving Lycia and streams of Xanthus,
       in winter, to visit Delos, his mother's home!
145   He starts the dancing; gathering round his shrine,
       islanders, mountaineers, painted plainsmen sing,
       while he climbs Cynthus. He braids his flowing hair
       and holds it in place with laurel and crown of gold;
       his arrows clang at his back. So fresh, alive,
150   was Aeneas, so matchless the glory of his face.
       They rode to the hills, to the wayless woods and marches.
       Look! Down from a rocky ridge leaped mountain goats
       to race downhill; on this side, where the plains
       lay open, a line of antelopes flashed past
155   away from the hillsides, trailing a swirl of dust.
       Ascanius—boy on a lively pony—loped
       up hill, down dale, with a laugh past these, past those.
       Such nerveless beasts! He wished a foam-flecked boar
       might come his way, or a lion charge from the hills.

160   Now thunder roared and rumbled across the sky;
       soon came black clouds, the hailstorm, and the rain.
       The Tyrian people and men of Troy broke ranks,
       and with them Venus' grandson ran for shelter—
       anywhere! Rivers in spate rushed down the slopes.
165   The prince of Troy and Dido both had come
       to a cave. The bride's attendants, Earth and Juno,
       gave signal: lightning and empyrean flamed
       in witness; high in the hills Nymphs made their moan.
       That was the day, the first of death and first
170   of evil. Repute, appearance, nothing moved

the queen; she laid no plan to hide her love,
but called it marriage, with this word veiled her shame.

At once Rumor went out through Libya's towns—
Rumor, than whom no evil thing is faster:
175 speed is her life; each step augments her strength.
Small, a shiver, at first, she soon rears high.
She walks aground; her head hides in the clouds.
Men say that Earth, in fury at the gods,
bore this last child, a sister to the Giants.
180 She is swift of foot and nimble on the wing,
a horror, misshapen, huge. Beneath each feather
there lies a sleepless eye (wonder to tell!),
and a tongue, and chattering lips, and ears alert.
By night she flies far over the shadowed world
185 gibbering; sleep never comes to rest her eyes.
By day she sits at watch high on a roof
or lofty tower, and terrifies great cities,
as much a vessel of slander as crier of truth.
This time she filled men's minds with varied gossip,
190 chuckling and chanting both false and true alike:
Aeneas had come, born of the blood of Troy;
Dido had deemed him worthy mate and man.
Now they were warming the winter with rich exchange,
forgetful of thrones, ensnared by shameful lust.
195 Such tales foul Rumor spread from lip to lip,
then turned her course straight off to King Iarbas,
heaped fire into his heart and raked his wrath.

Iarbas, son of a Nymph, raped by Hammon,
had raised in his broad realms a hundred shrines
200 to Jove, a hundred altars and vigil fires
with priests at perpetual prayer; the blood of beasts
fattened the soil, the doors were decked with flowers.
Maddened at heart, enflamed by bitter rumor
he stood at the altar amid the powers of heaven,
205 raised hands in suppliance, and prayed aloud:

"Almighty Jove, to whom the Moorish kind
on purple couches serve rich food and wine,
do you see this? Or are we fools to fear
your lightning bolt? Are cloud and fire blind,
210   that frighten our hearts, mere noise devoid of strength?
This woman, this immigrant in my bounds, who paid
to build her little town, to whom I granted
tidewater land on terms, rejects my hand
but takes my lord Aeneas to her throne.
215   And now that Paris and his half-male crew,
with perfumed hair and chin-tied Persian caps,
keeps what he stole, while I bring gifts to shrines—
your shrines—and worship empty shams of glory."

As with hand on altar he made this prayer
220   the almighty heard; his eye turned toward the palace,
toward two in love forgetting their better fame.
He spoke to Mercury then with this command:
"Go, son, summon the Zephyrs and take flight.
Our prince of Troy dawdles in Carthage now
225   and takes no thought for cities assigned by fate.
Fly with the wind, bring him my word, and speak:
'Such not the man his lovely mother promised,
nor such twice saved by her from Argive arms,
but one to rule a country big with power—
230   Italy, land of the war cry—to pass on
the blood of Teucer, and bring worlds under law.'
If none of these great glories fires his heart
and for his own renown he'll spend no toil,
does he begrudge his son a Roman fortress?
235   What plans, what hopes hold him on foreign soil,
blind to Ausonia and Lavinia's land?
'Sail on!' That is all. Bring him this word from me."

He ended. Mercury moved to carry out
the father's command. First he put on his sandals

240 golden, winged, that bear him swift as the wind
high over land and high above the sea,
then took his wand. With this he calls the ghosts
pale out of Orcus, or sends them sorrowing down,
grants sleep, withdraws it, unseals the eyes of death.
245 With it he drives the winds and sails the clouds.
Now flying he saw the cap and rugged flanks
of Atlas, whose granite shoulders prop the sky—
Atlas: his pine-clad head, forever crowned
with clouds, is buffeted by wind and rain.
250 A glacier clothes his back, and cascades course
down over his face; his beard bristles with ice.
Here Mercury hovering on both wings alike
stopped, then plummeted headlong toward the sea
just like a gull that, round the beaches, round
255 fish-haunted reefs, skims low across the waves.
So between earth and sky he flew along
toward Libya's sandy shore, cleaving the wind
eastward from Atlas—Mercury, son of Maia.
Soon as his winged feet touched settlement ground,
260 he saw Aeneas footing down forts and raising
new homes. The sword he wore was yellow-starred
with jasper, a cape of glowing Tyrian scarlet
hung from his shoulders—gifts the wealthy queen
had given, and broidered the cloth with thread of gold.
265 Up stepped the god: "Aeneas! In Carthage now
do you lay foundations and plan a handsome town
for a wife? *Your* throne, *your* state—are they forgotten?
From shining Olympus *he* has sent me down—
the king of gods, whose nod makes heaven roll.
270 He bade me fly with the wind to bring his word:
what plans, what hopes hold you at leisure here?
If nothing of promised glory moves your heart,
and for your own renown you'll spend no toil,
what of your son? He's growing! Your heir, Iulus:
275 what of his hopes? A kingdom—Italy—Rome:

these are his due!" With this, the Cyllenian god
left mortal sight, nor waited for reply;
beyond the eye he vanished into air.

Aeneas was frightened out of speech and mind;
280   his hair stood up in terror, his voice stuck fast.
He burned to go, to flee this pleasant land;
God's word, God's great commands had struck him hard.
But what should he do? How dare he tell the queen?
She was mad for love: how could he start his plea?
285   His mind turned quickly here, turned quickly there,
darting in different ways all round about.
As he weighed the matter this seemed the better course:
he called Sergestus, Mnestheus, Serestus the brave:
"Not a word! Prepare to sail! Call out our people!
290   To battle stations, all: coin some excuse
for these new orders." Meanwhile, let gentle Dido
know nothing, suspect no rupture of their love:
he now would test approaches, seek the time
and kindest way to tell her. Quickly all
295   in joy at his command obeyed his orders.

But still the queen (who can deceive a lover?)
foretold the scheme, caught contemplated moves,
feared even where all was safe. Then Rumor came
to report the fleet outfitted and ready to sail.
300   Her passion burst control; savage, aflame,
she raced through town, as, at an elevation,
the Thyiad who feels the spur of Bacchic hymns
and dances, and hears Cithaeron shout by night.
At last she addressed Aeneas; her words burst forth:

305   "You lied! You thought you could conceal a wrong
so vast, and leave my land without one word?
Our love, your right hand given in pledge that day,
a Dido to suffer and die—are these no check?
What? Fit out your fleet beneath a winter sun,

310 and hurry across the sea while north winds howl,
hard-hearted man? Were it no foreign land,
no unknown home you sought, but Troy still stood,
would you send ships through storms like these to Troy?
You run from *me?* In tears, I seize your hand
315 (what other solace have I left myself?)
and beg you recall our marriage, our wedding day:
if I have served you well, if you have found
delight in me, have mercy! My house is crumbling!
If prayer can still be heard, change, change your heart!
320 You made the Libyan tribes, the Nomad kings,
yes, my own Tyrians, hate me; lost for you
were honor and good repute, my only path
to glory. Cast off, fit only to die, who'll have me,
you whom I entertained—no more say, 'married.'
325 What now? Wait till Pygmalion levels my walls,
or the Moor Iarbas drags me off in chains?
If only before your flight I had conceived
your child, if only a baby Aeneas played
here in my court, whose face might mirror yours,
330 I'd feel less like one taken and discarded."
She finished. Aeneas, strengthened by Jove's words,
gazed steadily at her and suppressed his pain.
At last he briefly replied, "Speak! List them all—
your favors and courtesies! There is not one
335 I won't confess. I'll think of you with joy
long as I think at all, and live, and breathe.
But now to the point. I did not mean (believe me!)
to slip away by stealth, nor ever feigned
the wedding torch, or made such league with you.
340 If fate had let me govern my own life
and heal my troubles in the way I willed,
I would be living in Troy with what remained
of my people; Priam's halls would still be standing;
and we, though beaten, had built our walls anew.
345 But Apollo Grynean sent me to Italy;
'Find Italy! Win her!' the oracles declared.

My love, my home, lie there. You are of Tyre,
yet Libyan Carthage holds you, hall and wall:
why take it ill that Trojans look for homes

350   in Italy? We too may seek strange lands.
Whenever dewy night enshrouds the world
and fiery stars arise, Anchises' ghost,
murky and fearful, warns me in my dreams.
Ascanius, well-loved son: see how I wrong him,

355   cheating him of Hesperian land and throne!
Now comes a messenger from Jove himself
(I swear it!) ; he sped through air to bring command.
In the clear light of day I saw that god;
he entered these walls; my ears drank in his words.

360   Cease to enflame my heart and yours with plaints:
not by free choice I go to Italy."

Even as he spoke she turned her face away.
Glancing now here, now there, she viewed the man
from head to foot, wordless. Then speech flared out:

365   "No goddess your mother, no Dardanus sired your kind,
you liar! No! Caucasus got you on those cliffs
of jagged granite, and tigers suckled you there!
Dissemble? Why? To await some greater wrong?
I wept; he made no sound, nor turned an eye.

370   I loved him; where were his tears, his sympathy?
What else shall I say? Juno, lady and queen,
Jove, son of Saturn, can be unmoved no longer.
Good faith is folly! I saved him, castaway
and helpless, I made him partner to my power.

375   He'd lost his ships, his men; I rescued them.
My madness flames like fire: 'Apollo' now,
'the oracles' now; now 'sent by Jove himself
a messenger comes through air with dread commands.
This is the gods' life work! Such cares disturb

380   their peace! You're free; I'll not refute your claims.
Go! Find your Italian throne by wind and wave!
Midway, I trust, if God has power, you'll drink

requital on a reef and scream for Dido!
There'll be no Dido, but a funeral flame
385   will follow, and when death sunders soul from flesh
my shade will haunt you till my price is paid.
I'll know! Report will reach my ghost in hell!"
She broke off in mid-speech and, sickened, fled
the light of day—ran from his sight, from him,
390   while he stood trembling, groping, conning a flood
of words. She fainted. Her people raised her up
and bore her to her room and to her bed.

Aeneas the good, though longing to ease her pain
with words of comfort and turn aside her care
395   (his groans came deep, for love had racked his heart),
obeyed God's orders and sought his fleet again.
Then truly his men fell to; the shore was filled
with hauling of ships. Out swam fresh-painted keels;
men loaded oars still green, and from the woods
400   brought spars half-hewn in haste.
"Move out!" they heard. "All hands!" "Look lively, now!"
(As when the ants, mindful of winter, attack
a heap of grain and carry it home across
the fields: black goes the column; they bear their prize
405   down narrow grassy lanes. Some push big kernels
with heave of shoulders; some close the line of march
and hurry stragglers. The path is a froth of toil.)
Dido! What did you feel to see all this?
What cries did you utter when from tower's top
410   you saw the shore all seething, saw the sea
churned up before your eyes, and heard the shouts!
Shameless love, where do you not drive men's hearts?
Again she went and wept and begged, for try
she must; her pride must bend the knee to love,
415   lest for failing to move she die in vain.

"Anna, you see them rushing round the shore:
the crews are mustered; the canvas calls the breeze;
the men have cheered as garlands dressed the spar.

Could I have known such sorrow was to come,
420 I could have borne it; but now in tears I beg
one favor, Anna, of you: that faithless man
was always with you, told you his secret thoughts;
as no one else, you knew, his gentler moods.
Go, bring to our heartless guest this humble plea:
425 I joined no Greeks; I took no oath at Aulis
of death to Trojans, I sent no ships to Troy,
I never harried his father Anchises' ghost.
Why will he lock his ears against my words?
Why haste? Let a broken heart win one last grace:
430 Await a safer passage and favoring winds!
I'll not ask now for the wedlock he betrayed,
or that he resign his darling Latin throne;
I beg for time, an hour of rest from madness,
till fortune teach me how to lose and grieve.
435 This favor the last your sister asks: be kind!
I'll pay my debt with death to make full measure."

Such was her plea; such sorrows her grieving sister
reported, reported again. But nothing moved him;
no tears nor words could teach his heart to hear.
440 (Fate blocked the way; God closed his ears to pity.)
Like an oak tree, ancient, toughened by the years,
blasted by Alpine winds this way and that
contesting to uproot it; the North Wind howls,
the trunk is shaken, foliage strews the ground.
445 The tree holds hard; its crown lifts up toward heaven
far as its root grows down toward Tartarus.
Just so Aeneas, assaulted by pleas this side and that,
felt in his heart the thrust of care.
His mind stood firm; tears came, but came in vain.

450 Then Dido, luckless, by fortune terrified,
invited death: to view heaven's vault was pain.
To strengthen her resolve to leave the light,
she saw, when she offered her gifts and censed the altars

(dreadful to tell!), the holy water turn black
455 and the wine pour down in horrid clots of gore.
She told none, not even Anna, what she'd seen.
Besides, in her house there stood a marble shrine
to her former husband, which she kept sacrosanct,
festooned with white wool bands and feast-day flowers:
460 from it she thought she heard her husband's voice
calling her, calling, when darkness gripped the world.
And on her roof a lonesome owl sang songs
of death; its mournful cry trailed off in sobs.
Then warnings of long dead seers came crowding back
465 to fill her with fright. She dreamed herself gone mad,
with Aeneas in wild pursuit; then left alone
to travel, forever friendless, a long, long road,
seeking her Tyrians in an empty world,
like maddened Pentheus * seeing the rank of Furies,
470 seeing twin suns and a double Thebes displayed;
or like Orestes † racing across the stage
to escape a mother armed with torch and serpent—
and at Agamemnon's door the Dirae wait.

Filled with madness and prisoner of her pain,
475 she determined to die; and now, with how and when
planned in her mind, she addressed her tearful sister
(concealing intent behind a cloudless brow):
"Anna, I've found a way—applaud your sister!—
that will bring him back, or free me from my love.
480 Near to the ocean's edge and setting sun
lies African land's-end, where giant Atlas
bears on his back the spinning star-tricked wheel.

* A reference to a scene from a tragedy, possibly Euripides' *Bacchae,*
in which Pentheus is driven mad by Dionysus (Bacchus) for having
profaned his rites.

† Another reference to a scene from a tragedy, here possibly Aeschylus'
Eumenides, in which Orestes, having killed his mother, Clytemnestra,
in revenge for the murder of his father, Agamemnon, is driven mad by
the Furies at the instigation of his mother's ghost.

I've found a religious of that place—a Moor;
she served the Hesperides' temple, fed the snake,
485   and guarded the holy branches on the tree;
with honey and poppy she made the elixir of sleep.
She swears she can release what hearts she will
with spells, and freight still other hearts with care,
can stop the rivers and reverse the stars,
490   and raise the dead by night: you'll see the earth
groan at her feet and trees climb down the hills.
Sister, I tell you, by your life, by all
that's holy, I take to witchcraft against my will.
Slip into our inner courtyard and build there
495   a pyre; pile on it the arms that perjured man
hung in my house—take all he left, the bed
of marriage that brought me sorrow. I must destroy
his every devilish trace: so says my Moor."
This much, then silence, and her face turned pale.
500   Yet Anna never suspected that these strange rites
were cover for death; her heart grasped no such madness.
She feared no worse than when Sychaeus died,
and did as Dido asked.

In the inner court beneath the open sky
505   the pyre stood huge with pitch pine and with oak.
The queen hung garlands and wreathed the place with boughs
of death; atop, she laid his sword, his garments—
yes, and his image: she knew what she would do.
Ringed by altars the Moor let down her hair,
510   intoned three hundred gods, Chaos, and Hell,
three Hecates, Diana the triform virgin.
She sprinkled water labeled "from Avernus,"
selected hairy leaves by moonlight reaped
with brazen sickle (their milky juice turns black),
515   pulled out the membrane torn from a newborn foal
and snatched from its mother's mouth.
Dido stepped to an altar, blessed her hands,
took meal, slipped off one shoe, unlatched her gown,

then, ready to die, begged gods and prescient stars
520 to hear her prayer to any power just
and mindful, that cares for lovers wrongly matched.

It was night; all over the world the weary flesh
found peace in sleep; forests and savage seas
rested; the stars rolled on in middle course.
525 No sound from field, from herd, from painted birds
that swarm the liquid lakes or love the thorn
and thicket: they slept in silence of the night,
healing the heart of care, forgetting pain.
But never the broken-hearted, luckless queen
530 slipped off to sleep or took the night to eyes
and heart. Her torment doubled; desire rose
raging; she ebbed and flowed on waves of fury.
At last she paused and pondered inner thoughts:
"What shall I do? I'm scorned! Shall I turn and try
535 my earlier suitors, and beg a Nomad's bed?
I have disdained their hand—how many times?
Well, then, to the Trojan fleet? Hurry to catch
their final word? Because they prized my help
and remember that musty favor with gratitude?
540 Granted the will, who'd let an unloved woman
tread his proud deck? You fool! You still don't know,
don't see, how the sons of Laomedon can lie?
Well—? Trail his jeering crews, a lovesick girl?
Or board ship with my Tyrians, rank on rank,
545 around me—men I've just now saved from Sidon:
bid them make sail and put to sea once more?
No! Die as you've earned! Take steel and end your pains!
You, Anna, gave in to my tears, you topped my folly
with evil; you tossed me to our enemy!
550 I had not the will to pass my life unwed,
unstained, like some wild creature, untouched by guilt.
I did not keep my oath to dead Sychaeus."
Such were the sorrows that broke forth from her heart.

Aeneas knew he would go; on his tall ship,
his preparations made, he took his rest.
555 In his dreams a godly form appeared again,
just as before, and seemed to warn once more
(in all like Mercury, in voice, complexion,
in the flaxen hair and graceful limbs of youth):
560 "Goddess-born, can you sleep at such an hour,
and fail to see the dangers that surround you—
madman!—nor hear the favoring West Wind blow?
Dido devises malice and foul crime
(she knows she'll die) her fury seethes and surges.
565 Run! Leave in haste, while haste's within your power.
Soon you will see the ocean churned by ships,
the shore ablaze with savage torch and flames,
if Dawn shall touch you tarrying in this land.
Hurry, now! Ever a various, changeful thing
570 is woman." He spoke and mingled with black night.

This apparition terrified Aeneas.
He tore himself from sleep and harried his men
to haste: "Look lively, there, and man the thwarts!
Off buntlines! Quick! A god from heaven's height
575 again has bid us speed away and cut
our anchor-lines. We come, O sacred presence,
whoever you are! Again we hear your word.
Be with us in peace! Bless us! Show helpful stars
in heaven!" He spoke, and ripped his flashing sword
580 from sheath, and with the bared blade slashed the lines.
Like ardor held them all. They seized, they ran,
they emptied the beach; their vessels hid the sea.
Men heaved, churned up the foam, and swept the blue.

And now Aurora brought the dawn's new light
585 to earth, and left Tithonus' golden couch.
Dido was watching, and with the first pale gleam
she saw the fleet, yards squared and outward bound,
and marked the emptiness of shore and pier.

Three times and four she beat her lovely breast
590 and tore her golden hair: "What? Shall he go,"
she said, "and mock my power—that foreigner!
There'll be no general muster? No pursuit?
Will no one hurry to launch my ships? Quick, men,
bring torches, hand out arms, lean on your oars!
595 What's this? Where am I? What madness warps my mind?
Fool! Has your sacrilege just struck you now?
It should have, the day you offered a throne! Such honor!
And he, they say, brings with him his fathers' gods;
his shoulders carried Anchises, tired and old!
600 Why couldn't I hack his flesh, tear it, and strew
the sea with it? Slaughter his people and his son—
serve up Ascanius at his father's table?
But battle had been uncertain? Grant it so,
why fear, when I meant to die? I'd have thrown fire
605 and filled their camp with flame: father and son
and people had burned to death to make my pyre.
O Sun, who with your flame light all men's works;
you, Juno, who know my troubles and read them true;
Hecate, hailed at night by town and crossroad;
610 Dirae, gods of a Dido soon to die,
receive my prayer; turn sanction meet and right
upon these wrongs; hear me! If touch he must
on promised port and land—that man accursed!—
and so Jove's laws demand, this is decreed.
615 But let brave people harass him with war.
Driven from home, torn from Iulus' arms,
let him beg for help, and see his people die
disgraced. Make him surrender under terms
unjust, and know no happy years of rule,
620 but die untimely, untombed, in miles of sand.
This is my final prayer, poured with my blood.
And you, my Tyrians, hate his race, his kind,
all and always. On my remains bestow
this office: no love, no peace between our peoples!
625 And from my grave let some avenger rise

to harry the Trojan settlers with fire and sword—
now, some day, whenever we have the power.
Shore against shore, I pray, wave against sea,
sword against sword, fight, father and son, forever!"

630 So said she, and turned her thoughts this way and that,
seeking how soonest to end an unloved life.
She spoke to Barce then—Sychaeus' nurse
(her own lay buried in the fatherland):
"Dear nurse, bring Anna, my sister, here to me.
635 Tell her to hurry and wash in running water,
then bring the victims and holy things I showed her.
Come, both, with sacred ribbons in your hair.
I wish to do my office to Stygian Jove
(all duly prepared) to put an end to care
640 and lay that Trojan soul on funeral flames."

This much. In joy, the old nurse hobbled off.
Savage design drove Dido mad with fright.
Her eyes were wild and bloodshot; on her cheek
flush faded to pallor in terror of death so near.
645 She rushed to the inner court; madly she climbed
up the tall pyre and drew that Trojan sword,
gift that was never meant for such a use.
She saw his Trojan garment and their bed
well-known; then after a moment's tearful thought
650 lay down on the couch and spoke these final words:
"Here, trophies that I loved, while God allowed!
Oh, take my life and free me from my sorrow.
I've lived, and run the course that fate assigned;
my shade now goes in glory beneath the earth.
655 I built a splendid city and saw it walled,
avenged my husband, and made my brother pay—
blessed beyond measure, if only Dardan craft
had never touched upon these shores of mine."
She kissed the couch. "I'll die without revenge,
660 but die, and pass to darkness undismayed.

From shipboard let the heartless Trojan see
my flames! My death ride with him as he sails!"

While she yet spoke, her people saw her fall
crumpled upon the sword, the blade all frothed
665 with blood, her hands spattered. A scream rose high
in the hall; the city was stricken; Rumor ran wild.
Houses were filled with sobs and lamentations,
with keening of women: the sound rose to the skies—
as if an enemy had burst in, and all
670 Carthage or ancient Tyre were falling, while flames
rolled to the roofs, through homes of gods and men.
Anna, half-dead with fear, came running fast:
her fingers tore her face; she beat her breast.
She pushed through the crowd, calling her sister's name:
675 "Dido, was this what it meant? You lied? to *me*?
Was this the purpose of pyre, altar, and flame?
You left me! What shall I say? You died, but scorned
to take me? You might have let me share your death:
one hour, one stroke of pain had served for two.
680 These hands helped build—this voice of mine helped call
our gods—oh, cruel!—that I must fail you now!
You've killed yourself and me, your people, the lords
of Sidon, and your own city! Oh, let me wash
your wounds, and if some faltering breath remains,
685 let my lips take it!" With that, she climbed the pyre
and cradled her dying sister in her arms,
cried as she used her dress to stop the blood.
Dido would open her heavy eyes again,
but failed. The gash hissed in her wounded breast.
690 Three times she raised herself up on one arm,
three times fell back, then with an errant eye
sought light in heaven, and moaned that she had found it.

Then Juno in pity for her lingering pain
and laggard death, sent Iris down from heaven

695 to free her struggling soul from bonds of flesh.
(For not at her earned and fated hour she died,
but in a flash of fury, before her days:
Proserpina had not yet cut the lock
from her head, nor sentenced her to life below.)
700 But Iris flew down, dewy and golden-winged,
trailing a thousand colors against the sun.
She stopped over Dido's head: "This sacred lock
I carry to Dis, and from the flesh I free you."
With that she cut the wisp; at once all warmth
705 dispersed, and life retreated to the winds.

BOOK FIVE

Meanwhile Aeneas held a mid-sea course,
steadily cutting dark water before the wind.
A glance astern showed luckless Dido's walls
glowing with flame. What set a fire so vast
5   could not be seen—but passion wronged means pain
intense, and woman's fury has a power
men know: grim augury for Trojan hearts.
When Aeneas was far at sea, and no more land
was visible—water only, and only sky—
10 above him rose a thunderhead slate-blue
with night and storm; the waves turned rough and black.
Palinurus the pilot called from his quarterdeck:
"Why have these clouds so thickly wrapped the sky?
Lord Neptune, what do you plan?" With that he cried,
15 "All hands! Make fast! Lively! Lean on your oars!
Brace the yards for a reach!"—then turned and spoke:
"My lord Aeneas, if I had Jove's own pledge,
I'd never head for Italy with this gale.
The wind is roaring abeam and shifting west
20 where skies are dark and clouds are piling high.
We've tried but have not strength enough to hold
our course. Luck wins the throw: we'd best give in
and change course where she calls. Not far, I think,
is Eryx, Sicily's friendly port and shore,
25 if I recall my charts and stars aright."
Aeneas the good, then: "Yes, I've seen the winds
calling the turn, for all your work against them.
Haul sail about! What spot could please me more,
where would I rather moor my tired ships

30 than in the land that owns my Trojan friend
Acestes, and holds in its lap Anchises' bones?"
At this they swung toward land; the West Wind filled
their sails; their vessels trailed a boiling wake.
At last with a cheer they raised that well-known shore.

35 From a cliff Acestes, wondering, watched them come,
these friendly craft, and then ran down to meet them,
a-bristle with spears, rough in a bearskin coat.
His mother was Trojan; his father was the river
Crinisus. Mindful of them, his aged parents,
40 he welcomed the company back with simple gifts
and a smile; his friendly bounty eased fatigue.

At the next dawn, when day had put the stars
to flight, Aeneas called his people in
to meeting, and from a mound of earth addressed them:
45 "Children of Dardanus, sons of heaven's descent,
the months of one full year have run their course
since in the earth we laid my father's bones
and ashes, and hallowed here a shrine of sorrow.
And now, that day is near which by God's grace
50 I'll keep forever in honor and in grief.
If I were exiled on the Moorish coast,
or trapped on Argive seas or in Mycenae,
still I would hail this day each year with prayer,
processional, and gifts meet for the gods.
55 We've come unprompted to my father's grave;
yet not without God's wish and will, I say,
have we sailed here and entered this friendly port.
Come, then! In joy we'll join in solemn feast,
and pray for winds. Father, each year accept
60 our prayers in shrines we'll someday raise to you!
Acestes, son of Troy, has given two oxen
to each ship's company. Call to your feast
our gods of home, and those Acestes worships.
Nine days from now, if Dawn shall promise men

65 fair weather, and show a heaven bright with sun,
    I'll set us Trojan games: a ship race first,
    and then a foot race; next, the bold and strong
    in archery contest and the javelin throw;
    last, those who dare to fight with boxing thongs.
70 Come all! Expect the prize your merit earns!
    Now let us pray! Wear each his crown of leaves."

    So speaking he donned his mother's myrtle crown.
    So Helymus did, and Acestes—good old man!—
    so young Ascanius. All the young men followed.
75 Aeneas with his thousands then strode out
    to the tomb. Around him his vast company marched.
    With prayers he poured two cups of purest wine
    on the ground, next two of milk, and two of blood,
    then tossed a bunch of scarlet blooms, and spoke:
80 "Hail, sainted father, whom I saved in vain!
    Hail ashes, ghost, a father's empty shade!
    To search with you for Italy's fated fields,
    for Tiber lost in the West, was not to be."
    He stopped. From under the tomb a gliding snake
85 trailed seven huge circles, seven rolling coils.
    He rounded the tomb, slipped gently over the altar,
    his back picked out with turquoise and with gold,
    his scales alight and sparkling like the bow
    that casts the sun in colors on a cloud.
90 Aeneas fell back. The snake, in column long,
    slid between patens and polished chalices,
    tasted the food, then harmlessly withdrew
    beneath the tomb, leaving the tasted meats.
    With zeal increased Aeneas resumed the office:
95 the snake—was it local god or famulus
    to his father? He said the prayers and killed two sheep,
    two sows, and then two oxen with black hides;
    from the cup he poured out wine, and called the shade
    of Anchises: "Come, great ghost! Come up from hell!"
.00 His people, too, as best each could, in joy

brought gifts to load the altar, and slaughtered steers;
others ranged cooking pots, and round the lawns
set spits with fires beneath to roast the flesh.

The awaited day arrived; the ninth dawn came
105   riding the clear, bright car of Phaethon.
Acestes' name and fame had roused the tribes
nearby; in holiday mood they filled the shore
to watch the Trojans; some, too, joined the sport.
The prizes first were placed mid-field for all
110   to see: the holy tripods, wreaths of green,
palm branches (prize of victory), arms, and cloaks
dyed in deep scarlet, bars of silver and gold.
From a mound a bugle called. The games began.

First to enter the lists were ships, well matched:
115   four long-oared craft, chosen from all the fleet.
Mnestheus captained the "Pristis": fast, well manned
(Mnestheus: sire, one day, of Memmius' line);
Gyas, the giant "Chimaera": beamy, huge,
a floating city: a triple Trojan crew
120   rowed her with oars arranged in banks of three.
Sergestus (from whom the Sergii take their name)
rode the great "Centaur," while the blue-hulled "Scylla"
carried Cloanthus (of him Cluentius sprang).*

Well out to sea, far from the foaming beach,
125   is a rock, submerged at times, when swollen surf
is pounding and winter storms black out the stars;
in calms it rises noiseless from the waves,
a sunny roost and rookery for gulls.
Here Lord Aeneas set an oak branch, green
130   and leafy, to show the crews their turning point,
where they should haul round for the long run home.
The captains tossed for places, then stood high

---

* In mentioning the names in lines 117–123, Vergil is giving poetic
sanction to the tradition that these noble Roman houses traced their
descent from members of Aeneas' Trojan company.

on their quarterdecks in glory of red and gold;
the crews all shaded their heads with poplar fronds;
135   stripped to the waist, their bodies gleamed with oil.
They manned the thwarts; their arms stretched for the stroke.
Tense, they awaited the signal, hearts drained dry
with excitement, pulses pounding, eager to win.
Clear came the bugle call; at once the ships
140   leaped from their stations; the coxswain's loud command
struck heaven; taut muscles churned the sea to foam.
Bows even, they plowed ahead; the ocean's plain
was ripped and riven by oars and three-pronged rams.
Never so fast do chariots course the field
145   when two-horse teams leap from the starting pens;
never so free is the rein when drivers shake
the rippling lines, and lean to ply the whip.
Men clapped and cheered, and with their partisan cries
the forest rang; the circling shores rolled back
150   the sound, and shouts rebounded from the hills.

Amid the rush and roaring, Gyas slipped
to the lead; his wake was first. Behind him came
Cloanthus, better in oars, but heavy-sparred
and sluggish. Next, dead level, came the Pristis
155   and Centaur, pulling hard to gain the lead—
and now the Pristis held it, now the Centaur
passed her, now they both surged beam to beam,
their long keels plowing the salt sea, side by side.
Now they were nearing the rock, hard by the mark,
160   when Gyas, heading for victory at mid-course,
called to Menoetes, helmsman of his ship:
"Why hold so far to starboard? Alter course!
Haul close to shore! Let port oars scrape the reef!
The others can have their sea room!" But Menoetes,
165   fearful of hidden rocks, veered out to sea.
"Where are you heading? Menoetes, skin that rock!
Up helm! Up!" Gyas shouted, then turned to see
Cloanthus crowding astern and pulling close.

Cramping the helm, Cloanthus scraped the reef
170 inshore of Gyas, then shot ahead to win
the lead; he passed the mark and gained safe water.
In Gyas' heart frustration swelled and flamed;
tears of sheer rage poured down: "You fool, Menoetes!"
Forgetting his place and the safety of his crew,
175 he tumbled Menoetes head first over the stern,
then seized the helm himself and took command—
"All right, men: heave!" He swung the ship toward shore.
Up from the bottom Menoetes rose at last—
no young man, he. Dripping, his clothes all drenched,
180 he climbed the rock to a dry spot, and sat down.
The Trojans laughed to see him fall and swim,
and laughed as he coughed salt water from his throat.

And now the two tail-enders gained fresh hope
of beating Gyas, whose speed was far reduced.
185 Sergestus moved in first, tight on the reef,
but still not leading Mnestheus by a length:
the Pristis kept him covered, bow to beam.
But Mnestheus strode midships among his men
and urged them on: "Now lean! Lean on those oars!
190 You're Hector's men! In Troy's last hour I chose you
for my command; let's see that muscle of yours,
that spirit you showed once in the Moorish Gulf,
the Ionian Sea, and Malea's vengeful waves.
I, Mnestheus, no longer aim to gain first place,
195 although—well, let them win whom Neptune loves!
But, shame! Let's not be last! Win this, my friends;
prevent disgrace!" His men, with all their strength,
heaved hard. Huge oar-beats shook the brazen ship
and lifted her clear of water; the men breathed fast,
200 their mouths went dry, they shook; sweat ran in streams.
Sheer chance brought to the crew the place they wanted:
Sergestus lost his head: he nosed his ship
too close to the reef, too tight on the inside turn.
Bad luck! He struck a jutting rock and grounded.

205 The crag crashed; slammed on sharp barnacles, oars
shrieked and shattered; the bow crunched to a halt.
The crew leaped up and filled the air with shouts,
then they unlimbered boat hooks and long pikes
sharp-pointed, and gathered the broken, floating oars.
210 But Mnestheus, happy and heartened by events,
stepped up the oarsmen's stroke and prayed for wind;
he steered for the home stretch, running fast and clear.
Like a pigeon bursting suddenly from a cave
in porous rock, home for her precious nestlings:
215 she flies for the fields, and beating frightened wings
fills a whole house with noise; then swooping clear
she glides through quiet air with pinions spread:
so Mnestheus and his Pristis sliced the sea
of home stretch, slipping swift and effortless.
220 He passed Sergestus struggling on the reef
and in the shallows, shouting in vain for help,
and learning how to row with broken oars.
Next he caught up with Gyas and his huge
Chimaera; with helmsman lost, she'd fallen back.

225 Alone near the finish line remained Cloanthus:
Mnestheus pursued him, pushing with all his strength.
The shouts redoubled; every man cheered on
the challenger; heaven rang until it cracked.
One crew would never stand to lose a prize
230 already earned: they'd give their lives to win;
the other fed on a power born of success.
And bow to bow they might have tied to win
had not Cloanthus lifted both his hands
and poured out prayers, begging the gods to hear:
235 "Gods of the sea, who rule the course I run,
joy to us both! I promise to tie a bull,
pure white, to your seaside altar, and to throw
his vitals to your waves, and pour bright wine."
He spoke. Down under the waves they heard him: all
240 the dancing Nereids, Phorcus, Panopea,

and Father Portunus: with his huge hand he pushed
the passing ship. Fast as a feathered arrow
she fled toward shore and anchored safe in port.

Then, by the rules, Aeneas hailed them all
245 and cried, "Hear this! Cloanthus I declare
the winner!" He draped green laurel on his head,
and named the awards: each ship to choose three oxen,
take choice of wines, and win a silver talent.
To the captains then he gave especial prizes:
250 to the winner a gilded cloak rich broidered round
with twofold stripe in Meliboean purple—
the woven tale of Ida's woodland prince,*
who, spear in hand, ran down the speeding deer.
(He seemed alive, panting; from Ida stooping,
255 Jove's squire, the eagle, hooked him and bore him off.
His greybeard guardians stretched their hands toward heaven
in vain; his hounds barked fiercely to the winds.)
To him whose skill had won him second place
he gave a coat of polished mail, bound thrice
260 in gold (he'd won it himself at towered Troy
by Simois, when he killed and stripped Demoleos) —
both honor and bulwark to a fighting man.
Two slaves could scarcely raise the fabric up
though putting their shoulders to it, yet the Greek
265 had worn it to chase the Trojans far and wide.
Third prize, a pair of matching jugs of bronze
and cups of solid silver deeply chased.
All now had taken their prizes; rich and proud
they strode with purple ribbons round their heads.
270 Then in Sergestus came: sheer force and skill
had wrenched him from the reef; he limped along
propelled by a single bank of broken oars.
Like a snake so often trapped by a roadside bank,
and crushed by a brazen wheel, or left half dead
275 by a passerby with a stone and a heavy hand;

* Ganymede (see Glossary).

frightened, it twists long useless loops and turns.
With head still high and bold, and eye still bright,
it strikes and hisses; the wound has lamed and prisoned
its other parts: they knot and weave and writhe.
280 Such were the oars that moved the lagging ship;
still it made sail, came in with canvas flying.
Aeneas gave Sergestus the promised prize,
glad he had freed his ship and saved his crew.
The prize was a slave well-trained in household arts,
285 a Cretan girl, with twin babes at her breast.

This contest ended, Aeneas the good moved on
to a grassy field with wooded hills all round
curving to form a theater; in its midst
an oval track. Here thousands found their seats
290 while Aeneas climbed his mound and throne among them.
Here he sought to attract all who might wish
to run the foot race, and set out the prizes.
They came in crowds, both Trojans and Sicilians,
but Nisus and Euryalus first,
295 Euryalus handsome, in the bloom of youth,
Nisus for love of the lad; behind them came
Diores, prince of Priam's royal line,
Salius next, and Patron—one Acarnan,
the others Tegean, of Arcadian stock;
300 then two Sicilians, Helymus and Panopes,
men of the forests, squires of King Acestes;
and others too, whose fame has been obscured.
Aeneas rose and spoke among them all:
"Now hear this! Listen, and in your hearts be glad!
305 Not one shall leave without a gift from me.
To each I'll give two darts of Cretan steel,
to each a double ax inlaid with silver:
this compliment goes to all. The three who place
shall wear the olive crown and win awards.
310 First place shall have a horse with silvered gear;
second, an Amazon quiver filled with arrows

from Thrace. The strap around it is of gold;
its clasp is fastened with a rounded gem.
And third, this Argive helmet for his joy."

315 And now they were on the mark. The bugle call
sent them sprinting away and down the course
like a streak; each eye was on the finish line.
Nisus was leading; far ahead of all,
he ran faster than wind and winged lightning.
320 Second to him—second, but far behind—
came Salius; after him, by just a space,
Euryalus was third,
and next ran Helymus. Nearly up to him
Diores flew, now treading on his heels,
325 now touching his shoulder; another lap or two,
and he'd have slipped ahead or won a tie.
And now they were in the stretch, exhausted, close
to the finish line, when—bad luck!—Nisus slipped
and fell in a pool of blood some bull had shed
330 at the slaughter, making the green grass slick and wet.
So close to victory! He stepped down hard
but lost his footing and fell flat on his face,
down in the mud and slime and sacred blood—
but never forgot Euryalus, whom he loved!
335 He rose from the muck and tripped up Salius,
who stumbled, rolled, and sprawled in blood-soaked sand.
Euryalus streaked ahead, to win by gift
of his friend, his dash companioned by loud cheers.
Second was Helymus, third man now Diores.

340 But here came Salius, filling the huge arena,
the very seats of the chiefs, with shouts of rage,
demanding the prize he claimed he'd lost by fraud.
The people favored Euryalus' tear-stained face,
his body's budding grace and fresh young manhood.
345 Diores backed his claim with cheers and cries
(he'd just edged into place, and stood to lose

third prize if Salius now regained his first).
Then Lord Aeneas spoke: "Your prizes stay
unchanged; none shall disturb the lad's first place.
350 My friend was innocent; I may well console him."
So saying, he gave to Salius the huge hide
of a Moorish lion, shaggy, with gilded claws.
Then Nisus: "If such awards go to the losers
and you console the fallen, what fit prize
355 will come to me, whose merit had won first crown
if I, like Salius, had not had bad luck?"
As he spoke, he pointed to his face and limbs
all foul with muck. The great prince smiled at him
and called for a shield, the work of Didymaon,
360 once ripped by Greeks from Neptune's holy doors;
he gave the noble youth this splendid gift.

Then when the race was done and prizes paid:
"Now where are the men? Where are the ready hearts?
Let them step up and raise a thong-bound fist!"
365 He spoke, announcing the combat's twofold prize:
to the winner, an ox, horns gilt and ribbon-draped;
a sword and helmet to console the loser.
At once Dares—muscular, huge—looked up
and rose to his feet while all the company gasped.
370 He was the only man who'd boxed with Paris;
he, too, by the tomb where Hector lay in state,
knocked out the champion, Butes (heavyweight,
Amycus' son, of Bebryx—so he claimed),
and stretched him on the dark brown sand to die.
375 Such was Dares, who rose first challenger;
flexing broad shoulders, tossing lefts and rights
one after the other, he shadowboxed the air.
And now, an opponent? No one in all those ranks
dared rise to the man and bind his hands with thongs.
380 Dares grinned, thinking they'd all defaulted.
He strode to the platform, wasted no more time,
but, seizing the bull's left horn, addressed Aeneas:

"My lord, if no one dares to box with me,
when may I be dismissed? How long's to wait?
385   Present the award!" At once the sons of Troy
all shouted together, "Give him the promised prize!"

But now Acestes turned to chide Entellus
who sat beside him on the fresh green grass:
"Entellus, once held bravest, were we wrong?
390   Prizes like these—you'll see them carried off
without a fight? Where's Eryx now, the god
you called your teacher—rightly? Where's that fame
Sicily-wide, and the trophies that filled your house?"
Entellus replied, "I'm not afraid. I still
395   love praise and glory, but age has slowed me down;
my blood is sluggish, my muscles stiff and cold.
Had I what once I had, what that young fool
blusters and boasts of—had I my youth again,
it would have taken no prize, no fancy ox
400   to rouse me: gifts mean nothing to me." With that
into the ring he tossed twin boxing thongs,
thick and heavy, that Eryx the bold had worn
for combat—hard bull's-hide to wrap the wrists.
Men stood amazed: the things were seven hides thick
405   and stiff with insewn lumps of iron and lead.
Dares fell dumb; he shrank back and declined.
Aeneas, the great of spirit, tried their weight
and turned the long, thick leathers over and over.
Then the old champion spoke with vehemence:
410   "What if you'd seen the thongs of Hercules
himself, and the fearsome fight here on this beach?
These are the straps your brother Eryx wore
(you see them still all flecked with blood and brains) —
wore them against Alcides. I used them, too,
415   when I had strength and hotter blood, when years
had dropped no grudging grey upon my head.
If Dares of Troy declines these thongs of mine,
and Aeneas and Acestes so accord,

let's balance the boast. I yield the thongs of Eryx
420 (no fear!) ; you too strip off your Trojan straps."
With that he flung the tunic from his shoulders,
baring his massive muscles, arms, and wrists,
and took his stand, a mountain in mid-ring.
Then Lord Aeneas brought out thongs well-matched
425 and bound the hands of both with bands alike.
At once the two rose up upon their toes
and, fearless, raised their arms high in the air.
They held their heads back, sloping from the blows,
while fist feinted at fist to tempt attack:
430 Dares better at footwork, nimble, young;
Entellus tall and heavy, but slow, unsteady;
his knees wobbled; his breath came hoarse and gasping.
Many a punch they threw to no effect;
they beat tattoos on flank and chest—a huge
435 deep drumming; they landed blows all over ears
and temples; their teeth rattled beneath the thwacks.
Entellus stood there, monolithic, still,
watching for blows and swaying to avoid them.
Dares, like one who lays siege to a town
440 or sits in arms around a mountain fort,
tried here, tried there, attempted every point
of entry, bobbing and weaving, but gained no ground.
Entellus showed his right, rose up, and swung
from the floor, but Dares saw the blow beginning
445 and nimbly stepped aside to let it pass.
Entellus flailed the air and threw himself
off balance; with heavy thud his whole vast weight
fell flat, as some vast pine falls flat on Ida
or Erymanth, ripped rotten from its roots.
450 The men, Sicilians, Trojans, rose and cheered;
their shouts hit heaven. Acestes hurried in
and raised his poor old friend up from the ground.
Not slowed by the slip or scared, the champion
came back the keener, with strength refreshed by wrath
455 (shame fired him, too, and knowledge of his skill).

In a fury, he chased young Dares round and round,
now landing rights, now lefts—again! again!
No stopping, no rests: as when the clouds rain down
a hail that rattles the roof, Entellus punched
460   and pounded and punched and pommeled Dares dizzy.

Such anger Aeneas would not let proceed;
he could not condone Entellus' savagery.
He stopped the fight, pulled out the tired Dares
to save him, and soothed his feelings with these words:
465   "Poor boy! What madness had come over you?
He got fresh wind: you see? Your luck turned bad.
Give up!" He then declared the contest ended.
Good friends of Dares helped him away; his knees
were weak, his head was lolling, from his lips
470   he spat out clotted muck and teeth and blood.
They saw him home. Recalled, they took the sword
and helmet. Entellus, the winner, took the bull.
He boasted, proud of his victory and his bull:
"You, goddess-born; you, hear me, sons of Troy!
475   Learn now what strength I had when I was young
and from what death you won reprieve for Dares!"
With that, he took his stand by the ox's head
(his boxing prize), drew back his fist wrapped hard
in thongs, and struck from above between the horns,
480   crushing the skull and breaking out the brains.
The ox fell dying, shuddered, and lay still.
And then with words heartfelt, Entellus spoke:
"Eryx, I pay this better life in place
of Dares'. I won; now I renounce my craft."

485   Aeneas next announced the archers' match
for all who'd speed the arrow, and named awards.
With his great hand he heaved a ship's tall mast
erect, with a fluttering pigeon tethered fast
to its lofty tip—a target for their shafts.
490   The contestants gathered; each man tossed his lot

into a brazen helmet. The first chance fell
to Hyrtacus' son, Hippocoön (loud applause).
Next followed Mnestheus, victor just before
in the boat race—Mnestheus, wearing his olive crown.
495 Third, Eurytion, brother of that great man,
Pandarus (he, once bidden to break a truce,
whirled a first shaft against the assembled Greeks).
Last at the helmet's bottom lay Acestes,
for he too dared to try a young man's sport.
500 Then each with all his muscle bent his bow
to a curve, and poured the arrows from his quiver.
First from the twanging bowstring, through the sky,
the feathered shaft of Hippocoön whipped the air
to reach and strike and pierce the tree-high mast.
505 The mast vibrated; the frantic, frightened bird
filled the whole place with drumming of her wings.
Next Mnestheus rose and drew a skillful bow;
high aiming, he tensed alike both eye and shaft.
Poor man! To reach the bird itself, his arrow
510 had not the power, but severed the linen band
that tethered the bird's foot to the swaying mast.
She flew away to the winds and lofty clouds.
Eurytion moved fast. His bow was stretched,
his arrow ready. He called his brother in prayer,
515 aimed at the pigeon gaily winging the sky,
and struck her just as she drummed into a cloud.
She faltered and fell; her life she left on high
with the stars; but, falling, brought the arrow back.
The prize was lost; Acestes still remained.
520 Even so, he whirled an arrow through the air
displaying his skill—old sir!—and twanging bow.
Right then before their eyes was thrust a sign
portentous (history later proved its truth,
and prophets declared that fearsome things would be).
525 Up where the clouds were bright, the shaft took fire
and drew a trail of flame, then disappeared,
burnt out, into thin air—like stars that drop

from heaven and stream their flying hair behind them.
They stood there frightened, rooted, muttering prayers,
530   Sicilians and Trojans, but Aeneas hailed
the omen; he embraced a smiling Acestes
and loaded him with gifts, then spoke these words:
"Take them, good sir! Olympus' mighty king
meant by these signs a special prize for you.
535   This was Anchises', the long-lived; now it's yours—
a wine bowl carved in relief. Cisseus of Thrace
once gave it in generous gesture to my father
to be reminder and token of his love."
So speaking, he bound Acestes' brows with bay
540   fresh-greening, and named him victor over all.
Nor did Eurytion grudge him this preferment,
though he alone had shot the pigeon down.
Next prize was his who broke the cord, and last
his who had pierced the mast with feathered shaft.

545   The games were still not finished. Lord Aeneas
called to his side Iulus' constant friend
and tutor, Epytides, whispering in his ear,
"Go find Ascanius: are his boys' brigade
in marching order, his horsemen ready to ride?
550   Then say, 'In Anchises' name, move out, display
your drill!'" He bade the people all withdraw
and form a circle, leaving a wide clear field.
In marched the boys before their fathers' eyes,
parading on tight-reined horses; as they passed,
555   Sicilian and Trojan marveling, cheered aloud.
Each boy wore on his head a formal wreath,
each bore two cornel javelins tipped with steel.
Some carried polished quivers; each one wore
at his throat a braided circlet of soft gold.
560   There were three platoons; in all, three captains led
maneuvers, and each commanded twice six boys.
They marched in separate columns, each with a leader.
First came a line of youths led in review

by Priam—named for his grandsire, fine young son
565 of Polites, soon to be Italy's pride. He rode
a Thracian pony, dappled black and white:
white his pasterns, his proud head blazed with white.
Second came Atys—our Atii name him sire—
the young boy, Atys, whom young Iulus loved.
570 Last, but handsome beyond them all, Iulus,
riding a Tyrian horse that Dido the fair
gave him—reminder and token of her love.
The rest rode on Sicilian horses, gift
of Acestes, now grown old.

575 The nervous boys were hailed with joyful cheers
by the Trojans, who saw in them their fathers' faces.
They rode in proud review past all that crowd
and their parents' eyes; they halted. Epytides
from the sidelines shouted an order and cracked his whip.
580 They formed two columns, and then in groups of three
wheeled dancing from the line; then at command
re-formed and snapped their javelins to the ready.
The lines now faced each other across the field;
they marched and countermarched, then formed two rings
585 interlocking. Last, they simulated battle,
now wheeling in retreat, now leveling spears
for the charge, then making peace and marching off.
Men tell how once, in Crete, the labyrinth,
with its impenetrable walls and winding paths,
590 had a thousand tricky turns that made all guides
useless: the route could never be retraced.
Just so the sons of Troy performed maneuvers
intricate, interlocking, charge and retreat,
like dolphins swimming the waters of the sea,
595 cutting their capers off Crete or Libyan shores.
This riding contest later was revived
by Ascanius when he built the girdle walls
of Alba Longa. He taught the ancient Latins
to repeat what he and the Trojan boys had done.

600   The Albans taught their sons; from them, great Rome
       received it and preserved their fathers' game:
       the boys are "Troy" today, their band is "Trojan."
       Here ended the games in honor of Anchises.

       And here Dame Fortune changed and altered faith.
605   While yet they held their solemn funeral games,
       the daughter of Saturn, Juno, pondering much,
       her wrath not yet appeased, sent Iris down
       to the ships of Troy, and breathed her on her way.
       The maiden, gliding fast, ran down the bow
610   of a thousand colors, and no man marked her passage.
       She saw the vast assembly, viewed the shore,
       beheld the empty port, the fleet unguarded.
       On a distant lonely beach the women of Troy
       mourned for dead Anchises; they all looked out
615   to sea, and wept as one for the weary miles
       of water. "And so much still to sail!" they cried;
       "Oh, for a home! We're weary of life at sea!"
       Iris, no novice at troublemaking, joined
       their ranks; doffing her godlike form and dress,
620   she changed to Beroë, Doryclus' aged wife,
       of noble lineage, mother, once, of sons;
       and so strode out among the Trojan women.
       "Too bad," she cried, "that no Greek warrior dragged us
       to death beneath the walls of home! O sex
625   accursed, for what destruction were we saved?
       The seventh summer is passing since Troy fell;
       we've traversed lands and seas and hostile reefs,
       we've followed the stars across those endless miles
       of ocean, questing a land that's never there.
630   Here Eryx, our cousin, lived; here dwells Acestes:
       who now forbids us walls—a town—a home?
       My country! Gods of my fathers, torn in vain
       from the enemy, shall Troy never rise again?
       Shall I nowhere see the rivers that Hector loved?
635   No, come! Join me, and burn these luckless craft!

In a dream Cassandra the wise appeared to me
and gave me a flaming torch. 'Search here for Troy;
here,' she said, 'is your home!' Now is the hour!
Let's go! The omens are clear: look! Altars! Four
640 to Neptune! The god himself gives brands and courage!"

So speaking she took the lead, seized deadly fire,
and lifting it high in a swirl of smoke and sparks,
hurled it; the women forgot good sense and leaped
with excitement. One, the oldest of them all,
645 Pyrgo, once royal nurse to Priam's sons:
"Beroë, ladies? No! Nor from Rhoeteum,
nor Doryclus' wife! The signs of godlike grace,
those flashing eyes, mark them! Her fiery speech,
her face, the sound of her voice, her pace and step!
650 And Beroë? Just a moment ago I left her
sick, indignant that she alone had missed
the holiday and the honors to Anchises."
These were her words.
The women wavered at first; with angry looks
655 they eyed the ships, unhappily torn 'twixt love
for Sicily and the land where fate was calling,
when up on balanced wings the goddess rose
and sped off, tracing her rainbow on the clouds.
This frightening miracle drove the women wild;
660 they screamed; from family hearths they snatched up fire
(some robbed the altars) and threw it—flaming leaves
and branches. The holocaust spread wild, unchecked,
through spars and oars and decks of painted pine.

To Anchises' tomb Eumelus brought the word:
665 "The fleet's afire!" The company, turning round,
could see the cloud of smoke and flying sparks.
Ascanius wheeled; he'd led his cavalry show
with joy; no less decisive now, he spurred
to the camp, nor could his frightened tutors hold him.
670 "What madness is this? What can you mean," he cried,

"poor souls? This is no hostile camp of Greeks
you're burning, but your own hopes! I am your prince,
Ascanius!" At their feet he hurled the helmet
he'd worn when he had staged the game of war.
675 Just then Aeneas and all his men rushed in.
The women fled in fear all up and down
the shores, or slunk to the woods, to any hole
in the rocks, ashamed of the light, of what they'd done;
fresh loyalty drove Juno from their hearts.

680 Not for all that did flame and fire remit
their wild attack; beneath damp timbers, caulking
bubbled and belched thick smoke, a glow crept down
the keels; the plague gnawed everywhere at the hulls:
strong backs and water in floods were no avail.
685 Aeneas tore the garment from his shoulders,
spread wide his hands, and called the gods to help:
"Jove, if you loathe not every Trojan down
to the last, if your old justice still takes thought
for the troubles of men, rescue my fleet from fire!
690 Lord, save from death these meager scraps of Troy!
Or let it end: hurl your dread bolt and kill me,
if such I've earned. Your right hand bury me here!"
He scarce had done when rain poured down and clouds
came wild, swirling, and dark; the thunder shook
695 high hill and plain. Down from a turbid sky
all black and gusty, the floods came washing, rolling,
to fill the ships brim-over. Half-burned beams
were drenched till all the fire was out. Four ships
were lost, but all the rest saved from destruction.

700 But Lord Aeneas, hit hard by this harsh blow,
revolved vast cares at heart, now here, now there,
turning and changing: What? Settle in Sicily,
forgetting his fate? Or make for Italian shores?
Then Nautes the old, sole man whom Pallas taught
705 the riches of her art, and brought him fame

(she gave him the answers: what the wrath of gods
portended, or what the laws of fate required) —
he spoke these words of comfort to Aeneas:
"My lord, best follow Fate, to go or stay;
710   whatever happens, courage must meet all odds.
A Trojan is here, sprung of the gods—Acestes.
Take him to share your plans; he'll not object.
Give him the people from the four lost ships,
and those who've tired of pioneering with you—
715   greybeards and mothers weary of the sea,
the sick, the fearful of danger: call the roll.
In Sicily let the weary build a home,
a city that—with due leave—they'll call 'Acesta.' "

The old man's counsel seared Aeneas' heart
720   and left him deeply worried and distraught.
Now Night rode up and darkness gripped the sky;
just then from heaven he saw Anchises' form
float down and all at once burst into speech:
"Son, who were once my life, while life remained;
725   son, dearer with each ordeal Troy's death imposed,
I come by Jove's command: he drove the fire
from the ships; his mercy came at last from heaven.
Most wisely has old Nautes now advised:
obey him! The best young men, the bravest hearts—
730   take them to Italy. In Latium you must fight
a race of savages. Yet first come below
to the halls of Dis, and through Avernan depths
seek meeting with me. No sinful Tartarus
confines me, grim and dark; I live where meet
735   the good, in Elysium. Here the holy Sibyl
(when many black cows have bled) will bring you through
to behold your people and learn what walls are yours.
And now, good-by. Cool Night turns at mid-course;
I feel the breath of Dawn's wild panting steeds."
740   He spoke, and passed like smoke into thin air.
"Where are you rushing? Where?" Aeneas cried.

"Whom do you flee? Who keeps you from my love?"
So speaking, he roused the ash and sleeping fires
on Vesta's altar and to the Lar of Troy
745 made humble prayer and offered holy bread.

At once he summoned his friends, Acestes first,
to tell Jove's orders, his beloved father's
teachings, and what he now designed to do.
After brief thought Acestes gave assent.
750 They listed the women and all who volunteered
for settlement—souls not thirsting for great praise.
The rest hewed timbers and replaced the spars
flame-weakened, shaped new oars and rove new lines.
The men were few, but men who lived for war.
755 Meanwhile Aeneas plowed the city's bounds
and marked out homes: this place was Ilium, Troy,
he declared. The new domain pleased Lord Acestes;
he called the elders to meet and hear his laws.
Then on Mount Eryx a temple near the stars
760 was built to Idalian Venus; Anchises' tomb
was granted a priest and spacious sacred grove.

Now for nine days the people feasted; prayers
were said till peaceful breezes smoothed the waves;
the South Wind breathed again his call to sea.
765 Along the curving shore vast keening rose
as people filled day and night with fond embrace;
the very women, the men who once had thought
the sea's face harsh, its force too great to bear,
now longed to leave, to escape, to endure all hardships.
770 Aeneas the good consoled them with kind words,
commending them, with tears, to dear Acestes.
Three calves to Eryx, and to the Winds a lamb
he bade them slaughter, and then cast off the lines,
while he, crowned with the olive branch, stood high
775 on his deck and from his paten tossed the meats
to the salty waves, and poured out sparkling wine.

As they sailed out, the breeze rose brisk astern;
the crews vied stroke for stroke, and swept the sea.

Venus, meanwhile, concerned and troubled, spoke
780   to Neptune; such the complaints her heart poured out:
"The burden of Juno's wrath, her unslaked grudge,
compel me, Neptune, to stoop to any plea.
No length of time nor goodness softens her;
Jove's word and Fortune's blow leave her uncowed.
785   To eat out Phrygia's heart by foul ill will,
to drag the scraps of Troy through every torment
was not enough; now she attacks dead bones
and ashes. Let her justify such madness.
You saw her lately rouse the Libyan waves
790   to sudden hugeness, mingling sea and sky,
foolishly trusting the winds of Aeolus:
in your domain she dared this.
Now look once more! She's driven the women of Troy
foully to burn the fleet; this loss of ships
795   has made them leave their friends on foreign shores.
For the rest, I beg you, let them sail your seas
in safety, let them reach Laurentian Tiber,
if this be allowed, if Fate there grant them homes."

Then Neptune, deep-sea-tamer, thus replied:
800   "Cytherea, you have full right to trust my realm:
it gave you birth. I too deserve your trust
who often have calmed the fury of sea and sky.
On land—be witness, Simois and Xanthus!—
I loved Aeneas no less. Achilles had crushed
805   the half-dead ranks of Troy against her walls.
He'd killed his thousands; every stream was filled
and moaning; Xanthus could find no way to roll
to sea. Just then the brave Achilles met
with Aeneas, not half so strong or heaven-blessed:
810   in a pillar of cloud I saved him, though I longed
to tear down the walls I'd built for perjured Troy.

I feel as I felt then: forget your fears.
Safe, as you pray, he'll come to Avernus port.
One only shall you mourn—one, lost at sea;   *scapegoat*
815   one life shall pay for many."

With these soft words he filled her heart with joy,
then yoked his horses with gold, and slipped the bit
between their foaming lips, and freed the reins.
In sky-blue car he skimmed across the water.
820   The waves died down; beneath his thundering wheels
the sea was leveled; the clouds fled from the sky.
Behind him, many shapes: enormous whales,
old Glaucus' greybeard dancers, and Palaemon,
the speeding Tritons, Phorcus and all his host;
825   on the left came Melitë, Panopea, Thetis,
Cymodocë, Spio, Thalia, and Nisaea.

And now through Lord Aeneas' anxious heart
sweet joys came crowding; quickly he bade the masts
be raised and canvas spread upon the spars.
830   Together they all made sail, together filled
now port, now starboard luff; now braced, now slacked
the yards. A favoring breeze bore on the fleet.
Ahead of all, Palinurus led the line;
the rest, as ordered, shaped their course by him.
835   And now, cool Night had nearly reached mid-mark
of heaven; in peaceful sleep the sailors lay
under their oars, stretched out upon the thwarts.
Then down from the starry sky Sleep softly slipped
brushing aside dark air, dispelling shadows,
840   to find Palinurus and bring him deathly dreams,
that sinless man. The god perched on the stern
in likeness of Phorbas, and from his lips poured speech:
"Palinurus, the seas themselves bear on your fleet;
the wind blows fair astern; there's time for rest.
845   Lay down your head; steal tired eyes from toil.
For an hour I'll do your office in your place."

Palinurus, who scarce could raise his eyes, replied:
"Is it I you bid make light of ocean's calm
and peaceful face? You'd have *me* trust that fiend?
850 What? Leave Aeneas to faithless winds and sky,
I, who have learned so often how calms deceive?"
Such was his answer. Locked to the tiller, he held
fast, unyielding, his eye fixed on the stars.
Then Sleep took branches drenched in Lethe's dew
855 and drowsy Styx; over the helmsman's head
he shook them and washed resistance from his eyes.
Unwanted sleep had barely loosed his limbs
and set him nodding when the taffrail parted
and dropped him, tiller and all, into the waves,
860 headfirst and calling for help, but none could hear.
Like a bird the god flew off through empty air.
The ships meanwhile held safely to their course,
by Neptune's promise sailing fearless on.
And now they were hauling hard by Siren's Reef
865 (treacherous once, and white with bones of men,
its roaring rocks and waves were heard afar)
when Aeneas felt his ship broach to—her helmsman
lost! In the dark he hauled her back on course,
with a cry and ache at heart for a dear friend lost:
870 "For trusting too much in peaceful sea and sky,
Palinurus, you'll lie unburied on unknown sands."

BOOK SIX

He spoke, and wept, and gave the ships free rein
until they raised Euboean Cumae's coasts.
The bows were swung seaward; the anchor's tooth
grounded the ships, their curving quarterdecks
5   curtained the strand. The young men dashed like flame
to Hesperian shores. Part sought the seeds of fire
hidden in veins of flint, part raided forests,
the wild beasts' homes, found brooks, and marked them out.
But Aeneas the good looked for Apollo's hill
10 and castle, and near it the awesome cave where hid
the Sibyl, the terrifier, whose heart and mind
the Delian seer filled with prophetic speech.
They came to Trivia's grove and golden halls.

Men say that Daedalus, fleeing Minos' power,
15 dared put his trust in air and widespread wings.
He sailed unwonted ways toward Arctic cold,
and settled lightly, at last, on Cumae's heights.
Safe landed, he made thank-offering first to Phoebus—
the wings he'd used—and built an awesome shrine:
20 on one door, Androgeos' death; the penalty, next,
paid by a sorrowing Athens every year:
seven of her sons; the urn and lots were shown.
On the other side, the isle of Crete rose high;
here a bull's cruel and furtive act of love
25 with Minos' daughter, their twiform hybrid child,
the Minotaur, monument to love profaned.
Next came that winding, wearying, hopeless house;
but Daedalus pitied a princess lost for love

and solved the riddle and puzzle of those halls,
30   with thread to guide blind feet. You, Icarus, too,
had shared in the masterpiece, had grief allowed.
Twice Daedalus tried to carve your fate in gold,
twice fell a father's hands.
                 They had perused
each last detail, had not Achates joined them,
35   and with him the seer of Phoebus and Trivia,
Deiphobë, Glaucus' daughter. She hailed Aeneas:
"The hour allows no time for seeing sights!
Far better from virgin herd to slaughter seven
bullocks, and seven sheep, and make due prayer."
40   So speaking (the men at once performed the rites
as ordered), she called the Trojans to her shrine.

From Cumae's cliff was hewn a monstrous cave,
with hundred gaping mouths and hundred doors,
whence hundred words poured out, the Sibyl's answers.
45   As they entered, the priestess cried, "Now hear your dooms!
It's time! Behold my god!" And as she spoke
there at the door her face and color changed,
her hair fell in a tangle; she choked, she gasped,
her heart swelled wild and savage; she seemed to grow
50   and utter inhuman sounds, as on her breathed
the power of God. "Trojan," she cried, "you lag?
Aeneas, you lag at prayers? No other power
can blast agape these temple doors." She spoke
no further word. Through hardened Trojan hearts
55   ran shock and chill; Aeneas was roused to pray:
"Phoebus, help ever-present in Troy's dark days,
who guided the Dardan shaft and hand of Paris
against Achilles, through countless seas that block
vast lands you led me, and to Massylia
60   to tribes and tracts that border on the Syrtes.
At last we've reached elusive Italy's coasts:
so far, no farther, let Troy's fate pursue us.
You too may lawfully show us mercy now,
you heavenly powers who hated Troy and all

65 our Dardan glory. And you, most holy seer,
    who know the future, grant (the power I ask
    is not unsanctioned) that for Trojan gods,
    errant and battered, I find a Latin home.
    To Phoebus and Trivia then I'll build a shrine
70 of marble, and name a day 'The Feast of Phoebus.'
    You too shall find a temple in my realm;
    there I will place your lots and arcane dooms
    proclaimed to my people, and men shall be ordained,
    lady, to serve you. Write no more on leaves,
75 lest wanton winds make nonsense of your songs:
    let your lips speak!" He said no further word.

    Not yet possessed by Phoebus, the weird fay danced
    wild in the cave, if she might shake the god
    free of her heart; he harassed all the more
80 her lips, her savage soul, suppressing, molding.
    And now the temple's hundred mouths gaped wide
    of themselves; the Sibyl's answer rode the air:
    "My son, you have passed all perils of the sea,
    but ashore still worse await. To Latium's land
85 the sons of Troy shall come (this care dismiss),
    but coming shall find no joy. War, terror, war,
    I see, and Tiber foaming red with blood.
    You'll face a Simois, Xanthus, Greeks encamped;
    in Latium now a new Achilles lives,
90 he, too, a goddess' son. Troy's burden, Juno,
    will never leave you; humble, in need, you'll plead
    with every Italian tribe and town for help.
    Cause of disaster again a foreign bride,
    a match with a woman not of Troy.
95 Still, never retreat! Gain boldness from disaster!
    Where chance allows, march on! Where least you'd think
    a Greek town will reveal the way to safety."

In words like these the Sibyl from her shrine
sang riddles of terror and bellowed in her cave,
100 wrapping the truth in darkness; such the rein
and spur Apollo gave her maddened heart.
Soon as her lips, deranged and wild, found rest,
Aeneas began: "Lady, no face of peril
will strike me strange or rise up unforetold;
105 I've seized and pondered all things in advance.
One favor! Men say the infernal king here has
his gate; here hell's dark, swampy rivers rise:
allow me to see my well-loved father's face;
show me the way, spread wide the holy doors.
110 Through flames and thousand flying spears I saved him
on these shoulders, with enemies all around.
He shared the route through all those seas with me
and bore the threats of ocean and of sky,
more than the old and ill have strength to bear.
115 Still more: he used to plead that I seek out
your door in humble access. Lady, have mercy
on father and son! All power is yours; not idly
did Hecate lay Avernus to your charge:
Orpheus could hale a wife's poor ghost from hell
120 by power of music and his Thracian lyre,
and Pollux, saving his twin by altern death,
could pass and repass that road. Why tell of Theseus
or Hercules? * I too am of Jove's line."

So he petitioned, with hand on altar laid.
125 The Sibyl replied: "O child of blood divine,
Anchises' son, descent to hell is easy:
all night, all day black Pluto's door stands wide.
To recall the step, escape to air and sky—
this, this is task and toil! Some few—those loved
130 of Jove, those rapt to heaven by valor's flame,

* Orpheus, Pollux, Theseus, and Hercules all went to the Underworld
and returned again.

the sons of God—have done it. Between, all's forest
wrapped round with black Cocytus's coiling streams.
But if you have at heart such love and lust
twice to cross over Styx, hell's darkness twice
135   to behold, and this mad project gives you joy,
hear what is first to do. A dark tree hides
a bough whose pliant withes and leaves are gold,
sacred to hell's queen. Curtained by a grove
it lies locked in a shadowy, lightless vale.
140   But none may pass beneath this covering earth
till he has plucked the tree's gold-sprouted branch.
This must be brought to Pluto's lovely queen
as offering due. (Break one, a second grows
like it, with leaves and stems of purest gold.)
145   Search then the treetops; when you find it, pray
and pluck. The branch will come away with ease
if you are elect of Fate. If not, no force
of yours will break it, no cold steel hack it free.
Lastly: a friend lies now a lifeless corpse
150   (you did not know!) ; his death stains all your fleet
while you hang at my door to ask advice.
Now bring him home and lay him in the tomb.
Offer black beasts; be this your first atonement.
Then shall you see the grove of Styx, those realms
155   where the living never tread." She spoke no more.

Aeneas, with saddened face and downcast eye,
stepped from the cave, revolving in his heart
events beyond men's sight. Beside him walked
Achates the loyal, step by troubled step.
160   They spoke of many things, conjecturing much
what friend had died, whose body they must bury.
But high on the beach as they came in they found
Misenus, untimely taken off by death—
Misenus, son of Aeolus, best of all
165   at sounding the reveille or call to arms.
He had been Hector's man; by Hector's side

he'd marched to glory with trumpet and with spear.
But once Achilles had stripped his chief of life,
he'd joined Aeneas' corps, for he was brave
170 and a fighter, and would obey no lesser man.
But now with a conch he'd blared across the waves—
the fool!—and dared the gods contest his tunes.
Triton accepted and, if the tale be true,
caught him on foaming reefs and drowned him there.
175 Now, circling round, the company mourned his death,
Aeneas leading. Then, with tears, they turned
to the Sibyl's orders. Quickly they built a mound
and altar, and piled on logs to reach the sky.
They went to a wood, the wild beasts' mountain lair:
180 down came the pine, the oak rang to the ax,
the beech and holm were hewn and split to rail
and billet; great elms came rolling from the hills.

In this work, too, Aeneas took the lead,
urged on his men, and shared their tools and toil.
185 And yet discouragement circled through his heart
as he viewed the wood—so vast! He fell to prayer:
"Now be the golden bough revealed to us,
here in this endless wood! For all was true
that the seer has prophesied of poor Misenus."
190 Scarce had he spoken when a pair of doves
came flying down the sky before his face
and settled on the turf. Aeneas knew
his mother's birds, and said a joyful prayer:
"If path there be, lead me! Direct your flight
195 into the woods, where on the rich soil falls
the shade of the tree of wealth. Resolve my fears,
mother in heaven!" With that, he checked his pace
to see what signs they'd give, which way they'd go.
They stopped to feed, then flew on just so far
200 as could be seen by those who followed them.
Then as they reached Avernus' stinking throat,
they rose with a swoop and sailed through brighter air

to perch on the tree they loved, a pair at home;
but—strange!—through the branches came a flash of gold!
205 As in the winter's cold the mistletoe
grows leafy and green (no child of its parent tree)
and with its yellow fruit loops treetrunks round,
so in the darkness of the oak shone leaves
of gold, thin foil that tinkled in the breeze.
210 Aeneas seized the branch; it clung; he wrenched
it free and brought it to the Sibyl's home. ·

Meanwhile down on the shore the Trojans mourned
Misenus in thankless office for the dead.
They built his pyre with pitch-pine and split oak,
215 like one great torch, and then with dull dark leaves
they screened its sides. In front they set the cypress,
the death tree; shining armor graced the top.
Some set bronze pots of water over flame
to boil, then washed the body and embalmed it.
220 They wailed the dead, then laid him on the bier,
and covered him with the purple robe he'd known
and loved. They lifted high his heavy bed—
sad office—and in our fathers' way applied
the torch with averted face. Up went the pyre:
225 incense, food, and oil and wine commingled.
When cinders crumbled and the flames died down,
they quenched the dust and thirsty ash with wine.
Corynaeus gathered the bones in a brazen urn;
he bore pure water three times round his friends,
230 sprinkling them with hyssop of fertile olive,
to wash them clean, then said the last farewell.
Aeneas the good piled high a mounded tomb
(placing upon it the man's arms, oar, and trumpet)
beneath the crag that men now call, for him,
235 "Mount Misenus," to keep his name forever.

This done, they turned to do the Sibyl's bidding.
There was a cave, deep, huge, and gaping wide,

rocky, guarded by night-black pools and woods;
above it hardly a bird could wing its way
240   safely, such were the vapors that poured forth
from that black throat, and rose toward heaven's vault
(and hence the Greeks have named it "Birdless Cavern").
Here the Sibyl began by bringing oxen
four, black-hided. She sluiced their heads with wine;
245   between their horns she snipped the tips of bristles
to lay as first fruits on her altar fires,
then called on Hecate, power of heaven and hell.
Acolytes plunged their knives and caught the blood
hot in their salvers. Aeneas killed a lamb,
250   black-fleeced, for the mother of Furies and her sister,*
and for the queen of hell, a barren cow.
He built night-altars to the Stygian king †
and laid bull's vitals whole upon the flames,
drenching the sizzling meats with olive oil.
255   Just before sunrise and the dawn's first light,
the earth beneath them bawled, the wooded hills
opened, and in the shadows she-wolves howled.
"Here comes our lady! Fall back, unhallowed souls!"
the seer cried. "Out of the grove! Out! Out with you!
260   Aeneas, start down the road! Unsheathe your sword!
Now you need courage and now a steadfast heart!"
With one mad shriek she entered the cavern's mouth;
she led, he followed, step for fearless step.

O gods who rule all souls! O silent shades!
265   Phlegethon, Chaos, regions of voiceless night!
Grant me apocalypse! Grant me right and power
to show things buried deep in earth and darkness!

They walked obscure through night's dark loneliness
past Pluto's empty halls and vacant thrones:
270   as one might walk through woods beneath a moon

* Night and her sister Earth, both of whom were daughters of Chaos.
† Pluto.

malign and blotched, when Jove has hidden heaven
in shadow, and black night robs the world of color.
Right at the entrance, where hell's throat begins,
Sorrow, Vengeance, and Care have pitched their tents;
275   there pale Diseases live, and grim Old Age,
Fear, evil-counseling Hunger, shameful Want—
shapes terrible to see—and Death and Toil,
and Death's blood brother, Sleep, and Pleasures vile
even in thought. War, dealer of death, stands watch,
280   and Furies chambered in steel, while mad Sedition
leers through her bedlam braids of snakes and blood.

Midst all, an elm spreads wide her ancient boughs,
opaque and huge; men say this is the home
of Foolish Dreams: they cling beneath each leaf.
285   And there are wild beasts, monsters of mixed breed;
Centaurs and two-formed Scyllas haunt the doors,
hundred-handed Briareus, savage Hydra
horribly hissing, Chimaera armed with flame,
Gorgons, Harpies, the ghost of bodies three.*
290   In sudden terror Aeneas drew his sword
and showed the charging creatures his bare blade;
and had his guide, who knew, not warned that these
were lives unsubstanced, flitting empty shapes,
he had attacked and wasted blows on shadows.

295   Here the road leads toward hell and Acheron.
That mud-dark stream, wide, swirling, sucking down,
sinking and rising to belch Cocytus' sands.
A frightful ferryman keeps the river-watch,
Charon, a ragged horror, whose thick white beard
300   lies matted upon his chin. His eyes are flames,
and knotted rags hang filthy from his frame.
He poles his craft himself, he tends its sail,
and in its rusty hull he freights the dead—

---

* Geryon, a triple-bodied Giant, one of the company of the sons of
Earth who attempted to dethrone Jupiter, but were defeated by the gods.

old, but a god's old age is raw and green.
305   Toward him the whole crowd rushed to the river bank—
mothers and husbands, those that had lived the lives
of bold, brave fighters, boys, unmarried girls,
young men cremated before a father's face—
as many as forest leaves that flutter down
310   at the first autumn frost, or as the birds
that flock to earth from sea when winter's cold
drives them across the deep to sunny lands.
They stood there begging to be first to cross,
their hands outstretched in love of the other shore.
315   The glowering boatman took now these, now those,
but drove back others and blocked them from the strand.
Aeneas, amazed and moved by all the tumult,
said, "Tell me, why this gathering at the river?
What do the souls want? Why do some fall back
320   from shore, while others cross the lead-gray stream?"
Briefly the aged priestess spoke to him:
"Son of Anchises, prince of blood divine,
you see dark, deep Cocytus and swampy Styx,
names not even the gods dare take in vain.
325   The boatman: Charon; his passengers: the entombed.
Those others are all unburied, a hapless host;
they may not pass the shore, the hoarse, wild waters,
until their bones have found a home and rest.
A hundred years they flutter round this beach,
330   then finally may approach the longed-for stream."
The son of Anchises checked his pace and stopped,
puzzled and grieved at death's inequities.
He saw, embittered for lack of funeral rites,
Orontes, the Lycian admiral, and Leucaspis.
335   These two, sailing the wind-swept seas from Troy,
were lost when a Norther sank them, ship and crew.

Then toward them came the helmsman, Palinurus
(plotting his course from Libya by the stars
he'd slipped from his quarterdeck far out at sea);

340 Aeneas scarce recognized his face, so dark
and bitter. He spoke: "Palinurus, what god did this?
Who stole you from us and drowned you in mid-sea?
Tell me! I've never known Apollo lie
till this one message that betrayed my trust.
345 He said you'd be unharmed afloat, and come
to Italy. Is this then his word, his promise?"
Palinurus answered: "Apollo told no lie,
my lord Aeneas. I was not drowned at sea.
In a sudden lurch, the helm was cast adrift,
350 with me fast to it, for it was in my charge.
Overside I carried it. By all storms I swear
that for myself I feared not half so much
as that your ship, with helm and helmsman lost
overboard, might founder in the rising seas.
355 Three winter nights I drifted endless miles
of wind-torn water; when the fourth dawn came
from crest of a wave I raised the Italian coast.
I floated ashore by inches, made it safe,
and was clawing my way, slowed by dripping clothes,
360 uphill across sharp rocks, when tribesmen killed me.
(They did not know me, but thought I was fair game.)
And now I lie awash in wind and surf.
And so, by the sky, the light, the air we love,
by Anchises, by all you hope for young Iulus,
365 rescue me from this misery. Find the bay
of Velia and—for you can!—toss earth upon me.
Or, if your goddess mother show some way
(for not without the nod of heaven, I'm sure,
you sail the boundless pools and streams of hell),
370 give me a hand to cross the waves with you,
that here at last I find my peace, and rest."
Such was his plea, and this the seer's reply:
"Palinurus, whence this blasphemous desire?
Shall you, unburied, look on Styx, the stream
375 of stern requital—you, pass this beach unbidden?
Think not to change the law of God by prayer.

But hear! Note well! Be solaced, injured soul!
A nearby people, frightened by signs from heaven
all up and down their land, will bury your bones,
380 raise you a mound, do office for the dead,
and name that spot 'Palinurus' for all time."
These words resolved his care; for a time he ceased
to grieve, in joy that earth should bear his name.

They resumed their journey then and neared the stream.
385 But when the boatman saw them from the Styx
moving through voiceless trees on toward the shore,
he started up and challenged them, and shouted:
"You with the sword, who trespass toward my river,
halt! What are you doing here? Stop where you are!
390 This is the vale of Shades, Dreams, Night, and Sleep.
By law, no flesh may ride the boat of hell.
Alcides? Theseus? Pirithous? 'Twas no joy
to me to see them come and cross my swamp—
'Son of the gods'? 'Unconquered heroes'? Hah!
395 That first one snapped hell's watchdog to a leash
and dragged him whimpering from the royal door;
the others tried to kidnap Pluto's bride."
To him the Amphrysian * seer gave brief reply:
"Here are no schemes like those (cease your concern),
400 nor does that sword mean war. Your ghostly guard
may bark forever to frighten bloodless ghosts,
your queen keep undefiled her uncle's house.
Aeneas of Troy, the good, the great in arms,
has come to the shadowy pit to find his father.
405 If goodness and greatness leave you unconcerned,
this bough" (she showed it, hidden in her gown)
"you'll know." His hostile, puffed-up fury died,
and with it, debate. He stood amazed and humbled
to see the wand of fate so long unseen;
410 he swung his dead-blue craft stern-on to shore.

* The epithet means "belonging to Apollo"; it derives from a river in
Thessaly which was associated with that god.

The other souls who sat along the thwarts
he herded out and cleared the decks, then called
Aeneas aboard. With groans at his weight, the scow
took water at every ragged, gaping seam.
415 Slowly it ferried them, seer and man; still whole
it dropped them in foul muck and dry, grey reeds.

At once the world burst round them with wild barking,
for Cerberus crouched there, huge beside his cave.
But when the seer observed his snake-ruff rise,
420 she tossed him sleeping drugs tucked in a ball
of crumbs and honey. He stretched three greedy throats
and wildly gulped; his weird dog's-body crumpled
and sprawled from wall to wall across his cave.
Quickly Aeneas passed the sleeping guard,
425 and hurried away from the waters of no return.

Now they heard voices, sobs, a strange vast noise
of ghostly babies crying: just at the door
of life they'd lost their share; pulled from the breast
they'd sunk in darkness down to bitter death.
430 Next, those whom perjured witness sent to die.
(Due process, here, and justice fix their homes:
Minos is judge; he draws the lots and holds
assize of the dead, to hear defense and charge.)
Next came the gloom-filled strip of suicides.
435 Sinless, they'd tossed their own dear lives away
for loathing of the light. Now, just to see
the sky, they'd gladly work for beggar's bread.
The law says no; the grim and loveless stream
prisons them: Styx enfolds them nine times round.

440 Nearby, the plains ran wide in all directions;
these were the Fields of Mourning—such their name.
Here dwell Love's lepers: wasted, ulcered cruel,
they slink down private paths, and hide in thickets
of myrtle; even death brings them no cure.

445 Aeneas saw Phaedra, Procris, Eriphylë
    (tearfully showing the gash her son had made),
    Evadne, Pasiphaë, Laodamia too,
    all in a group, and Caeneus (once a boy,
    but now by fate returned to woman's shape).
450 There too among tall trees walked Punic Dido,
    faltering, for her wound still bled. Soon as
    the lord of Troy came near and saw her darkly,
    midst shadows—as one sees the young new moon
    (or thinks he saw it) rising through the clouds—
455 he dropped a tear and spoke with gentle love:
    "Poor Dido! Then the news I heard was true,
    that with a sword you'd made an end of life?
    Your death—was I its cause? By heaven and gods
    I swear, by every oath that hell can muster,
460 unwillingly, Lady, I parted from your shore.
    The law of God—the law that sends me now
    through darkness, bramble, rot, and night profound—
    imperious, drove me; nor could I have dreamed
    that in my leaving I would hurt you so.
465 Wait! Let me see you! Do not shrink from me!
    Why run? Fate will not let us speak again."
    He talked; she watched him, but with eyes of hate
    and scorn, for all his soothing words and tears,
    then looked away, her gaze fixed on the ground.
470 He tried to plead; her face remained unchanged
    as if she were carved of granite or of flint.
    At last she drew erect and turned unsmiling
    back to the shadowed grove where her first love,
    Sychaeus, gave her comfort in his arms.
475 Aeneas, hard-struck by unkind fate, still watched her
    and pitied and wept until she disappeared.

    The Sibyl led him farther. Soon they reached
    Plain's-End, preserve where meet the great in arms.
    Here Tydeus ran up, Parthenopaeus, too,
480 and Adrastus (poor, pale ghost!)—famed soldiers, all;

here, much bewailed on earth, the sons of Troy
fallen in war. Aeneas wept to see
that long parade: Glaucus, Thersilochus, Medon
(Antenor's sons), Polyboetes, priest of Ceres,
485   Idaeus, armed and gripping his chariot pole.
The souls thronged round him, pressing left and right.
Nor was one look enough; they tried to stop him,
to walk with him and learn why he had come.
But the Argive chiefs, Agamemnon's fighting men,
490   soon as they saw Aeneas and caught the flash
of arms, panicked. Some turned their backs and ran,
as once they ran to the ships; some gibbered and squeaked:
a jaw slack-fallen was all their battle cry.

Here too he saw Deiphobus, Priam's son,
495   his body one bloody wound, his lips hacked off—
his lips and both his hands; his ears were torn
from his head, his nose was lopped—unkindest cut.
He hardly knew him, for he cowered and tried
to hide his gashes. Aeneas addressed him gently:
500   "Deiphobus! Captain! Prince of Teucer's line!
Who felt impelled to such bloodthirsty blows?
Who thought himself so free? On that last night,
I heard, you killed Greeks till you fell exhausted
to die on your dead all helter-skelter piled.
505   On Cape Rhoeteum I raised your cenotaph—
I took that time—and thrice invoked your ghost.
Your name and armor mark the spot; I found
no trace of you to bury before I sailed."
Deiphobus answered: "You left no work undone;
510   you paid me every due the dead may ask.
Fate and that murdering she-devil * from Sparta
gave me these wounds: these are her souvenirs.
That final night: you know how gay we were,
such fools! You must remember all too well.

* For the story of Deiphobus and Helen, see "Deiphobus" in the Glossary.

515 Even as that deadly horse came bounding up
Troy's hill, its belly big with men-at-arms,
she led our women in the fire-dance round,
'to honor God.' She held the biggest torch
and from a high point signaled to the Greeks.
520 I'd come home tired, worried, dead for rest,
to my ill-starred bedroom; there I lay in sleep
so sweet, so deep—most like the peace of death.
My noble wife now stripped my house of weapons;
from under my pillow she even slipped my sword. ≠ Penelope
525 She called Menelaus in, threw wide my door—
thinking this lovely gift would please her darling
and make him forget old tales and ugly talk.
In short, the two burst in (he had a friend
to abet his crime, Ulysses): God give the Greeks
530 as much, if I may justly ask revenge!
But you're alive! Come, tell me now: What chance
has brought you? Did you lose your course at sea?
Did God command? Tell, by what blow of fate
you've come to this grim, sunless, fogbound place?"

535 As they talked, Aurora with her rosy team
had passed the mid-point of her course in heaven,
and the time allowed might all have been so spent,
had not the Sibyl uttered admonition:
"Night's coming, Aeneas; we're wasting time on tears.
540 The road splits here and leads in two directions.
the right fork stretches beneath the walls of Dis
to Elysium: this is our route. Left runs the road
to Tartarus, where the vile atone their crimes."
Deiphobus then: "Don't chide me, reverend lady!
545 I'm going—back to my company, back to night.
Go, glory of Troy! Have better luck than I!"
With that last word he turned and walked away.

Aeneas looked quickly round. To the left, he saw
a cliff; at its base, broad battlements triple-walled.

550 A river of swirling flame flowed all around—
Phlegethon, rolling a rubble of grinding rocks.
A gate rose huge, by granite columns flanked;
no mortal power—not even gods at war—
had strength to force it. Its tower of steel stood tall,
555 and at its gate, Tisiphone, bloody-garbed,
kept sleepless watch eternal, night and day.
From here came forth wild screams, the savage whistle
of whips, the hiss of irons, the rattle of chains.
Aeneas stopped short. He listened and turned pale:
560 "What shapes of sin are here? Speak, Sibyl! What pains
pursue them? The noise is deafening to my ears!"
Then spoke the holy seer: "Great prince of Troy,
no guiltless man may pass the door of sin.
When Hecate laid Avernus to my charge
565 she showed me the place, and how God punishes.
This kingdom of torment Rhadamanthus rules;
he hears and chastens fraud; all must confess
their sins committed on earth and tucked away
for atonement (death seemed pleasantly remote).
570 At the word 'Guilty!' Tisiphone lifts her lash
and leaps to snap it; her left hand holds out snakes
poised to strike; she summons her savage sisters.
Then only the hellish gates are opened wide
on shrieking hinges. You see what kind of guard
575 sits at the entry? What shape patrols the door?
Inside is the Hydra's post; her fifty mouths
gape still more black and monstrous. Then the pit
opens toward darkness downward twice as far
as eye looks up toward heaven and Olympus.
580 Down at the bottom the ancient sons of Earth,
the Titans, wallow where the lightning hurled them.
I saw the sons of Aloeus, giant twins,
who attacked high heaven and tried to tear it down
barehanded, and pull Jove from his royal throne—
585 saw Salmoneus in torment of the damned
for mocking the flame and thunderbolt of Jove.

Driving a four-horse team and shaking a torch
he'd marched in pride through Greece and down the streets
of Elis, demanding honors due a god,
590 the fool: he'd made a lightning bolt of brass
and fashioned his horses' hooves to drum like thunder.
But the father almighty massed his clouds and whirled
his bolt—no pitch pine and no smoky flame
of torch; a fireball rode the pretender down.
595 Tityus, too, the child of Earth all-mother,
was there to see: his body filled a field
nine acres broad; with curving beak, a vulture
fed on his deathless liver (fertile food
for pain), probing his vitals, making his ribs
600 her home; his flesh, reborn, could never rest.
Why tell of the Lapiths, Pirithous, and Ixion,
. . . .*
over whom a black flint, ever about to fall,
hangs menacing. Brightly shines the wedding couch,
deep-cushioned, gilded; royal is the feast
605 he sees laid out. But there she lies, the worst
of the Furies, and will not let him touch the food:
she jumps to her feet, lifts up her torch, and snarls.

"They too come here who, living, loathed a brother,
drove out a father, or tricked a poor man's trust;
610 who, finding wealth, sat lonely brooding on it
with never a share for a neighbor (legion, they!);
and those for adultery killed, and those who raised
rebellion, heedless of oath and service due;
here they are jailed and wait their dooms. Don't ask
615 what doom, what shape, what lot entraps them there.
Some roll great boulders; some, spread-eagled, hang
on whirling wheels. One sits, forever sits:
Theseus the luckless; one—poor, wretched Phlegyas—

* A line appears to have been lost here. The reference seems to have been to Tantalus, who was punished in the manner described in lines 602–603.

repeats in the gloom his warning to all men:
620 'Hear this: learn justice; never scorn the gods!'
Here is the man who for a tyrant's gold
enslaved his country; here, the peddler of laws;
here, one who raped his child and called it marriage:
all monsters of insolence, monsters in success.
625 Had I a hundred tongues, a hundred mouths,
and chords of steel, I could not tell the forms
of all their crimes, nor list the penalties."

When Phoebus' aged seer had thus concluded,
"Come now," she said. "Move on! Complete your task!
630 Let's hurry! I see the walls forged on the hearths
of the Cyclops. There's the arch and there the gate,
where we must place our gift, as we were ordered."
Then, walking together over a lightless road,
they covered the mid-space and approached the door.
635 Aeneas stood close and with fresh water sprinkled
his body, then set the bough against the door.

Thus with their liturgy to the goddess ended,
they came to the place of joy, the pleasant lawns,
the groves of the lucky, and the blessed homes.
640 These lands are clothed in larger air and light
the color of life; they see their sun, their stars.
Here, figures were training on the grassy grounds,
some playing games, some wrestling in the ring,
and some were treading the dance and singing songs.
645 There stood, the priest of Thrace,* in poet's gown,
playing his instrument of seven strings
(he plucked with fingers now, and now with plectrum).
Here, Teucer's ancient line, his splendid sons,
greathearted heroes, born in happier days:
650 Ilus, Assaracus, Dardanus, founder of Troy.
Aeneas was startled: there lay cars and arms
at rest, spears stacked, and horses running free

* Orpheus.

grazing the field. The joy the living knew
in arms and car, their love of grooming horses
655 to sleekness, followed them beyond the grave.
Aeneas saw others about him on the grass,
feasting and singing cheerful songs of praise.
Above them hung sweet bays, and from a hill
Eridanus tumbled his waters through the grove.

660 Here were the band who for their country bled,
here priests who in the world led saintly lives,
prophets of truth, who spoke as God would speak,
those whose discoveries made a better world,
those who by doing good earned men's remembrance.
665 Each one wore snow-white bands about his head.
The Sibyl addressed them as they gathered round,
Musaeus first (the crowd surrounded him
and watched him towering shoulder-high above them) :
"Tell us, O blessed souls, tell, best of bards,
670 where we may find Anchises? To see him
we came and crossed the floods of Erebus."
Then from the great man came this brief reply:
"None has a place assigned. We live in groves;
our beds are the riverbanks and fields made fresh
675 by springs. But if you wish so much to find him,
climb up this hill; I'll set you on your way."
He walked ahead, and from the hilltop showed them
the garden lands. They left the summit then.

Deep in a grassy valley stood the souls
680 mustered for life on earth. With eye alert
Anchises surveyed them, checking off the roll
of all his cherished line: his sons, their sons,
their luck, their destinies, their works and ways.
But when, across the fields, he saw Aeneas
685 coming, he stretched out both his hands for joy;
tears washed his cheeks; words tumbled from his lips:
"You've come at last! Your father waited long

for love to conquer hardship! Oh, my son!
Do I see your face? And may we talk once more?
690   I knew it would happen! In my heart I knew!
I reckoned the hours with care and told them right.
Over what lands, what endless seas you traveled,
harried by countless dangers, and now you've come!
In Libya, disaster was close: I feared for you."
695   Aeneas replied: "Father, your tear-stained face,
so often in my mind, compelled me here.
Our fleet is in Tuscan waters! Give me your hand,
let me embrace you, father: don't slip away!"
So speaking, he let the tears course down his face.
700   Three times he tried to fold him in his arms;
three times an empty shade escaped his grasp,
light as the air, most like the wings of sleep.

Just then, far down a slope, Aeneas saw
a grove apart, with foliage thick and rustling:
705   this was the haven of peace, where Lethe flowed:
about it flitted the nations of mankind
like bees in a meadow on a summer's day
(they stop at bright-hued blooms and cluster close
around white lilies; their humming fills the field).
710   At the sight Aeneas was puzzled and stopped short:
"What did this mean? What river," he asked, "was that?
Who were those people that swarmed about its banks?"
Then Lord Anchises: "Those are souls whose fate
binds them to flesh once more. At Lethe's waters
715   they drink and forget past years of care and fear.
I've longed to show them to you and tell their names—
the line of my children, the muster of my heirs—
that you may rejoice with me for Italy found."
"What, father? Must I think men's souls rise up
720   from here to the air, and to the sluggish flesh
return? Poor fools! Whence this mad lust for life?"
"I'll speak at once, dear son, and ease your mind,"
Anchises answered, and told the order of things.

"To begin: the heavens, the earth, the watery wastes,
725 the lucent globe of moon, the sun, the stars,
exist through inward spirit. Their total mass
by mind is permeated: hence their motion.
From mind and spirit comes life—of man, of beast,
of bird, of monsters under the foam-flecked seas.
730 Life is from heaven—a seed of fire that glows
bright, so far as flesh cannot repress it,
or earthly, death-bound bodies dull its glow.
From flesh come fear, desire, pain, and joy:
its pitch-dark prison blinds us to the light.
735 And even on that last day when life departs,
not all our evil, all the body's foul
corruption leaves us: deep ingrained, in ways
past comprehension, much has hardened fast.
Our souls, then, suffer pain, and pay the price
740 for wrongs done years before: some, like a cloak
laid off, hang to the winds; some lose their stains
by flood and swirl, or cautery of fire.
We suffer, each, our ghostly selves, then pass—
some few—to gain Elysium's fields of joy.
745 The years go by; Time makes his cycle just,
our hardened filth is sloughed; intelligence
pure, as of heaven, is left, and breath, and fire.
After a thousand circling years, God calls
these souls to Lethe in a long parade
750 to gain forgetfulness, then view the sky
once more, and wish to put on flesh again."

Anchises spoke no more, but led his son
and the Sibyl, too, deep into the rustling throng,
then up on a mound where they could see the files
755 approaching and watch the faces as they passed.

"Now you shall see the glory that awaits
the children of Troy and their Italian sons—
all souls of splendor, who shall bear our name.
Hear their story, and learn your destiny.

760 That young man—see him, leaning on his staff?—
by lot will be the first to rise to light
and air with blood of Italy in his veins.
His name is Alban, 'Silvius,' your last child,
born in your old age to your wife, Lavinia,
765 bred in the forest, king and sire of kings;
through him our line shall rule in Alba Longa.
Next him is Procas, pride of the race of Troy,
and Capys and Numitor and—named after you—
Aeneas Silvius, famed alike for valor
770 and goodness—if ever he gain the Alban throne.
What fine young men! Look at the strength they show!
See how they wear the oak-leaf civil crown!
They'll found Fidenae, Gabii, Nomentum,
and build Collatia's castle on the hills,
775 Bola, Cora, Pometii, and Castrum.
(Great names they'll be; now they are nameless lands.)

"There's Romulus, son of Mars; with Numitor
he'll take his stand (through Ilia, his mother,
he's of our blood): see, on his head, twin plumes,
780 sign of a father's favor, mark divine.
With him Rome will begin her march to glory,
to world-wide rule, to spirit that rivals heaven.
She'll throw one wall around her seven hills;
she shall be rich in sons, like that great mother*
785 who, mural-crowned, rides through the Eastern world,
god-bearer triumphant; a hundred sons of sons,
all gods, a heavenly host, are in her arms.
But look, now! Look! Here comes your family,
your Roman children: Caesar and all the sons
790 of Iulus who'll come beneath the vault of heaven.
Here is the man you've heard so often promised:
Augustus, son of godhead. He'll rebuild
a golden age in Latium, land where once
Saturn was king. Past India, past the Moor

* Cybele.

795 he'll spread his rule to zones beyond the stars,
    beyond the ecliptic, where Atlas carries heaven,
    and bears on his back the spinning, star-tricked wheel.
    Against Augustus' advent, even now
    God's oracles have panicked Eastern steppes
800 and roiled the outlets of the seven-twinned Nile.
    Not even Hercules crossed so much land
    to shoot the bronze-hoofed hind, or bring back peace
    to Erymanthan groves, or frighten Lerna;
    nor Bacchus, when he drove his tiger team,
805 with vines for reins, in glory down from Nysa.*
    (And still we hesitate to fight and win,
    or fear to make our stand in Italy?)

    "But who is that? He wears the olive crown
    and carries hallows. White hair and beard—I know him:
810 that king † whose code gave Rome a base of law.
    He'll come from little Cures, poor-man's land,
    but rise to royal heights. Succeeding him,
    Tullus will shatter our peace and lead to war
    a people soft, unused to battle line
815 and glory. Ancus next—a boastful man,
    too much enamored of the people's whims.
    And there the Tarquins—see?—and their avenger,
    Brutus the proud, who'll give us back our power.
    He first will rule as consul, first will take
820 the axes; when his sons rise in revolt,
    in liberty's name he'll see them put to death
    (unhappy father, however the tale be told!)
    bested by love of country and lust for praise.

    "See—back there!—Decius, Drusus, and Torquatus
825 the savage headsman, Camillus with his standards,
    and, just this way, two souls in polished armor,
    full of good will while night entombs them here;

* For information on Hercules' labors and on Bacchus, see the Glossary.
† Numa.

but oh, if they see the light, what wars, what strife
they'll set afoot, what battle lines and death:
830   from Gaul and the Alps the father-in-law * will march
against the son † with Eastern legions massed.
(Children, never grow hardened to wars like those;
against your homeland raise no hostile hand!
Oh, take the lead, show mercy, child of heaven,
835   throw down that sword, son of my blood!)

"That man will slaughter Greeks and conquer Corinth,‡
then ride in triumph up high Capitol Hill;
this one § will pull Agamemnon's Argos down,
and a king who boasts the blood of brave Achilles—
840   vengeance for Troy and Pallas' temple defiled!
Who'd pass by Cato or Cossus without a word?
Who the Gracchi, or those twin thunderbolts,
the Scipios, bane of Libya? Who Fabricius,
whose need spelled might, or Regulus, sower of seed?
845   The Fabii rush me, yet he'll be their greatest
'who lone by laggard tactics saves our state.' **
Others will forge the bronze to softer breath,
no doubt, and bring the sculptured stone to life,
show greater eloquence, and with their rule
850   map out the skies and tell the rising stars:
you, Roman, remember: Govern! Rule the world!
These are your arts! Make peace man's way of life;
spare the humble but strike the defiant down."

* Julius Caesar.
† Pompey, who married Caesar's daughter, Julia.
‡ Mummius, the Roman general who had the dubious distinction of
destroying the beautiful old city of Corinth in 146 B.C.
§ L. Aemilius Paulus. He defeated King Perseus of Macedon in the
battle of Pydna in 168 B.C. Perseus claimed descent from Achilles.
** There were so many famous Fabii that Anchises must hurry to tell
of them all; yet the greatest of them was a "delayer" (see "Fabii" in the
Glossary).

So Lord Anchises; then to their wonder, added:
855 "See, there: Marcellus, splendid in the spoils
of war, in victory tall above his troops.
In the great conflict, he'll set Rome aright
once more, bring down rebellious Gaul and **Carthage**,
and a third time offer captured arms to Mars."

860 Beside him, Aeneas saw, there walked a man
handsome and young, with armor shining bright,
but brow not joyful, face and eyes downcast.
"Who, father, walks there at Marcellus' side?
His son? Some other of his glorious line?
865 See how his friends press close! There's greatness **there**,
yet shadows black as night hang round his head."

Anchises answered as tears rose in his eyes:
"Don't seek to know your people's deepest sorrow!
The world will see him—only that, for Fate
870 will grant no more. The gods had deemed
our power too great, if we had kept this gift.
Mars' people, in his field, beside his city—
how they will grieve! What mourners you will see,
Tiber, as you glide past that new-raised mound!
875 No child of Trojan blood will raise such hopes
among his Latin sires, nor rouse such pride
of offspring in the land of Romulus.
Ah, loyalty, ancient honor, hand unbeaten
in battle! If he'd borne arms, no enemy
880 had faced him and lived, whether he went on foot,
or spurred a foaming horse against the lines.
Poor boy! If you should break the bars of fate,
you'll be Marcellus. Bring lilies! Fill my hands!
I'll scatter scarlet blooms: so much, at least,
885 I'll give a grandson's ghost, and do my office,
though vain." Thus over all that place they walked,
through broad and airy fields, and saw the sights.

After Anchises had shown his son each thing
and fired his heart with love of fame to come,
890   then he recounted wars that must be waged,
told of the Rutuli, of Latium's city,
and how he'd bear, or how escape, each blow.

Twin are the gates of sleep; men say that one
is of horn, a ready exit for real shades;
895   the other is white, of flawless ivory:
this way the dead send false dreams to the world.
Anchises' tale was told. Taking his son
and the Sibyl, he sent them through the ivory gate.
Aeneas made for the ships and joined his friends.
900   Then straight upshore he sailed to Port Caieta.
Out went the anchors; the fleet lay moored to shore.

BOOK SEVEN

Caieta, nurse of Aeneas, your death, too,
brought everlasting glory to our shores.
Your place is honored, and your grave still bears
your name, on a western shore—if that be glory.

5 Aeneas the good paid honors due the dead
and raised a barrow. When the sea turned calm,
he set his course, made sail, and left the port.
The winds held into night; a bright moon marked
the way; the ocean shone in shimmering light.

10 They skirted the beaches close to Circe's land
where she, the gilded daughter of the Sun,
filled pathless woods with music, and by night
burned sweet cedar to light her haughty halls
while she wove silken fabrics on her loom.

15 From here they heard the moan of angry lions
fighting their chains and roaring all night long,
heard bristled boars, and bears growling in cages,
and heard the savage howling of huge wolves.
These had been men, but with her magic herbs

20 Circe the savage had shaped them into beasts.
That Trojans should endure no such weird fate
by being tricked to land on deadly shores,
Neptune filled their sails with following winds
and sent them speeding past those boiling reefs.

25 The waves were red with sunlight, and in heaven
the Dawn rode golden in her rose-pink car,

when the wind dropped, and all at once each wave
fell flat; oars pulled against a sea becalmed.
On deck, Aeneas scanned the shore and saw
30   dense forests. Through them, Tiber's pleasant stream,
swirling and swift, dyed rich with golden sand,
burst out to sea. All round, bright-colored birds,
lovers of riverbank and river course,
flocked through the trees and sweetened the air with song.
35   "Put about!" he cried. "Men! Swing your bows toward land!"
Up the dark stream Aeneas sailed in joy.

Come, Erato, now! I'll tell of days long past,
of kings, conditions, times, when Latium first
saw strangers land in force on Western shores;
40   I'll call to mind how conflict first arose.
Blest lady, instruct me as I sing of wars
and wounds, of kings whose courage was their doom,
of Tuscan bands, of all the Westland forced
to fight. My greater history, greater work,
I now begin.
45   Latinus ruled the land,
a king grown old in years of peaceful reign,
the son of Faunus and the nymph, Marica.
(Faunus was son of Picus; Picus claimed
Saturn as father and founder of his line.)
50   Latinus had no sons; his only one
had been in childhood stolen away by fate;
one daughter alone kept to his stately house.
She was of nubile years, full ripe for men;
many from Latium and all Italy
55   sought her—the handsomest was Turnus, prince
of an ancient royal line. Latinus' queen
with love and wonder seconded his suit,
but portents, terrors, omens, blocked their plans.
In a court within the house, a laurel stood,
60   held in religious awe for many years.
(Surveying his castle, the king had found it there

and called it sacred to the Lord Apollo;
from it, men say, Laurentum took its name.)
Wonder to tell bees swarmed about the treetop;
65 with a loud hum they'd sailed the clear, bright air
and formed a cap, then, locking foot to foot,
dropped like a curtain from a leafy branch.
A priest looked up: "I see it! A foreigner
is coming! His army will attack *this* place,
70 and come *that* way, to master our citadel!"
And as Latinus piled an altar high
with holy brands, Lavinia stood beside him:
with shock men saw her long, long braids catch fire
and all her ribbons crackle and turn to ash.
75 Her hair was burned, her royal crown was burned
bright with its jewels; smoke and sooty flame
engulfed her, sparks flew all about the shrine.
Men spoke of the sight with wonder, awe, and fear:
they said that for the princess fame and glory
80 waited, but for the people, years of war.

The king was troubled; he sought the oracle
of Faunus, father and prophet, whose shrine lay near
Mount Albunea—wooded, full of the roar
of sacred streams, dark, and reeking of death.
85 Here the Italians, all Oenotria,
came to resolve their doubts: the priest received
their gifts; he slaughtered sheep, then on a night
of silence lay on their spread-out hides to sleep.
Thousands of shapes flew weirdly through his dreams;
90 he heard strange tongues, held converse with the gods,
and, deep in Avernus, spoke to hell itself.
Here, then, Latinus came to seek God's word.
He prayed, and killed a hundred thick-wooled sheep,
spread out their fleeces to make his bed, and there
95 lay down. At once a voice came from the woods:
"Seek not a Latin marriage for your child,
my son, and do not trust the match you've made.

Husbands will come from abroad; their blood will bear
our name to heaven; sons of their line will see
100   all earth beneath their feet: wherever Sun
returning lights the ocean, they shall rule."
These words, that Faunus spoke in night and silence,
Latinus could not keep locked upon his lips;
Fame, flying wide throughout Ausonia,
105   had spread them, when Laomedon's young men
made fast their fleet upon the grassy shore.

Aeneas with his chiefs and young Iulus
lay down beneath a tall and branching tree;
beginning their meal, they spread flat cakes about
110   to hold their food (so Jove himself directed)
and on this wheaten base piled rustic fruits.
They'd eaten all of these, when gnawing hunger
drove them to bite the poor thin cakes as well,
with reckless hand and jaw to break the rounds
115   of fateful crust, and crumble the broad, flat board:
"Look!" cried Iulus. "We're eating our tables, too!"
He stopped; he'd meant to joke, but that word marked
where trouble's end began. Straight from his lips
Aeneas seized it, but dared not speak, for awe.
120   And then "Hail, land by Fate ordained for me!"
he cried. "Hail, home gods, faithful friends of Troy!
Here is your hearth and home! For so my sire
Anchises (now I recall) phrased Fate's enigma:
'My son, when you have sailed to unknown shores
125   and hunger drives you to eat both food and tables,
then think of rest for the weary, remember there
to build new homes and pile a rampart high.'
This was that hunger, this the finish line
destined to mark our wandering's end.
130   Let's greet tomorrow's dawning sun with joy,
and then make search: What place? What men live here?
Where are their towns? We'll fan out from the shore.

Now pour libation to Jove, pray in the name
of father Anchises, then serve the wine once more."

135   So speaking, he crowned his head with fresh green leaves,
and prayed to the local god, to Earth (the first
of gods), to Nymphs, to rivers yet unknown,
to Night, and to Night's rising constellations,
to Jove of Ida, to Phrygia's mother of gods,
140   to mother in heaven and father beneath the sod.
Thrice in a bright, clear sky the almighty father
thundered, and brandished in his heavenly hand
a cloud shot through with golden, flaming light.
At once through Trojan ranks the rumor spread:
145   the day had come to build their long-due walls.
The omen set them feasting; filled with joy
they stationed the mixing bowls and crowned the wine.

The next day's lamp had brought the light of dawn
to earth when they spread out to learn the land—
150   cities, peoples, coasts. Here was "Numicus"—
a pond; a river—"Tiber"; here Latins lived.
The son of Anchises chose a hundred men
from all the ranks to approach the king's great walls;
each was to wear an olive crown, bear gifts
155   for the king and plead the cause of peace for Troy.
They obeyed at once, marching with rapid pace.
Aeneas drove a furrow to mark his walls,
then built his fort: this first, this seaside home,
he ringed with stakes and earthworks, like a camp.
160   And now, their journey done, the embassy
saw Latin towers and roofs, and neared the walls.
Before the town, a company of young men
rode horses and drove the dusty chariot race,
stretched a taut bow, or tensed to send a spear
165   spinning, or raced on foot, or boxed and sparred.

One leaped to horse and brought the aged king
the news that tall men dressed in foreign garb
were coming. The king bade bring them to his house,
then took his place on his ancestral throne.

170   The house was like a temple, columned, huge,
high on a hill—the palace of King Picus,
whose ancient trees inclined the heart to prayer.
Here only could the scepter be received
by holy rite; here were both court and temple,
175   here was the house of feasts; here, month by month,
the elders killed a ram, then sat in council.
Within the door stood antique cedar masks
of men and gods: Italus, Lord Sabinus
the vintner, his pruning hook still there to see,
180   Saturn the old, Janus the double-browed,
row after row of kings, since time began,
and bands of those who bled to save their country.
And from the holy doorposts, too, hung spears
by the hundred, captured chariots, curve-blade axes,
185   plumed helmets, timber-balks from city gates,
arrows and shields, and rams wrenched out of ships.
There, too, holding the augur's crook and clad
in a long purple coat, with shield on arm,
sat Picus, breaker of horses: his lustful wife,
190   Circe, with golden wand and magic drug,
had made him a bird with particolored wings.

Within this temple, on his father's throne,
Latinus sat, and called the Trojans to him.
They entered: he started the parley with a smile:
195   "Sons of Dardanus—for we know your home
and lineage: all the world marked how you sailed—
what do you wish? What cause, what need has brought you
to Italy's shore, through all those deep blue seas?
Are you off course? Did storm winds drive you here?
200   (Mishaps like these plague sailors everywhere!)

You've stepped ashore, made camp beside our river:
be welcome! Know that Latins are the sons
of Saturn—just, but not by bond or law;
rather, by nature and God's timeless code.
205   Yes! I remember (the years had dimmed the tale):
Auruncan elders told how Dardanus,
born in our land, had sailed to Phrygia, Ida,
and Thracian Samos—now called 'Samothrace.'
He came from here—from Corythus, Tuscan town.
210   And now the golden house of star-flecked heaven
enthrones him: one more god, one altar more."

He ended, and Ilioneus replied:
"My lord, great son of Faunus, no black wind
nor winter wave forced us to haven here;
215   no star nor shoreline tricked us from our course.
We sailed here by design, with full good will,
forced exiles of a kingdom once the greatest
the Sun shone on from tall Olympus' top.
From Jove, our eponym, and Dardanus
220   our proud line runs; our king is of Jove's blood—
Aeneas of Troy: he sent us to your door.
How great the storm that swept from savage Argos
across the plains of Ida, how fate drove
Asia and Europe to clash—two worlds at war—
225   is known by men even beyond the sea
at earth's last limit, and by men sequestered
where suns are heartless, mid-zone of the five.
Out of that deluge, across vast deeps, we sailed;
we ask a patch of land for our gods, a beach
230   out of the way, and man's right: water and air.
We'll not disgrace your throne; your kindness here
will earn no trivial honor, soon forgotten;
Italy won't regret embracing Troy:
by Aeneas' life and strong right arm I swear it.
235   All who have tried our honor or fighting power,
people on people, nation (never scorned us

because we plead humbly, with signs of peace!)
on nation, have sought to make us their ally.
But God and Fate have bid us seek your land;
240 such were the orders! Dardanus came from here;
here he returns, by weight of God's vast will,
to Tuscany's Tiber, and Numicus sacred spring.
Aeneas sends you gifts, the poor remains
of prior glory, saved from Troy in flames.
245 This was Anchises' gold libation cup;
this was King Priam's vestment, when he called
his nations to hear the law; his mace, his crown,
his robe, work of the daughters of Troy."

Now as Ilioneus spoke, Latinus watched him
250 with gaze intent, fast rooted to the spot,
his eye alive and darting. Vestment, mace,
all Priam's purples moved the king far less
than nagging thoughts of daughter, marriage, bride.
His mind kept turning back to Faunus' words:
255 was this the fated man come from abroad,
this the husband of prophecy called to share
his throne, the man whose children, great and good,
should bring a universe beneath their power?
At last he cried, "God bless what we do now!
260 Blessed be the signs! Trojan, you have your wish.
I accept your gifts. Your people, while I rule,
shall have the fat of the land—true Trojan wealth.
But Aeneas himself, if he so much desires us,
and is eager to know my house and share my throne—
265 let him come: a friendly face should cause no fear.
His royal hand in mine will seal our peace.
And now go tell your king what I propose:
I have a daughter, but marriage within our clan
is not for her; the signs, my father's oracle,
270 forbid it. 'Husbands will come from foreign shores'
(so run our prophecies); 'their blood will bear
our name to heaven.' This is that fated man,

I think, I pray—if my heart tells me truth."
With that, the king chose horses from his stable
275   (three hundred stood there, sleek, in royal stalls)
for all the Trojans—bade them be led out
prancing, gay in purple caparison
(gold were the chains that hung about their necks;
they wore gold armor and champed on solid gold),
280   but for Aeneas a chariot and matched team,
a pair of fire-breathers, breed divine
(Circe had got their bloodline: bastard foals
born of a seed she'd put her mare to steal).*
The Trojans took Latinus' gifts, and high
285   in the saddle rode back to bring the word of peace.

And now from Argos of Inachus returned
Jove's savage wife, riding a steady wind;
from Sicily's Mount Pachynus, high as heaven,
she saw Aeneas jubilant, and his men
290   building houses: sure that this land was home,
they'd left the ships. She stood transfixed with pain,
then, shaking her head, burst out in angry words:
"I hate that tribe! Their fate runs ever counter
to mine! They fell in battle, but did they die?
295   They lost, but were they lost? Troy burned—but they?
Where are their ashes? Through combat line, through fire
they found a way. But I? Must I admit
my powers exhausted, my fury slaked and dulled?
I boldly pursued those homeless fugitives
300   across the waters, and harried their flight by sea.
I wore out wind and wave against the Trojans.
What use were Syrtes, Scylla, vast Charybdis?
They've found their longed-for haven by the Tiber,
free of the deep and me. Mars could destroy
305   the monster Lapiths; the father of gods resigned
his old haunt, Calydon, to Diana's wrath—

* Circe, daughter of the Sun, had secretly bred her own mortal mare
with one of her father's immortal stallions.

and for what crime of Calydon, of the Lapiths? *
But I, the queen of heaven, must fall back
on last resorts, on scheme and subterfuge—
310   only to lose again. So! Majesty
is not enough! I'll beg—beg anywhere!
If I cannot bend heaven, I'll stir up hell!
We may not deny Aeneas his Latin throne;
Lavinia stands firm as his fated wife:
315   so be it! But we'll hold back his day of glory
and extirpate the peoples of both kings.
Let marriage join them, and let the nations pay!
Italian and Trojan blood shall dower the bride,
and War attend her. Venus, like Hecuba †
320   bedded by fire, has borne a nuptial flame
again. Her child, a Paris of latter day,
shall once more burn to the ground a Troy reborn."

She swooped to earth (men shuddered as she passed)
and called Allecto from the dreadful hall
325   of Furies and hell's black night: she loves grim war,
anger, treachery, charge and countercharge.
Her very father in hell, her hell-born sisters
hate her, a formless thing of thousand shapes,
savage, alive with black and writhing snakes.
330   Juno spoke, and her words were like sharp spurs:
"Daughter of Darkness, help me. You will find
the task not hard! I must not be displaced
or fail of honor; the Trojans must not win
Latinus to marriage, nor burden Italy's bounds.
335   You cause devoted brothers to seize the sword,
fill homes with hate, bring lash and brand and death

---

*Jupiter had permitted both Mars and Diana to cause suffering and
death for no reason other than bloodthirstiness and hurt vanity.
† Before the birth of Paris, Hecuba dreamed that she had been made
pregnant by a flaming torch—an omen of Paris' role in the destruction of
Troy.

under men's roofs. You have a thousand names,
a thousand deadly arts. Rise up, rich heart!
Tear up their treaty; tempt them to acts of war!
340   Let will and cry and leap to arms be one!"

Allecto, slaked with Gorgon-poisons, leaped
to Latium, to the king's Laurentine halls;
soundless she stopped by Queen Amata's door
(poor soul! The Trojans' coming, Turnus' wedding
345   had filled her woman's heart with fire and fear).
From hell-blue hair the goddess hurled one snake
at the queen's breast, to lie close to her heart,
and witch her to fury—her and all her house.
Beneath her gown, past a smooth breast it slipped,
350   coiling but never touching; unperceived
it breathed her a snake's mad breath, then coiled about
her neck like a golden collar, then entwined
her hair and trickled oil-smooth down her flesh.
While yet the deadly poison slowly seeped
355   into her brain, and first flamed round her heart,
and fire had not yet filled her, soul and body,
she pleaded gently and in a mother's way,
with tears for her child and this outlandish match:
"Shall Trojan outcasts have Lavinia's hand?
360   Have you, her father, no pity? no self-concern?
no thought for her mother? The first fair wind will take
that pirate off to sea. He'll steal our daughter!
Just so the Phrygian shepherd came through Sparta
and kidnaped Leda's Helen off to Troy!
365   What of your word? Your ancient loyalties?
The hand you held so often out to Turnus?
Must Latins seek a prince of foreign blood?
So Faunus commands? Such is his fixed decree?
I think all lands not subject to our throne
370   and free are 'foreign.' This is what God meant!
Trace Turnus' line back to its origin:
his sires? Acrisius, Inachus! Where? Mycenae!"

She attacked Latinus thus, but to no end:
he stood his ground. The madness of the snake
375 now reached her vitals and flowed through every vein.
Helpless, driven by wild hallucinations,
a lunatic possessed, she ranged the city.
Like a top spinning beneath the braided lash:
absorbed in play, boys send it circling wide
380 around an empty room; whipped on in arcs
it travels across the floor. The children hang
in innocent wonder over the whirling toy
and lash it to life—just so she dashed and darted
through city streets and crowds of angry people.
385 Then on to the woods! Pretending Bacchic frenzy,
and spurring herself to madder sacrilege,
she hurried her daughter away to tree-clad hills:
she'd steal the bride and stop that Trojan wedding!
"Bacchus!" she cried, "you only deserve my child!
390 Glory! See how she holds your vine-wand high,
and dances, and trains a sacred curl for you!"
Word spread; soon all the women's hearts were fired
with mad and flaming passion to seek new shelter.
They ran from home: their hair streamed on the wind.
395 Still others filled the air with pulsing shrieks,
and, dressed in hides, carried the vine-wrapped spear.
Amata, waving her pine torch, flashed among them
intoning, "Lavinia! Turnus! Bless their banns!"
With bloodshot eye and wild, bloodcurdling screams
400 she shouted, "Mothers of Latium! Hear me, all!
If I, your luckless queen, can yet command
your love, and mother's rights can grip your hearts,
then loose your hair; join in these prayers with me!"
So down the lonely forest tracks, Allecto
405 harried the queen with Bacchic sting and lash.

Now that she'd put the first sharp point on madness
and set Latinus' house and plans at odds,
the goddess soared on dark and deadly wings

to walls of Turnus the bold, a town that once
410 Danaë built, men say, for Argive settlers,
when south winds blew her there. (Our forebears named it
Ardea, and its name is Ardea still,
but its day is past.) Here Turnus in his halls
was taking his rest through dark night's middle hours.
415 Allecto dropped the dreadful face and shape
of madness and took an aged woman's form.
Deep wrinkles furrowed her brow; in hair turned white
she bound a fillet and tucked a sprig of olive;
now she was Calybë, Juno's ancient priestess.
420 She appeared to the prince and spoke these words to him:
"Turnus, must all your will and work be wasted,
your throne signed over to immigrants from Troy?
Blood bought that match and dowry; now the king
reneges, and seeks his royal heir abroad.
425 Go on! Let mockery pay you for your pains,
you terror of Tuscany, bulwark of the Latins!
There, now! I've said it, just as Juno told me,
frankly and openly, while you slept at night.
Come now! Be quick! Get ready! Arm your men!
430 Move out! Those gilded captains camped beside
our river: burn them! burn their pretty boats!
So God commands! Let King Latinus know:
unless he listen to you and allow the match,
he'll feel it! He'll meet a Turnus, sword in hand."

435 So spoke the aged priestess; Turnus smiled
and answered: "Ships bound up the Tiber? Yes!
That news has not escaped me, as you think.
Don't dream up tales of terror. Juno the queen
has not forgotten me.
440 You're worn out, old, past your prophetic days,
mother; your worries are foolish. When kings make war,
servants may well fall prey to groundless fears.

Go dust your images! Keep your temples clean!
Leave war and peace to men. We'll keep that trust."

445   At this, Allecto's wrath burst into flame.
Turnus fell to his knees, trembling and mumbling,
his eyes staring: there stood the frightful Fury
with all her hissing snakes. Thick-tongued, he tried
to stammer on, but with a fiery glance
450   she stopped him short. Twin snakes rose from her hair;
she cracked her lash and slavered and shrieked and screamed:
"Worn out, am I? Old, past prophetic days?
Victim of groundless fears when kings make war?
Look at me: I am a Fury, straight from hell;
455   my hand wields war and death."

With that she threw a torch; it caught the man
full in the chest with a ball of smoke and flame.
A formless fear jerked him from sleep, while sweat
burst out of every pore and drenched his flesh.
460   "My sword!" he shouted all through the house. "My sword!"
He raged, bloodthirsty, murderous, mad for war,
ruled by his anger: as when faggots flame
and crackle under a brimful brazen pot;
heat sets the water leaping; it goes wild
465   and bubbles up from the bottom, foam and steam,
until it boils over and black smoke fills the air.
Peace was a ruin! He sent his officers
to King Latinus, ordered his men to arms.
He would guard Italy, beat her enemies off;
470   he'd be a match for Trojans and Latins both.
So he proclaimed, and summoned the gods to help.
The Rutuli rushed in concert to his standards,
some for love of his beauty, strength, and youth,
some for his royal blood and bold right arm.

475   While Turnus was rousing his men to fever pitch,
Allecto, on hellish wing, flew to the Trojans.
She tried new strategy—sought out the shore

where Iulus was snaring and running down wild game.
At once the maid of moaning drove his hounds
480 stark mad: with well-known scent she touched their nostrils
and sent them hot after deer. This was first cause
of trouble; this fired the farmers' hearts for war.
There was a fine, tall stag with branching antlers;
the sons of Tyrrhus had torn him from his dam
485 and raised him—Tyrrhus, herdsman to the king,
whose trust it was to guard his grazing lands.
Their sister Silvia taught him to come at call
and loved to wreathe his antlers with fresh flowers,
brush his wild coat, and bathe him in clear springs.
490 He suffered her touch, stood always by her table,
ran free in the woods, but then came back again
to the door he knew, however late the hour.

He was far afield when Iulus' maddened hounds
startled him as he floated down a stream
495 and sought a cooling shade along the shore.
Ascanius, eager to earn uncommon praise,
bent his horn-bow and let an arrow fly.
Some god guided his shaking hand: the shaft
with a loud whistle pierced through flank and loins.
500 The wounded beast ran bleating to the home
he knew; there in the barn he lay and bled,
filling the place with pitiful, helpless cries.
Silvia found him. Beating her hands, she called
for help: "Does no one care? Come, people! Come!"
505 They appeared like magic (for in the voiceless woods
Allecto skulked), one with a blackened stake,
one with a huge knobbed cudgel: wrath found arms
in every corner. Tyrrhus mustered the files
(he had been quartering oak with sledge and wedge;
510 with one great roar he'd seized an ax and run).

Allecto spied a moment ripe for mischief.
She flew to the stable roof and from its ridge
sounded the shepherd's call, and on her trumpet

blew one long, hellish note that shook the trees
515   all round, and made the forest deeps resound.
Far off, Lake Nemi heard it, and the Nar,
pale white and sulphurous; Lake Velinum heard;
mothers in fear pressed babies to their breasts.
At the terrible bugle cry the peasants ran
520   where the signal called, seized arms and joined the ranks,
angry and bold. The Trojans, too, poured out
through open gates to bring Ascanius help.
The lines were formed. This was no farmer's fight,
no skirmish, now, with clubs and charred vine-props.
525   Men fought with two-edged steel; the field turned black
and bristling with naked swords; bronzes flashed
in the sun and cast reflections on the clouds:
as, when a wind first turns the waters white,
the seas rise higher and higher until the waves
530   are huge and from the bottom reach toward heaven.
Here, in front of his men, young Almo fell—
the oldest son of Tyrrhus: an arrow sang
and struck him full in the throat. His cries were drowned
and the slender path of life locked off by blood.
535   Dozens fell round him, even old Galaesus,
who ventured to offer peace—the justest man
who lived in Italy, and her richest lord.
He owned five herds of bleating sheep, and five
of cows; a hundred plowshares tilled his land.

540   The fight surged over the field, an even match.
Allecto's task was done: she'd spilled first blood,
she'd seen the war begun, the first men fall.
Leaving the West, she rode the winds of heaven
to Juno; proud, successful, she addressed her:
545   "There, see it? Done—your hatred, sorrow, war!
Now bid them join in friendship and make peace!
I've spattered the Trojans with Italian blood;
now I'll do more, with your consent and will:
I'll talk the nearby nations into arms,

550 and fire their hearts with love of Mars the mad.
They'll join the fighting; I'll scatter the seeds of war."
Juno replied: "Enough of fear and fraud!
They've cause for war; there's fighting, hand to hand:
chance drew the sword, and now new blood has stained it.
555 Be this their marriage, this their wedding feast—
this son of love divine, that royal Latin!
You must not walk so free through heaven's air:
the lord of Olympus' top would disapprove.
Leave us! If further trouble chance this way,
560 I'll put it to use." So spoke the child of Saturn.
Allecto flew on hissing serpent wings
to her home in hell, leaving the world above.
Deep in the mountains of Italy is a spot,
matter for story and myth in many a land:
565 All-Hallows' Vale. Pitch-dark beneath dense leaves
it lies pressed in by wooded flanks; a stream
roars down it, swirling and crashing against the rocks.
An awesome cave, vile Pluto's breathing-hole,
is there: hell's roof has cracked, to open wide
570 a deadly, gulping throat. Down sank Allecto,
spirit of hate, and eased both heaven and earth.

Meanwhile the daughter of Saturn gave the war
a final push. From battle, into the town
the shepherds all came rushing with their dead:
575 young Almo, old Galaesus, slashed and bloody.
"O heaven, see this!" they cried. "See, King Latinus!"
Midst fiery shouts of "Murder!" Turnus came
to touch off panic: "A foreigner on our throne?
Our bloodstream mongrelized? And me—dismissed?"
580 Then the young men whose mothers, in Bacchic dance,
were ranging the wild wood (Queen Amata's name
was not unweighty) joined the demand for war—
unholy war, forbidden, by God's fate
and omens! As if possessed, they called, "To arms!"
585 Outside, the people thronged the palace round.

Like a sea cliff unmoved Latinus sat,
like a sea cliff when breakers come crashing in:
it stands, a solid mass, though wave on wave
howl round it, though the reefs and foaming rocks
590 make moan, and battered kelp festoon its flanks.
But when no power remained to contravene
madness, and savage Juno had her way,
the old king cried, "Hear, heaven! My words are wind!
Fate has destroyed me; I must ride the storm.
595 You'll pay the price with sacrilegious blood,
you fools! For you, Turnus, there's crime ahead,
and grim requital; you'll pray, but pray too late.
My peace is made; standing within death's door,
I'm robbed of a blessed grave." He said no more.
600 Locked in the palace, he dropped the reins of state.

There was a Latin custom (Alban cities
preserved it piously; now imperial Rome
follows it when hostilities begin—
when tragic war moves toward the Getic North,
605 or east toward Mede and Arab and Indian,
or against the Parthian, to reclaim our standards):
the double doors of war (such is their name)—
held sacrosanct through fear of Mars the cruel
and locked by hundred deathless bars of bronze
610 and steel, where Janus keeps eternal watch—
soon as the elders in council vote for war,
must be unlocked. The consul, in the dress
of citizen-soldier, draws the shrieking bolts
and cries, "War is declared!" The people cheer,
615 and brazen trumpets blast their hoarse assent.
Thus, then, Latinus was ordered to declare
war on the Trojans, and open the doors of dread.
The old king shrank from touching them, turned, and fled
that foul office. He hid where he could not see.
620 Then heaven's queen flew down; with her own hand
she struck the laggard doors. The hinges turned:

Saturnia burst the steel-bound gates of war.
Up flared an Italy always slow to anger.
Some marched to fight on foot; some leaped to horses
625   rearing and raising a dust. All cried, "To arms!"
Some shined the shields and polished the lance heads bright
with fine oils, and whetted the ax blades sharp;
they raised their banners and cheered at the bugle call.
And five great cities set their anvils out
630   to forge new swords: Atina, Tibur the proud,
Crustumeri, Ardea, tower-tall Antemnae.
They hollowed helmets and braided willow withes
as frames for shields; others forged bronze cuirasses
or from soft silver fashioned gleaming greaves.
635   The honored plow, the well-loved scythe made way
for heirloom swords retempered on the hearth.
Now bugles blared; the word was passed for war.
Here trembling hands seized helmets; here they forced
snorting horses to harness, shouldered shields,
640   or strapped on gold-bound armor and faithful swords.

Now, Muses, unveil Helicon! Start your song!
What monarchs marched to war, what men behind them
filled fields with battle lines? What soldiers then
were Mother Italy's pride, what swords flashed fire?
645   You, holy ones, remember; you can tell:
fame's fitful breeze scarce whispers to my ears.

First to the war came that rough Tuscan lord,
Mezentius, scorner of gods, with his armed bands;
beside him his son, Lausus, than whom no man
650   was handsomer, save Turnus the Laurentine:
Lausus, tamer of horses, battler of beasts.
He led (to defeat) an army from Agylla
a thousand men—he'd earned a kinder fate,
a better father than that stern Tuscan tyrant.

655   Next came a team and chariot marked with palms
of victory; Aventinus showed it, son

of Hercules. He bore his sire's device:
a hundred snakes, and Hydra, serpent-girded.
(On wooded Aventine the priestess Rhea
660 had covertly brought him to the coasts of light—
woman coupled with god, when Tiryns' son,
with Geryon beaten and killed, came to Laurentum
and bathed his Spanish cows in Tuscan stream.)
His men brought spears and deadly pikes to war,
665 and fought with swords and with Sabelline darts.
The prince, afoot, was wrapped in a lion's hide;
its shaggy, bristling mane and ivory fangs
covered his head. Into the palace he tramped,
a barbarous figure, garbed like Hercules.

670 Twin brothers marched in from the walls of Tibur
(their brother, Tiburtus, gave the place its name):
Catillus and Coras the brave, Argive by birth.
They strode to the front ranks, where the spears stood thick:
like Centaur twins come down from some high mountain,
675 from Homolë, mother of clouds, or snow-clad Othrys—
come at a gallop, and as they pass, tall trees
make way, and crashing thickets yield them room.

Nor did Praeneste's founder stay away—
Caeculus, son of Vulcan, king, but born
680 by a campfire while the stupid cattle watched
(so all believed). His regiment were peasants—
men from Praeneste's hills, from Juno's lands
at Gabii, from cool Anio or the rocks
and rills of Hernica, from Anagnia's fields
685 from Amasenus. Not all had swords and shields
or rode the rumbling chariot: most were slingers
who hurled grey lumps of lead; some carried darts,
two to a hand. They wore rough wolf-hide caps
to cover their heads; they pressed the left foot bare
690 to the ground; a rawhide sandal shod the right.

Messapus, breaker of horses, son of Neptune,
whom none had power to kill by fire or steel,
haled into battle a folk long since grown soft
and unused to war. He drew the sword again.
695 His people—Faliscans—came from hill and plain,
from Mount Soractë, the Flavinian fields,
Mount Ciminus and its lake, and from Capena.
They marched to the beat and hailed their king in song.
Like snow-white swans sweeping through sunlit clouds
700 back from their feeding grounds, from graceful throats
they pour sweet music to make the Asian pools
and rivers echo far.
So vast their number, none had thought them mustered
for arms and battle line; they seemed a cloud
705 of screaming birds pressing from sea to shore.

And here came Clausus, prince of the Sabine blood,
leading his army, himself a host in arms.
From him come all the Claudii, now widespread
in Latium, since Sabines gained a share in Rome.
710 He led Amiternum's hordes, the old Quirites,
the men of Eretum and olive-crowned Mutusca,
Nomentum, and the rose fields of Velinum,
the men of Terror Cliffs and Mount Severe,
Casperia, Foruli, Himella's waters,
715 Tiber and Fabaris, Nursia of the snows,
the captains of Horta and their Latin troops,
those whom Allia (luckless name!) divides
(their number as the Libyan waves that roll
when savage Orion sets in winter seas,
720 or as the grain heads parched by summer sun
on plains of Hermus or Lycia's golden fields).
They clanged their shields; their marching shook the earth.

Nearby, Agamemnon's man, that foe of Troy,
Halaesus, harnessed his team. He rushed to Turnus

725   a thousand fighters, men who tilled the vine
       on rich Mount Massic, from Auruncan hills
       or from Teanum's plain (their elders sent them);
       people from Cales, men who lived beside
       the shallow Voltur, rough Saticulans,
730   a troop of Oscans, who threw nail-studded clubs
       like spears, but fastened them to leather thongs.
       The left arm bore a targe; they used hooked swords.

       Nor will you fail to find place in my song,
       Oebalus, gotten by Telon on Sebethis,
735   a nymph, when he was old—king of Capri
       of Teloboës. But the father's lands
       did not content the son: he held in fee
       Sarrastis and the plains that Sarnus watered,
       Rufrae, Batulus, and Celemna's fields,
740   the towns beneath Abella's apple yards.
       His people, like the Teutons, whirled the sling.
       Their helmets were of bark torn from a tree;
       their shields and swords were made of sparkling bronze.

       You, too, from hilly Nersa came to war,
745   Ufens, called "the great" and "lucky warrior."
       His men, Aequiculans, loved to hunt all day
       in the woods: a rough lot from a crabbed land.
       They armed to work the fields; their joy, to rustle
       cattle in endless herds and live by plunder.

750   Here, too, came Umbro, priest, Marruvian,
       his helmet topped with fruitful olive branch.
       King Archippus had sent him, his bravest man:
       to snakes and vipers of the deadly breath
       he could bring sleep with gesture and with song;
755   his art could calm their fury and cure their bites.
       But he could not heal the slash of Trojan spear,
       and against wounds his song of sleep, his herbs,
       hunted on Marsian mountains, could not help.

Angitia's forest, Fucinus clear as glass,
760 and bright blue lakes bewailed him.

Up marched Hippolytus' brilliant warrior-son,
Virbius, sent by Aricia to her glory,
reared in Egeria's grove and on her shores
sea-washed, where dwells Diana of good will.
765 So runs the tale: Hippolytus, put to death
by Phaedra's art, shed blood to pay his father
(wild horses tore him to bits), but rose again
to the fiery stars and to the air of heaven:
Apollo's herbs, Diana's love recalled him.
770 The father almighty, angry that mortal man
should rise from the shadowed pit to light and life,
blasted the finder of this healing art—
the son of Phoebus *—down to the waves of Styx.
But Trivia, loving Hippolytus, hid him away
775 in secret exile in Egeria's grove,
to live unknown and lonely in the woods
of Italy, changing his name to Virbius.
This is why horn-foot horses may not enter
Diana's groves and temples: on that shore
780 they threw the lad when some sea monster scared them.
Yet nonetheless his son, on level field,
trained horses and drove a chariot into battle.

And there stood Turnus, giant among the chiefs,
holding his spear, head-high above the rest.
785 His helmet bore a triple plume and showed
Chimaera breathing out Aetnean fire:
she roared and flamed with wilder savagery
the more the battlefield grew raw with blood.
His polished shield showed Io, done in gold—
790 horns, hairy hide and all, a cow full-formed
(baleful tale!) —and Argus, guard of her virtue,
and Inachus, pouring a river from his urn.

* Asclepius, founder and god of the art of healing.

Behind him, his men were a cloud; shield crowded shield
in rows across the field: the Argive levies,
795   Auruncans, Rutuli, and old Sicani,
Sacrani, and Labicans' painted shields,
men from the fields by Tiber and Numicus,
and farmers who put the Rutulan hills to plow—
Circeii, too; and men who worship Jove
800   at Anxur, or in Feronia's leafy groves;
men from Satura's fens, men from the draws
where icy Ufens finds his way to sea.

Lastly there came Camilla, the Volscan maid,
with her column of horse, platoons abloom with bronze—
805   a fighter. Hers were no woman's hands, attuned
to distaff and wool; her young girl's heart endured
bloodshed and war; her feet outran the winds.
She might have sped across a virgin field
of grain and not have bent one tender stalk,
810   or flitted across the wide sea's swollen waves
as down a path, nor moistened a speeding foot.
From home, from field, the people rushed to see her—
both men and women—and marvel as she rode by.
They stared in wonder at her royal beauty—
815   purple on pure white shoulders, golden clasp
locked in her hair, but arrows at her back,
and in her hand a steel-armed shepherd's crook.

BOOK EIGHT

Now Turnus on Laurentine tower unfurled
the war sign, and let loud-voiced bugles blow;
and now he lashed his team and clashed his arms.
At once men's hearts beat fast; all Latium roared
5 the oath of terror and riot, as men went wild
and savage. Messapus, Ufens, and Mezentius,
scorner of gods—the generals—mustered troops
from everywhere; they stripped the fields of farmers.
Venulus they dispatched to Diomede's town
10 to ask for help: The Trojans were in Latium—
Aeneas had landed; he'd brought his conquered gods
from home and claimed the crown by right divine.
And tell him: many people had joined the prince
of Troy—his name was spreading all through Latium—
15 what his intent, what outcome he might wish
for the war (if fortune bless him), Diomede
would know far better than Turnus or Latinus.

So Latium moved. Laomedon's fighting son
saw it, and ebbed and flowed on waves of care—
20 his mind turned quickly here, turned quickly there,
darting in different ways all round about:
as light shimmers on water in brazen urns
when struck by the sun or by the moon's bright face;
the flash flits to far walls, then climbs the air
25 and strikes the high beams of a coffered ceiling.
It was night; all over the world, tired creatures,
both bird and beast, were held in profound sleep,
when on the shore, under the sky's cold vault,

167

Aeneas, disturbed by thoughts of war and death,
30   lay down past midnight and let peace enfold him.
A vision rose up from the pleasant stream
through poplar leaves—a gray-haired local god,
Tiber himself, clothed in a thin gray gown
and wearing a crown of reeds to shade his head;
35   he spoke, and with his words removed all care:

"O son of heaven, who bring our homeland back
from enemy hands, and save eternal Troy,
O long-awaited in Latium and Laurentum,
hear and be sure: This is your house, your home!
40   And fear no threats of war: the gods have dropped
all anger and resentment.
And that you may know this is no empty dream:
where oaks grow on the shore, you'll find a sow
huge lying, having borne her thirty young—
45   white she will be, and white her suckling young.
Here build your city, find peace and labor's end.
From there, when thrice ten years have circled round,
Ascanius will found his famous 'Alba.'
My song is true. Now, how you best may win
50   through trials ahead, hear, while I briefly tell.
In this land live Arcadians, sons of Pallas;
coming as friends and followers of Evander,
they chose a spot in the hills to build their town,
Pallanteum—for Pallas, their ancestor.
55   With Latium they engage in constant wars:
bind them by treaty; join them to your camp.
With my own hand I'll lead you straight upstream,
that you may conquer the current with your oars.
Up, son of heaven! When the first stars fade,
60   say prayers to Juno; with humble offerings
subdue her angry threats. When you have won,
pay honor to me. You see me in full flood,
washing my banks and cutting through fertile fields,

the sky-blue Tiber, river that heaven most loves.
65 Here is my home, source where tall cities rise."

So speaking, the River dived deep in his pool
and faded from sight. Night fled; Aeneas woke.
He rose, and watching the sun light up the sky
in the East, he prayed, and in his hollowed palm
70 scooped up the stream, then sent these words toward heaven:
"Nymphs of Laurentum, from whom our rivers rise,
you, Father Tiber, you and your holy river,
receive Aeneas; grant, grant him danger's end.
Have mercy, for I have suffered! Whatever pool
75 or fount or spring-fed spot may be your source,
you shall have honor on honor, gift on gift,
O horned king of waters of the West!
O, stand by me! More nearly state your will!"
He spoke, and chose twin biremes from his fleet,
80 put oars in locks, and called his men to arms.

At once, before their eyes, a miracle!
A white thing in the woods! White young ones, too!
She dropped to the grassy bank—yes, see! A sow!
Aeneas the good, with rite and prayer, dispatched her—
85 her and her brood—to Juno, lady of might.
That night was long, but Tiber checked his stream
flood-swollen: his waves dropped lower and were still;
he smoothed his waters like a gentle lake
or peaceful pond, that oars meet no resistance.
90 The Trojans pressed their course. With friendly sound
the oil-smooth keel slid through the stream, while wave
and forest wondered at the strange, new flash
of shields, at men and painted ships afloat.
They rowed through all a weary night and day,
95 pulled past long curves, found shelter under trees,
and cut through forests where the stream ran still.
The fiery sun had climbed to heaven's mid-orb

when far ahead they sighted walls, a fort,
and homes (now raised to heaven by Roman might,
100 then a mere village, Evander's sparse domain).
They hastened oar-stroke and approached the town.

It happened this day the Arcadian king paid honor
out in a park to Amphitryon's great son
and to the gods. With him Pallas, his son,
105 his generals, and his senate—plain folk, all—
reverenced the altar where the warm blood streamed.
They saw tall mastheads moving through the trees,
then out of the shade slipped hulls and muffled oars.
The sudden sight unnerved them; they leaped up
110 from the board. But Pallas boldly shouted, "No!
Don't stop the prayers!" He seized his sword and ran
to a rise, then called out, "Halt! You men: what made
you travel an unknown route? What is your goal?
Where is your home? Do you bring peace or war?"
115 Then Lord Aeneas from his quarterdeck
held out an olive branch of peace and spoke:
"We're sons of Troy, armed now against the Latins,
whose pride thrust war on us, war's fugitives.
We seek Evander. Call us ambassadors
120 come to ask you to join your arms with ours."
Troy! The name meant greatness! Pallas fell back:
"You, sir! Come ashore," he said, "and meet my father.
Enter our home; speak. You are welcome here."
He offered Aeneas a hand; his grasp was firm.
125 They walked off through the trees and left the shore.

Aeneas addressed the king with friendly words:
"Noblest of Greeks, God willed that I appeal
to you, and show you this beribboned branch.
Afraid? Not I, though you were lord of Greeks,
130 Arcadian, blood-kin to the twin Atrides!
No, courage and God's holy will revealed,
our fathers' kinship, your world-wide repute,

my fate—all brought me gladly to your side.
Dardanus, father and founder of Ilium,
135   by Greek account Electra's son, sailed off
to the Teucri. Electra's father, now, was Atlas
the mighty, whose shoulder holds the vaulted sky.
Your sire is Mercury, son of Maia the fair,
who bore him on Cyllene's snow-capped peak:
140   Maia (if we may trust the tale) was child
of Atlas—Atlas, who bears the stars of heaven.
You see: we are two branches of one line!
For this I dispensed with plot and go-between
and feeling-out; I wagered self and life
145   to come myself a suppliant to your door.
Alike on you and us the Latins wage
cruel war; if they defeat us, they are sure
to bring all Westland underneath their yoke—
to hold the Upper and the Lower Sea.
150   Here is my pledge; give yours! We have brave hearts
and men whose courage has passed the test of battle."

As Aeneas spoke, Evander watched his face,
his eyes, surveyed his person, head to foot,
and then replied, "Welcome, bravest of Trojans!
155   What joy to find in you the speech and voice
of Anchises the great, and to recall his face!
Yes! Priam, son of Laomedon, on his way
to Salamis, stayed with Hesione, his sister,
then came to visit Arcadia's wintry hills.
160   Youth's early bloom had then just clothed my cheeks.
What men, those Trojan princes! What a king
was Priam—but towering far above them all,
Anchises! How my youthful heart beat high
to address the man and take him by the hand!
165   All eagerness, I led him within our walls.
Then when he left he gave me a handsome quiver
and Lycian arrows, a cloak with threads of gold,
and a bit my son now owns—of solid gold.

Here, then, is the hand of friendship that you sought,
170   and when tomorrow's light dawns over earth
I'll send you away cheered by my aid and comfort.
And now—for you are friends—come join with us
in making this yearly feast, which we dare not
postpone. Grow used to this, our common board."

175   So speaking, he ordered food and drink brought back,
and showed the men their places on the green.
He led Aeneas to the seat of honor,
a bench of maple spread with lion skins.
Young men stepped quickly forward; with the priest
180   they served the altar meats; they filled the trays
with gift of the kneaded Grain, and poured the Vine.
Aeneas and all his Trojans ate their fill
of rib and chine and consecrated vitals.

With hunger appeased and appetite repressed,
185   Evander spoke: "This solemn feast of ours,
these sacramental foods, this hallowed altar,
are not imposed by fear and ignorance
of God. No; we were spared a hideous death,
and hence, in thanks, we make this yearly office.
190   You see, my Trojan friend, this crag-hung cliff,
with boulders scattered about, this houselike hole
where the hillside has collapsed in shapeless ruins?
There was a cave here, vast and deep recessed,
where Cacus lived—a dread, half-human shape.
195   No sunlight entered; the floor was ever warm
with new-shed blood, and at the tall, cold doors
hung dead men's faces blotched with ugly gore.
The monster's father was Vulcan, whose pitch-fed flame
he belched from his mouth when he moved, mountain-huge.
200   'Some day—!' we hoped; and time did bring us help:
the great avenger arrived, the god Alcides,
proud for his killing of triform Geryon.
He drove the spoils of victory: great bulls

and a herd of cows that filled both vale and stream.
205 Cacus—that thieving savage!—could not let pass
untried a chance for villainy or deceit.
From the corral he herded off four bulls—
pick of the lot—and four fine cows to match.
So that their hoofs should not leave telltale tracks,
210 he turned them around and dragged them by the tail
into his lightless cavern, and hid them there:
no signs would lead a searcher to his cave.
Meanwhile the herd had fed. Amphitryon's son
made ready to move them out and drive them on.
215 As he rounded up the cows, they bawled and filled
forest and hill with lingering, loud complaint.
Deep in the vast cavern, a lone cow answered:
she bawled, and blasted Cacus' hopes and plans.
The god flew into a rage; he flushed, and roared
220 with fury, grabbed his sword and heavy mace
all knotted, and rushed right up the high, steep hill.
That day our people first saw Cacus maddened
with fear: he ran—yes, ran!—fast as the wind
back to his cave; sheer terror winged his feet.
225 He ducked inside, ripped a chain free, and dropped
a boulder balanced by his father's art
on a spike. It blocked the door; he braced it there.
Up came the lord of Tiryns, raging mad;
he searched the approaches, looking this way and that,
230 grinding his teeth. Three times, in boiling fury,
he searched the hill, three times in vain attacked
the stony door, and thrice fell back exhausted.
A tall rock spire stood sculptured sharp and clear
atop the cave (men looked sky-high to see it) —
235 a handy nesting-place for carrion birds.
It leaned to the left, inclining toward the stream;
he stood on its right and pushed, then jerked it loose
and tore it free of its base, then tensed and heaved
and crashed it—crashed it to make the heavens ring.
240 The embankments burst; Tiber flowed back in terror.

But there the cave lay open—Cacus' proud
palazzo—deep, dark tunnels all revealed:
as if the earth in agony should split,
unlock the halls of hell, reveal the realm
245 of pallor (hated of heaven), and men should see
the pit, with ghost-things scurrying from the light.
The sudden light caught Cacus unprepared;
trapped in his hiding-hole, he howled in panic.
Alcides cornered him, jabbed him, pommeled him
250 with sticks and stones—whatever came to hand.
Now Cacus had nowhere to run from death;
he belched, and (wonder to tell!) out of his throat
poured clouds of smoke that wrapped the place in murk
and stole all sight away; a great black ball
255 of darkness, shot with sparks, rolled through the cave.
Alcides could not stand this; headlong he leaped
down through the fire where smoke rose up in billows
and the great cave was one black, boiling cloud.
Cacus spat fire, but despite flame and smoke
260 Alcides grabbed him, tied him in knots, dug thumbs
in eyes, then throttled him, till he screamed and died.
Now the black house lay open, its doors ripped loose.
There in broad daylight stood the stolen cows,
things Cacus had sworn he never touched; out came
265 his ugly corpse, dragged by the feet. Men gaped
at the terrible eyes, the face, the hairy body
('half wild beast!') and the jaws still stained by fire.
Since then, each generation has made this day
a holiday. Potitius was first founder;
270 the Pinarii now keep feast for Hercules.
In the park here stands his altar, styled 'the great'
by us forever—and ever 'the great' shall be.
So come, my men! Make the great act of praise!
Bind wreaths in your hair; the festive cup raise high!
275 Pray to the god we share; pour glad libation!"
So speaking, he veiled his head with poplar leaves
two-tinted, the sheltering crown of Hercules,

and took up the cup and blessed it. Then they all
poured out libation, and sang glad hymns of praise.

280   Meanwhile, where heaven rode low, the evening star
shone brighter. In marched the priests, led by Potitius.
Their vestments were of leather; they carried lamps.
They started the feast again, with tasty foods
for the table, and for the altar, gifts galore.
285   The Salii then danced round the altar fire
(they, too, with wreaths of poplar on their brows):
the young men here, the old men there, sang songs
of Hercules' glorious deeds: first how he crushed,
with baby hands, his stepmother's twin snakes;
290   then, how he destroyed two cities great in war,
Troy and Oechalia, and bore a thousand toils,
by Juno's cruelty, under King Eurystheus:
"Almighty, your hand struck down the twiform sons
of the cloud, Hylaeus and Pholus, and that weird creature
295   in Crete, and the Nemean lion in his cave.
You set the Styx to trembling, and hell's watchdog
crouched in his bloodstained hutch on half-gnawed bones.
No sight—no, not Typhoeus, mountain-tall
and armed to the teeth—could scare you, nor the snake
300   of Lerna, for all its heads that ringed you round.
Hail, very son of Jove, new light of heaven!
Bring us good fortune! Bless us! Bless these rites!"
Such were their songs; for closing hymns, they sang
"The cave of Cacus" and "Cacus, whose breath is fire."
305   The whole grove rang; the hills gave back the sound.

When feast and prayers were ended, all returned
to the city. There walked the king beset with years;
he kept his son and Aeneas at his side
and lightened the way with talk of many things.
310   Aeneas cast looks of wonder and delight
about him; in fascination at each sight
he asked its story, and heard the old, old tales.

Then spoke Evander, who laid Rome's cornerstone:
"The natives in these woods were Nymphs and Fauns,
315 and men, sons of the oak tree, tough and hard.
They were wild wanderers—never yoked the ox
nor knew of harvest or barn or husbandry:
they lived by hunting and gathering coarse, wild foods.
Saturn from tall Olympus first came down
320 (an exile, his kingdom lost) in flight from Jove.
He brought these ignorant, scattered mountaineers
together and taught them law; he named this place
'Latium'—since it was here that he lay safe.*
The Golden Age men tell of—that took place
325 while he was king: he ruled the world in peace,
until men worsened and an impure age
went wild for war and learned the love of gain.
Then came Ausonian and Sicilian hordes,
again and again. 'Saturnia' † lost her name.
330 Next there were tyrants, and rough, misshapen Thybris
(for him, we Italians later called our stream
'Tiber,' replacing the true name, 'Albula').
Exiled from home, I sought the ocean's end,
but Fortune almighty and a scapeless Fate
335 set me down here; so, too, my mother, the Nymph
Carmentis, ordered; so ran Apollo's word."

So speaking, the king walked on and showed the altar
and gate we Romans still call "Carmentalis"
to honor Carmentis, Nymph of a day long past.
340 (Prophetic soul, she first dared call the sons
of Aeneas "great," and Pallanteum "famous.")
He showed a forest (which Romulus would declare
"Asylum") and that cold vault, the Lupercal
(Arcadian name, called for Lycaean Pan).
345 He showed the sacred grove of Argiletum

* Vergil here alludes to a popular etymology, by which "Latium" was derived from *latere*, "to lie hidden."
† I.e., "land of Saturn"; hence, "land of peace."

(the "Death of Argus," for here that stranger died),
and led to Tarpeia's place and Capitol Hill—
glorious now, then rough with thorny brush,
a mystic, eerie spot that even then
350   frightened the peasants, fearful of cliff and woods.
"This forest," he said, "this tall and leaf-crowned hill
is home to a god—which one, unknown; my people
think they have seen Jove there in frequent storms
when his aegis flashed and thundered, and black clouds rolled.
355   And there—see?—are two forts, all ruined now,
remnant and proof of men of an older day.
Lord Janus built the one, Saturn the other.
Their names? 'Janiculum' and 'Saturnia.'"

As thus they talked, they reached Evander's house—
360   a poor man's; cows were grazing there, they saw,
in the Roman Forum and fashionable Carinae.
At the door, Evander said, "The great Alcides
passed this threshold; this palace welcomed him.
Be bold, my friend: scorn wealth! Earn, even as I,
365   a god's esteem: be gracious to the poor!"
So speaking, under his narrow roof he led
Aeneas the great, and showed him to a couch—
a pile of leaves, spread with a Libyan bear hide.
Night came and folded earth in dusky wings.

370   But Venus felt cause for fear; her mother's heart
was troubled by Laurentine threats of war.
She spoke to Vulcan, in his golden hall
breathed on her husband words of godly love:
"While Argive kings laid Pergama waste in war—
375   that citadel doomed to fall to enemy flames—
I asked no help for the suffering, no, nor arms
of your art and making. Dear my lord, I'd never
put you to vain trouble or useless toil,
for all the debt I owed the sons of Priam,
380   and all my tears for Aeneas' cruel mischance.
Now by Jove's order, he stands on Rutulan soil;

this time I come to beg your sacred power
for arms—mother for son. The tears of Thetis
and of Tithonus' wife could touch your heart.

385 See what peoples have gathered! They've barred their gates;
they whet the steel for me—for those I love!"

With that, her snow-white arms went round his neck—
gently, warmly. He tensed, then felt a burst
familiar of flame, a well-known warmth that pierced

390 his heart, then ran like a shock through all his frame,
as when the thunder rolls, the sky lights up,
and the clouds are split by jagged streaks of fire.
His wife smiled at the ruse; she knew her charms.
Then Vulcan, prisoned by boundless passion, spoke:

395 "Why all these farfetched pleas? How have you lost
your trust in me? If you had been concerned
then, too, as now, I could have armed the Trojans.
Neither the father almighty nor fate forbade
Troy and Priam to live for ten years more.

400 And now, if you want war, if such your thought
and concern, whatever my skill has power to give
that lies in the province of molten steel and bronze,
all that forge and bellows can make—stop begging!
Don't doubt your influence!" With that, he gave her

405 a lover's kiss, and melting in the arms
of his wife, sought limb by limb release and rest.

When night had passed mid-course, and the early hours
of ease had thrust off sleep, when woman wakes,
whose distaff and poor household arts perforce

410 sustain her life—she stirs the drowsy coals
and adds night to her day; through lamplit hours
she and her girls work on, ever the chaste
and dutiful wife, the fruitful mother of sons.
Just so, the fire god, at no lazier hour,

415 rose from bed and turned to his metal craft.

Off Sicily and the island of the winds
rises a rock, abrupt and wreathed in smoke;
beneath it, a cave—the echoing foundry hall
gouged out for the Cyclopes. Here can be heard
420   the clang and crunch of hammer and anvil, the hiss
of ingots of steel, the gasp of furnace and bellows.
The place is called Vulcania—Vulcan's home;
here came the fire god now, down from high heaven.

In the great cavern the Cyclopes were working,
425   Brontes, Steropes, and Pyracmon, stripped.
They held in hand, partly in final polish,
a thunderbolt—the kind that heaven hurls down
by thousands to earth. Part still was incomplete:
they'd fitted three coils of rain, and three of cloud,
430   three of red fire and three of winged wind;
now they were adding the awesome terror of flash
and crash to the bolt, and the fury of racing flame.
Elsewhere, for Mars, they'd started a chariot
with winged wheels—scourge to the world of men.
435   An aegis, too, weapon of Pallas aroused,
they were making glitter with gold and serpent scales;
snakes ringed it round, its breastplate was the Gorgon,
lopped from her body, but with eyes alive.
"Everything out," said Vulcan, "all you've started!
440   Hear me now, sons of Aetna, Cyclopes:
a brave man needs our arms. Gather your strength,
put speed in your hands, use all your master craft,
waste never a minute!" That was all. They bent
at once to the task and in fair measure shared
445   the work. Bronze flowed in rivers, and bright gold;
the steel that kills turned liquid on the hearths.
They shaped a shield portentous—one to stop
whole arsenals of spears—its seven orbs
all interlocked. Some filled the bellows-bags
450   with air, and emptied them; some tempered bronze

in water. Out came the anvils; the cavern groaned.
One by another, they raised their brawny arms
in rhythm, and turned the ingot with the tongs.

While Vulcan, far to the south, pushed on this work,
455 Evander was wakened by sunlight in his house,
and by the birds that sang beneath his rooftree.
The old king rose and shrugged a tunic on,
then strapped Etruscan sandals on his feet.
To shoulder and flank he laced a Tegean blade
460 and over his left side draped a panther skin.
He had a bodyguard, too: from his tall door
they stepped to his side—twin dogs, their master's escort.
He made for the guest hall where Aeneas slept:
he remembered his promised help—that great, good man.
465 But Aeneas, too, was up and moving about:
Evander, Pallas, Aeneas, Achates—all
met in the central hall, shook hands, found seats,
and then at last found time to hold converse.
The king began:

470 "Commander of Troy, never, while you yet live,
will I count Troy or Trojan power defeated.
For offering aid to you, a name so great,
our strength is slender. Here, the Tiber checks us;
there, Prince Turnus, whose arms clang round our walls.
475 But I've an ally for you—a warlike nation,
populous, rich, and royal, whom pure chance
declares our saviors. Fate brought you this way.
Not far from here, built on an ancient crag,
is a city, Agylla; Lydians, years ago,
480 a nation of warriors, settled those Tuscan hills.
For years they flourished; then a barbarous king,
Mezentius the proud, ruled them by force of arms.
How tell of the horror, bloodshed, tyranny,
atrocity? Such be on him and all his kind!
485 He even lashed the living to the dead:

hand to hand he bound them, and lip to lip
('torture,' this was) ; streaming with rot and gore
in horrid embrace, inch by inch, they died.
In the end, his people sickened. For all his ranting,
490 they took up arms, surrounded his house and him,
cut down his guard, and fired his palace roof.
While men were dying, he slipped to the Rutuli
and escaped; his 'dear friend' Turnus now protects him.
All Tuscany rose in outrage to demand
495 return of their king for judgment—or they'd fight!
Aeneas, I'll name you general of these thousands.
Their fleet has gathered; along the docks they fume
and call for attack. An aged priest restrains them,
chanting the dooms: 'You men, Maeonia's best,
500 pride of an ancient race! Your wrath is just:
Menzentius rightly stirs your indignation.
But hear God's word: bow down to no Italian!
Find foreign leaders!' At this, the Tuscan army
camped in the field, in terror of God's command.
505 Tarchon himself sent ministers to me
to offer me scepter and crown—the badge of rule:
'Come to our camp! Ascend the Tyrrhene throne!'
But I am cold and torpid, tired and old.
I will not command; my fighting days are past.
510 I might have named my son, but through his mother,
a Sabine, he's part native. You are blessed
by fate in years and blood; heaven calls on you.
Step forward, prince of Troy and Italy!
And see! I give you Pallas here, my hope
515 and comfort. Be his teacher! Let him learn
to bear the soldier's burden, and observe
your acts of war. Be pattern to his youth!
I'll give two hundred horsemen, young and strong—
our best—and Pallas as many in his own name."

520 At this, Aeneas and his loyal friend,
Achates, fixed their eyes upon the ground,

dwelling in thought on peril, sorrow, pain.
But then from a clear sky Venus sent a sign:
Suddenly, high in heaven, the lightning flashed,
525   the thunder rumbled as if worlds were tumbling
while Tuscan trumpets blew a brazen·blast.
They looked up: once and again came flash and roar:
arms moved across the sky from cloud to cloud,
blood-red and bright; they saw them meet and crash.
530   The rest were terrified, but Troy's great man
knew that the sound was his mother's promised word.
He spoke: "No need, my lord, no need to ask
what that sign means: it points to me. My mother
in heaven declared she'd send this omen to me,
535   if war should threaten, and promised to bring me arms
made by Vulcan, down through the skies.
Pity Laurentum! How her sons must die,
how Turnus make atonement! Those brave dead,
and shields, and helmets Tiber shall roll down
540   his bed! Let them break truce and call for war!"

Thus having spoken, he stepped from his high throne
and stirred the embers on Alcides' altar,
then turned exultant to the little gods
of home. Evander said the prayer and killed
545   his chosen sheep; the Trojans killed theirs, too.
Aeneas returned then to his ships and men.
Those who stood tall in courage he chose to be
companions in arms; the rest rode with the current
and floated slowly down the stream, to bring
550   news to Ascanius of his father's acts.
The Trojans bound for Tuscany got horses—
Aeneas, the finest: his blanket a lion skin
tawny and huge, with shining golden claws.

Report spread quickly through the little town:
555   "Horsemen are riding to the Tuscan king!"
Mothers in fear said prayer on prayer; bad news

brought panic; the face of Mars loomed **larger and larger.**
Then Lord Evander seized his son's right hand,
held it and spoke, while tears streamed down his face:
560 "If only Jove would give me back past years—
as I was, when, at Praeneste's walls, I won
first victory, and stacked their shields and burned **them,**
and sent King Erulus down to Tartarus—
his mother Feronia bore him with three lives
565 (terror to tell: three times to take up arms,
three times to fall in death!), yet my right hand
took off all three, thrice stripped him of his arms—
then I should not be torn from your embrace,
my son, nor had Mezentius dared attack
570 me, his neighbor, or bring death by cold steel
to thousands, and strip our city of her men!
O gods! O ruler of heaven, Jove supreme!
Have mercy, I pray, on this Arcadian king,
and hear a father's prayer: if 'tis your will
575 for Pallas, if fate reserves him safe for me,
if I am to see, to meet him once again,
then let me live, whatever I must endure.
But if events unspeakable are in store,
now—let me now break off a heartless life
580 while what I must fear and dread are still **unknown,**
while yet, dear son, sole joy of my last years,
I hold your hand. Let no news of disaster
deafen my ears." This was his final prayer.
He faltered; his people led him to his house.

585 And now the gates were opened; they rode away,
Aeneas and loyal Achates in the lead,
then other Trojan chiefs, and in mid-rank
Pallas, splendid in cloak and painted shield—
like Lucifer risen all streaming from the sea
590 (of all star fires, Venus loves him the most);
his glance divine toward heaven dispels the dark.
On the walls, mothers with fear-filled **eyes pursued**

the troop—the cloud of dust, the flash of bronze.
With lances braced, the column rode cross-country,
595   their quickest route. Commands passed down the lines,
and four-foot hoofbeats drummed on the fertile field.
Near Caere's ice-cold stream a forest grows;
generations have held it holy. Curving hills
ring it around with dark and pine-clad slopes.
600   Men say Pelasgians hallowed it to Silvanus,
god of the flock and field, and named its day
(they lived in prehistoric times in Latium).
Close by it, Tarchon and his Tuscans held
their stronghold; from its high point could be seen
605   all their legions encamped across the plains.
Here now Aeneas and his chosen troops
rode in, stabled their horses, and took their rest.

But Venus, fair-white among the clouds of heaven,
came with her gifts. In a secluded valley
610   far from the icy stream she found her son;
she approached him and addressed him with these words:
"Here are my promised gifts, by Vulcan's art
perfected. Challenge the proud Laurentines now,
or savage Turnus, dear son, and have no fear."
615   So spoke Cytherea, and sought her son's embrace.
On a nearby oak she propped the shining arms,
gift of a goddess; they filled his heart brimful
with honor and joy. His eye caressed each piece;
in wonder he touched them, turned them, held them up—
620   the helmet horror-plumed and bright as flame,
the sword doom-dealing, the corselet of bronze mail
with sanguine gleam, as when some great gray cloud,
catching the sun, glows red and rayed with fire;
the greaves, too, smooth to the touch, all gold and silver,
625   the spear, the shield—its fabric who could tell?
There stood Italian history, Roman triumphs
portrayed by the fire god (for he knew the prophets
and what would be), there all the future line

of Ascanius, and their yearly tale of wars.
630 There in the verdant cave of Mars was shown
the pregnant she-wolf; at her proffered teats
the twin lads tugged and played and sucked the breast
without a tremor. She turned her smooth neck round
and nuzzled each one, shaping them with her tongue.
635 Rome came next, and the Sabines rudely raped
there as they sat and watched the great spring games:
war flared then 'twixt the sons of Romulus
and Tatius the old, king of the stern Curetes.
Later, these same two kings laid quarrels by;
640 armed, they stood at the altar of Jove, and raised
their patens; a slaughtered pig confirmed the peace.
Nearby was Mettus, torn apart by teams
lashed to lungeing (he should have kept his word!) —
the scene showed Tullus dragging that liar's guts
645 off through the woods; the trees were flecked with blood
There cried Porsenna, "Take back your exiled Tarquin!"
as he laid the city under heavy siege:
the Romans, in liberty's name, ran for their swords.
He looked like fury and threat personified,
650 because Horatius dared to break the bridge
and Cloelia burst her bonds and swam the stream.
Atop the Tarpeian Rock stood Manlius
by the temple, and held the lofty Capitoline;
and there was the house of Romulus, freshly thatched.
655 Here were the gates, in gold; a silver goose
with wings outspread, hissed that the Gauls were coming.
The Gauls crept through the brush and gained the fort
protected by the darkness—gift of night.
Gold was their hair, and they were clothed in gold.
660 Their cloaks were gaily striped; on their white necks
lay golden cords. Each held two heavy pikes
that glittered; long oval shields were their protection.
And there the Salii danced, and nude Luperci;
there were the woolen caps, and the shields that fell
665 from heaven; in solemn pomp the matrons pure

rode to their prayers. Down near the base was shown
the home of the dead and hell's high entrance hall,
the torments of the damned, and Catiline
hung from a cliff and shuddering at the Furies;
670   the saints apart, with Cato as their judge.
Midst all, the ocean flowed, a band of waves
all golden and yet blue, with hoary foam;
round it, in shining silver, dolphins swam
sweeping the seas and cutting through the waves.
675   The center showed the battle of Actium—
the bronze-clad ships attacking in a line,
Leucata seething, and billows bright with gold.
Augustus led the Italians into battle
with Senate and people, with gods both small and great.
680   He stood in the sternsheets. Flame poured from his brows
exultant; above him dawned his father's star.
Elsewhere, Agrippa, blessed by gods and winds,
swooped down with his fleet; that proud ensign of war,
the naval crown, shone bright upon his brow.
685   There Antony, like some savage, gaudy sheik,
hero of Araby and the Sea of Pearls,
led Egypt, the lords of the East, and Bactria;
behind him (God forfend!) his Gypsy Queen.
The fleets advanced full speed; then oars aback
690   in a welter of foam, while spiked rams ripped the wave.
Then—out to sea! As were the Isles of Greece
torn loose and floating, or Alp attacking Alp,
so huge, so tall, were the battling men-o'-war.
Men lobbed the fireball; iron spear-points fell
695   like rain; fresh bloodshed reddened Neptune's realm.
Her majesty rang her gong for battle stations,
not yet aware of twin asps at her back.
Weird gods, fantastic shapes, the dog Anubis,
stood in phalanx against Minerva, Neptune,
700   and Venus. Mars raged up and down the lines,
chiseled in steel; the Dirae hung in heaven,
and Discord in torn gown strode grinning by,

trailed by Bellona with her blood-stained lash.
Apollo of Actium watched and bent his bow
705 above the scene: Egyptians, Indians all,
Sabaeans, and every Arab fled in terror.
Her Majesty herself prayed for a wind,
made sail, cast off the sheets, and let them run.
Amid the carnage Vulcan had carved her pale
710 with impending death, riding the wind and wave.
And there, to the south, the Nile, grief-stricken, great,
offering haven, waving the conquered home
to hiding spots in his blue creeks and bays.
But Caesar, riding through Rome in triple triumph,
715 promised immortal gifts to Italy's gods:
three hundred major shrines in all the city.
The streets were loud with cheers and joyful noise.
Women filled every temple with hymn and prayer,
and slaughtered oxen strewed the altar grounds.
720 Caesar, sitting by Phoebus' marble threshold,
canvassed the gifts a world by that proud door
had laid. Long files of captive peoples passed,
in speech outlandish, as in dress and arms.
Here were Numidians, Berbers in burnoose,
725 Levantines, bowmen from the steppes, all carved
by Vulcan; there Euphrates (gentled now),
men of land's end: Walloons, the horned Rhine,
proud Cossacks, Araxes grumbling at his bridge.

Such were the scenes on Vulcan's shield: Aeneas
730 saw only art, not history, and in joy
shouldered the fame and fortune of his sons.

BOOK NINE

While this was happening at a distant spot,
Juno, Saturn's daughter, sent Iris down
to Turnus the bold (he, so it chanced, was sitting
in a wooded vale Pilumnus had consecrated).
5   To him the daughter of Thaumas spoke these words:
"Turnus, if you were on your knees, no god
would dare to grant what circling time has given!
Aeneas has left his camp, his men, his fleet
to go to the Palatine and Evander's throne.
10 Still more: he's pushed far into Tuscany
to levy and arm the Lydians and their peasants.
Why wait? Now is the time! To horse! To arms!
Hurry! The camp is leaderless! Seize it now!"
So speaking, she spread her wings and rose toward heaven
15 trailing her rainbow vast against the clouds.
Turnus acknowledged her. He raised both hands
above him, and with these words pursued her flight:
"Iris, glory of heaven, who sent you down
to earth, to me? Whence comes this sudden burst
20 of light? The vault of heaven has split in two!
I see the wandering stars! A sign! I follow,
whoever calls to arms!" With that he strode
to the riverbank, took water in his hands
and prayed and burdened heaven with his vows.

25 And now the troops came marching down the field,
both horses and men splendid in gold and purple.
Messapus headed the column; in the van,
the sons of Tyrrhus. Prince Turnus rode mid-rank,
holding his spear, head-high above the rest:

30   as when the Ganges, stilling his seven streams,
     runs deep and silent, or when the Nile, silt-laden,
     flows off the fields and draws back to his bed.
     The Trojan sentries saw a dust-cloud rise,
     black and sudden, to plunge the plain in darkness.
35   From his rampart post, Caicus first called out:
     "Look, men! What is that dark, advancing mass?
     To arms; hurry! Pass weapons! Stations, all!
     Here come the enemy! Ho!" Midst loud commands
     the Trojans ran through the gates and manned the walls.
40   For when Aeneas, the master strategist, left,
     he gave his orders: If anything should occur,
     they must not chance a fight in open field,
     but only defend the camp and hold the walls.
     And so—though anger and shame declared, "Attack!"—
45   they barred the gates and carried out commands;
     armed, in their towers, they watched the enemy come.
     To Turnus, the march was slow; he raced ahead
     with twenty chosen horsemen. All at once
     he was at the walls. His horse was black and white,
50   (a Thracian), his helmet gold with scarlet plumes.
     "Men! Who is with me in the first attack?
     Let's go!" he shouted. His spear whirled through the air,
     first act of war. He cantered onto the field.
     His company raised a cheer; with berserk yells,
55   they charged—then halted. What? Were Trojans cowards?
     Fair field, yet still no sally, no attack?
     Men huddling in a camp? Puzzled, he searched
     the unbroken walls for a breach, this way and that.
     Just like a wolf stalking a crowded fold:
60   shivering in the midnight wind and rain
     he howls at the cracks; lambs cower beneath their mothers
     and bleat. His ruff stands up; his ugly fury
     rages against the unreachable. Starved for days,
     his throat gone parched for blood, he dare not rest.
65   Just so, as Turnus searched the camp and walls,
     his fury flared and seared his heartless soul.

How should he find ingress? How shake them loose,
those Trojans, from their walls, and force them out?
The ships! Next to the camp, they skulked at piers
70   protected by walls and by the river's wave.
As his men cheered, he advanced, calling for fire;
afire himself, he seized a blazing torch.
Where he was, there were his men; they all set to,
and armed themselves with scorched and smoking brands.
75   They plundered hearths; the pitch-pine torch gave light
all smoky; flame and ash rose toward the stars.

What god, O Muses, stopped the holocaust?
Who saved the Trojan ships from sheets of flame?
Tell us! (A strange old tale, but it persists!)
80   When Aeneas was laying keels near Trojan Ida
and readying ships to sail across the sea
men say our lady of Phrygia, mother of gods,
uttered these words to Jove: "Son, hear the plea
of your mother, who won Olympus to earn your love.
85   For many a year I loved my evergreens—
that grove on the mountaintop, where men said prayers
(half-hidden, it was, by dark blue spruce and maple) —
but gladly I gave them when that prince of Troy
needed a fleet. Now grief and fear assail me,
90   and I need help. Grant me, your mother, the power
to save my trees from ruin by wreck and storm.
My mountain was their home: be that their blessing."
Her son, who spins the stars of heaven, replied:
"Mother, you wrench the law! What will you ask?
95   Those ships are of man's making: shall they own
eternity? Life is risky: shall Aeneas
run never a risk? What god may claim such power?
No: some day, when they've done their work and reached
the Westland, all that have escaped the waves
100   and brought our Trojan prince to Italy's plains
I'll strip of mortal shape and bid them be
nymphs of the ocean, like the Nereids

who breast their way across the foaming sea."
He sealed his promise by the shores of Styx,
105 his brother's pitch-black, swirling, sucking stream.
He nodded; his nod made all Olympus tremble.

Now came the day; the Fates had counted out
their tale of years, when Turnus attacked the ships.
This warned the mother to save them from the torch.
110 First a strange brilliance shone into men's eyes,
and then in the East a huge cloud crossed the sky,
trailed by wild dancers. A voice of doom came down
and echoed through Rutulan and through Trojan lines:
"Trojans, don't trouble to keep my ships from harm;
115 don't rush to arms! Turnus will set the sea
afire before my ships! Go free, my craft,
be nymphs of the sea: your mother speaks." At once
each single ship broke moorings from the shore;
like dolphins of the deep, they turned head-down
120 and sounded. Then (a miracle!) for each ship
that once was moored, bronze-armored, by the piers,
the shape of a girl rose up and swam away.

The Rutulans were awed; Messapus shook,
his horses bolted. Tiber slowed his streams
125 and, hoarsely roaring, shrank back from the sea.
But Turnus the bold lost nothing of his courage;
he spoke; his words both heartened and chastised:
"For Trojans, this means ruin! Jove has wrecked
their well-known refuge. Neither spear nor torch
130 of ours was needed. The sea is closed to them;
they've lost all hope of escape, and half their power.
The land is in our hands; men by the thousands
bear arms for Italy. Oracles? Who fears them
or these degenerates and their 'word of God'?
135 Troy touched Ausonia's fertile plain: enough!
Fate and Venus are paid! And now, my 'fate'—
to cut to pieces the hellish tribe that stole

my bride! Not only Atreus' sons can know
that pain, nor only Argos wage that war!
140 'Once dead is dead enough?' Why not, 'Once *sinned?*'—
unless toward all of womankind they bear
pure malice. The wall between us makes them bold;
the ditch detains us and postpones their death—
hence, they are brave! Did they not see Troy's walls,
145 built by the hand of Neptune, fall in flames?
You are picked men! Who'll take the sword with me
against their wall, and charge their coward's camp?
I need no thousand ships, no Vulcan's armor
against the sons of Troy. Let Tuscans all
150 join them! I'll not sneak in by night and steal
their 'Pallas the Less,' nor knife their temple guards—
no fear! No horse shall hide us in its belly!
In broad daylight I'll circle their walls with fire.
We are no Greeks—no pale, Pelasgian boys
155 (they'll see!), that Hector held off for ten years.
But now the best part of the day is past.
For what remains, enjoy the rest you've earned.
Dismissed! Tomorrow, men, we'll hope to fight.
Messapus! Station sentries near their gates,
160 and build a ring of watchfires round their walls!
Twice seven Latin captains and their men,
a hundred each, were set to keep surveillance—
dressed for parade: all purple plumes and gold.
The men fell out and scattered; on the grass
165 they rested and drained their brazen bowls of wine.
The watchfires flared; the sentries kept awake
that night by gaming.

High on the walls, the Trojans manned their posts
armed and alert; uneasy, they kept patrols
170 checking the gates, laid planks, built battlements,
stocked weapons. Orders came from brave Serestus
and Mnestheus: Aeneas had named them to command

of camp and men, in all emergencies.
Every last man was stationed on the walls,
175   and squads by turns kept watch at danger spots.

Nisus guarded a gate. (Ida the huntress
had sent him, son of Hyrtacus, to Aeneas—
a fighter, nimble with arrows and with spear.)
Beside him stood Euryalus, handsomest
180   of all who fought for Troy and wore her arms,
a boy whose beardless face proclaimed his youth.
A close-knit pair, inseparable in the fight,
and now on watch inseparable at the gate.
Said Nisus: "Is it a god that fires my heart,
185   Euryalus, or does Wish become man's god?
My heart drives me to battle or some great act
of daring. It will not stop nor let me rest.
Look at the Rutuli! Such bold confidence!
Hardly a spark of light! Drunk, sound asleep,
190   they lie there—never a noise: I wonder, now!
Listen: a thought keeps rising in my mind.
All ranks demand Aeneas be called back,
and men dispatched to bring him true report.
If they'll reward you as I ask (for me,
195   fame is enough), I think beneath that hill
I'll find a path that leads to Pallanteum."
Euryalus was dumfounded. Lust for fame
beat at his brain. He addressed his eager friend:
"Nisus, you'd risk your life, and not let me
200   share danger with you? You'd go out alone?
That is not how my father Opheltes taught me
'midst Argive terror and travail of Troy
when war was habit; that is not how we've shared
the day of death as Lord Aeneas' men.
205   My heart—mine, too!—can scorn this world, and hold
life well lost for the glory you hope to gain."
Nisus replied: "I never doubted that—
believe me, never! So may Jove bring me back

in triumph—or any god who knows the right.
210   But if—you see the risks, the many dangers—
if some mischance—some god—should take me off,
I'd want you safe. You're younger: you should live
to drag my body from battle, or buy it back
for burial, or—should fate forbid me this—
215   to say last rites and raise my cenotaph.
Nor would I cause your mother so much sorrow,
she who alone of many mothers dared
to follow you, 'spite all Acestes offered.''
Euryalus then: "Your chain of argument
220   is vain. My mind's made up and will not change.
Let's hurry.'' With that, he woke the watch. They came
to stand their turn. Euryalus and Nisus
strode off to find the officer in command.

All over the world creation lay asleep,
225   with worry banished and hearts released from care.
But Trojan generals, leaders, chosen men,
were meeting for high counsel and debate:
What move to make? Whom send to Lord Aeneas?
Leaning on spears, they stood there, shield in hand,
230   at center of camp and field. Nisus approached,
Euryalus, too, and begged for admission: "Quickly!''
"Important matter!'' "Well worth the time!'' Iulus
moved to admit them: "At ease, Nisus! Speak!''
Nisus replied: "Be patient and hear us out,
235   my lords, and by our years do not adjudge
our offer. The Rutuli are drunk, asleep,
dead to the world! We've found a secret route.
Near our rear gate the road forks toward the sea;
the line of fires is broken, but dark smoke rolls
240   toward heaven. If you will let us try our luck,
we'll find Aeneas and Pallanteum's walls,
collect huge spoils, kill soldiers right and left.
You'll see us return, for we'll not lose our way.
We've hunted in those valleys: often we've seen

245 where the city begins; we know that river's course."
Here spoke Aletes, wise old counselor:
"Gods of our fathers, who govern Troy forever,
you think not yet to end the Trojan race,
since you have put such spirit and such heart
250 into our boys!" He gripped their hands and shoulders
while tears poured down in floods across his face.
"You men! What can we offer, what reward
pay for your exploit? God and your own goodness
will compensate you best. But there'll be more,
255 at once, from Aeneas the good; and his young son
Ascanius never will forget your courage."
"No, as my life hangs on Aeneas' return,"
Ascanius said, "I swear by our ancestral
great gods, Nisus, by white-haired Vesta's shrine:
260 all of my hopes and all my sacred honor
I give into your hands. Bring back my father;
show me his face! No fears, once he returns!
I'll give two cups—pure silver, carved and chased:
spoils from Arisba that my father won—
265 two tripods, matched, two talents of pure gold,
an antique wine bowl, gift of Punic Dido.
Then if we conquer Italy, if we win
her throne, and I may parcel out the spoils:
you saw Turnus—his horse, the golden armor
270 he wore: that horse, that shield, that scarlet plume
I'll set aside. Nisus, they're yours right now!
Besides, my father will give twelve women, choice
and fecund, and prisoners, too, with all their arms,
plus all of King Latinus' private lands.
275 For you, Euryalus, whose span of years
mine nearly matches: be my honored friend,
my heart's companion, always at my side.
I want no power, no glory, without you.
In war or peace, you'll have my highest trust,
280 in word and act." Euryalus replied:
"No day shall charge that I have lost the courage
I show today, if only Fortune bless

and not desert us. But past all awards,
one thing I ask: My mother, of Priam's house
285 a princess, would not stay on Trojan soil
nor in Acestes' town, but came with me.
I leave her now without farewell or word
of this adventure (night and your right hand
be witness!), since I could not bear her tears.
290 I leave her: help her, comfort her, I pray!
Assure me of this, and I'll more boldly face
all dangers." Every Trojan heart was struck;
they wept—Iulus most, who saw and felt
the image of the love he bore his father.
295 Then he spoke out:
"Be sure your bravery shall have full reward.
Your mother shall be mine but for the name
Creusa: she has earned no niggard love
with such a son! Whatever the event,
300 by my own life (so swore my father always):
all that I promise you if things go well,
your mother and your kindred shall possess."
So speaking, he stripped his shoulder of the sword
(work of Lycaon, master smith of Crete),
305 gilded, and with a well-matched ivory sheath.
To Nisus, Mnestheus gave a lion's skin,
prize of the hunt; Aletes traded helmets.
Thus armed, away they marched. All the high lords,
both young and old, walked with them to the gates
310 to wish them well. Iulus joined them, too,
sober, concerned, a man beyond his years,
with messages for his father; but the wind
scattered them to the clouds, an empty gift.

They crossed the moat and, in the dark of night,
315 made for the enemy camp, but on their way
brought death to many. They saw them drunk, asleep,
stretched on the grass, their chariots up-ended,
a tangle of wheels and harness, weapons, men,

and bottles of wine. Nisus was first to whisper:
320   "Euryalus, now's our chance: be bold and strike!
Here is our path. So no attack spring up
behind us, you stand guard and watch far back.
I'll cut a swathe of death; you follow me."
He spoke, laid finger to lip, then drew his sword
325   and went for Rhamnes the proud: on rugs piled high
he lay, breathing the deep full breath of sleep,
a prince, friend to Prince Turnus—a prophet, too,
but powers prophetic could not ward off his death.
Nearby three sentries slept beside their arms;
330   he killed them, and Remus' squire and charioteer—
reached under the horses to lop their lolling heads;
beheaded their master, too, and left his corpse
pulsing out blood; dark red and hot, it soaked
blanket and soil. He next killed Lamyrus, Lamus,
335   and young Serranus (he'd heavily won that night
at dice; a handsome lad, who'd drunk too much
and lay there sodden—happy if he had gamed
the whole night through until the daylight came).
Like an unfed lion loose in a full-packed fold,
340   mad hunger drives him to slash the gentle sheep
and drag them, mute with fear; he roars and slavers.
Euryalus killed no fewer. He too, hot
with blood-lust, cut through lines of nameless men
to catch Herbesus, Fadus, Abaris, Rhoetus.
345   Rhoetus had been awake and seen it all:
in mortal fear he'd hidden behind a wine bowl.
Euryalus faced him, pulled him erect, and sank
a sword's length in his ribs, then drew it out
scarlet with death. As Rhoetus, vomiting blood
350   and wine, fell dying, Euryalus, eager, silent,
came to Messapus' company. There he saw
the last of the watchfires, saw the horses staked
and tethered to graze. Nisus spoke briefly then
(he sensed the too strong grip of murder-madness):
355   "Let's stop, for dawn—no friend of ours!—is near.
They've paid blood price enough. We've cleared a path."

They left behind much solid silver work,
weapons and wine bowls, rugs of rich design.
Euryalus did take Rhamnes' gilded belt
360   and breastplate (sent by Caedicus, years before,
to Remulus, pledge of mutual good will;
he at his death bequeathed them to his grandson;
the Rutuli took them later as spoils of war).
He buckled these trophies on, so foolish and brave,
365   and donned Messapus' helmet, polished, plumed,
and fine. They left the camp and made for safety.

Meanwhile a company of horse rode out
from the Latin city (the main force lay encamped
afield): they brought dispatches to Prince Turnus—
370   three hundred men, with Volcens in command.
They had approached the camp, close by its walls,
when off to the left they saw the pair turn past;
the helmet betrayed Euryalus, for it shone
and flashed in the half-light: he had forgotten it.
375   Something was wrong! Volcens called from the line:
"Halt, men! What are your orders? Who are you?
Where are you going?" They offered no reply,
but ran for the woods and for the cover of night.
The riders wheeled to the forks on right and left
380   (they knew them well), and ringed each exit round.
The woods were wide and cluttered with scrub oak
and undergrowth of briars everywhere;
pathways were few and hidden, and hard to trace.
Confused by shadows and loaded down with spoils,
385   Euryalus panicked and ran. Nisus was clear
of the paths, and now unknowing had run past
the enemy, and the plot now called the Alban
(then known as King Latinus' Hill Corral);
he stopped, looked back: where was his friend? Nowhere!
390   "Euryalus, my poor friend, where were you lost?
Where should I turn?" He traced his tangled route,
his trail of footprints through the baffling woods,

backward; he searched the brush but found no clue.
Then he heard horses, heard the searchers call.
395 Hardly a moment had passed when loud cries came
to his ear; there was Euryalus, captive, caught
by darkness and terrain, noise and confusion:
he fought and struggled, but horsemen hemmed him in.
Nisus debated what feat of arms might save
400 the boy—or should he run against their swords
to die in a flash a hero's bloody death?
Instead, he gripped his lance, drew back his arm,
looked toward the moon in heaven, and voiced this **prayer**:
"Come, lady! Help me in this troubled hour,
405 Latonia, glory of heaven, watch of the woods!
If ever Hyrtacus, in my name, has brought
gifts to your shrine, if I too have hung spoils
of the hunt to deck your walls or holy rooftree,
send my shaft straight! Help me break up that crowd!"
410 With every ounce of strength he tensed and hurled
the spear. Whipping the shades of night, it flew
and struck Sulmo, whose back was turned: the point
broke off; the splintered shaft passed through his chest.
He toppled, coughing a hot flood from his lungs,
415 twitching, gasping, and moaning till he turned cold.
The riders looked wildly round. Nisus drew back
still keener, and whirled a second spear away.
While they stood shaking, the shaft impaled the head
of Tagus, and stopped, warmed by the brain it pierced.
420 Volcens went wild; he could not see who'd hurled
the weapons nor where to launch his counterattack.
"But you!—" he said, "your life's blood still shall **pay**
the price of both!" With that, he drew his sword
and went for Euryalus. Terror drove Nisus mad.
425 He shouted aloud; he could no longer hide
in shadow, nor longer bear such savage pain:
"Here, here I am! I did it! Direct your blades
at me, you men! I tricked you—never that boy:
how could he? Be heaven and all the stars my witness!"

430 (So great his love for his unlucky friend.)
Still as he spoke, a strong arm drove the sword
through the boy's ribs and laid his body open.
Euryalus toppled and died. The blood ran down
his smooth, young limbs; his head dropped on his chest,
435 as, when the plow has nicked a scarlet flower,
it wilts and dies, or poppy stems grow tired
under a burden of rain, and bow their heads.
Nisus rushed at the Rutuli, but attacked
Volcens alone—Volcens his only aim.
440 The enemy swarmed around him, parrying, jabbing,
pressing him back, but he pushed on, his sword
flashing, until he faced Volcens and drove
the blade in his yelling mouth and took his life.
Then, dying himself, a mass of wounds, he fell
445 on his dead friend, and there at last found peace.

O blessed pair! If power lies in my song,
no day shall steal you from the hearts of men,
long as Capitol Rock shall house the sons
of Aeneas, and Father Rome shall rule the world.

450 The Rutulan victors gathered up the spoils,
then sadly bore dead Volcens back to camp.
There they saw no less grief: for Rhamnes found
lifeless, for all the chiefs dead by one sword,
for Numa and Serranus. Crowds had gathered
455 round dead and dying, where the ground was warm
with slaughter and streams ran bubbling full of blood.
They examined the spoils: there was Messapus' helmet
and Rhamnes' breastplate, recovered with so much sweat!

And now Aurora brought the dawn's new light
460 to earth, and left Tithonus' golden couch.
The sun poured down; his beams revealed the world.
Turnus put on his arms and roused his chiefs
to arms; each ranged his men in battle line,

bronze-clad, and told tall tales to rouse their spirits.
465　They even paraded heads impaled on spears
　　　(pitiful sight!) ; men cheered as they passed by:
　　　Euryalus' head, and Nisus'.
　　　The sons of Aeneas grimly ranged their troops
　　　on their left flank (the right lay next the river) ;
470　they manned the moat, the walls, the tops and towers,
　　　and stood in sorrow for those poor heads impaled
　　　(how well they knew them!) and streaming with black blood.

　　　Meanwhile Report ran through the worried camp
　　　and slipped with her news into a mother's ears—
475　Euryalus'. Suddenly warmth fled from her bones,
　　　the shuttle shook from her hands, her yarn rolled down.
　　　She rushed away, wailing in woman's way
　　　and tearing her hair; half mad, she ran toward walls
　　　and battle line, heedless of men, of spears,
480　of danger, and filled all heaven with her cries:
　　　"Do I see you thus, Euryalus? Thus you ease
　　　the last days of my life? Heartless, to leave
　　　me alone, to go and face dangers so great
　　　and give your mother no chance for one last word!
485　In a foreign land you lie a feast for dogs
　　　and Latin birds. Your mother, I never led
　　　your funeral, closed your eyes, or washed your wounds,
　　　or covered you with the coat that, night and day,
　　　I hurried to finish weaving, to calm my fears.
490　Where shall I turn? What spot now holds your body,
　　　your poor, torn flesh? Is this all you bring back,
　　　son, to your mother? For this, I crossed a world?
　　　If you know kindness, Rutulans, kill me now!
　　　Throw all your spears; let cold steel take me off!
495　Or do you, father of heaven, have mercy! Hurl
　　　your bolt and banish my hated soul to hell:
　　　how else can I break off an anguished life?"
　　　Her tears struck every heart; a moan passed through
　　　the ranks; men's will to fight failed and grew cold.

500   She fired their sorrow; then Actor and Idaeus,
      at word from Ilioneus and tear-stained Iulus,
      raised her and carried her back to her own house.

      Just then the bugle blasted its brazen note
      of terror; men raised a shout that roared toward heaven.
505   The Volsci marched a "tortoise" up, full speed,
      ready to fill the moat and breach the wall.
      Some sought a place to set their scaling ladders,
      where gaps were found in the thin-stretched line of guards,
      and no massed men appeared. The Trojans, too,
510   let go a flood of missiles and pushed with pikes:
      long war had schooled them in defense of walls.
      They rolled down murderous rocks, trying to crack
      the "tortoise," but still the enemy's locked shields
      let them take cheerfully every kind of blow.
515   But finally they gave way, for where they massed
      thickest, the Trojans rolled a boulder down
      that crushed and scattered their ranks, and broke their cover
      of shields. Brave Rutulans!—still, they cared no more
      to fight where they could not see, but tried to drive
520   their foe from the wall with missiles.
      Elsewhere, Mezentius, brandishing Tuscan pine
      (a fearful sight), attacked with smoke and fire;
      but Neptune's son, Messapus, tamer of horses,
      trying to breach the walls, called for the ladders.

525   Now, Muse, I pray, breathe on me while I sing
      the wounds and death that Turnus dealt that day,
      what man each man sent with his sword to hell,
      and with me list the vast confines of war.
      (You, holy ones, remember, for you can!)

530   A tower tall of access and of view
      stood at a critical spot; with all their might
      the Rutuli sought to storm it, or with lever
      to overturn it. The Trojans fought with stones

to defend it, and crowded the ports to throw their spears.
535 Turnus began by hurling a flaming torch
at the tower's flank. It clung; a breeze sprang up
and spread the fire to sheathing and to joists.
The men inside panicked and tried in vain
to escape danger. They all rushed to the side
540 away from the fire; with all weight on one side,
the tower toppled and heaven echoed the crash.
Men fell half-dead; huge timbers followed them down.
Men fell transfixed by their own spears, or gouged
by splinters. Helenor, Lycus—scarce these two
545 escaped. (Helenor was the older, born
bastard of Lydia's king by a female slave;
despite his father's injunction, gone to Troy—
young fool!—with his naked sword and flat, blank shield.)
When he found himself hemmed in by Turnus' hordes—
550 lines of Latins to left, and lines to right—
as a wild beast, tight-fenced by hunters massed,
lunges and snarls at the spears, then, sure of death,
hurls itself high to fall upon the points—
just so Helenor rushed at the hordes around him
555 to die, right where the spears stood rank on rank.
Lycus, nimbler by far, had run straight through
the enemy lines. Reaching the wall, he tried
to grasp its top or his friends' outstretched hands.
Turnus had paced him along with weapon poised;
560 the winner now, he shouted: "Fool! You thought
to escape my hands?" He seized him as he hung
and tore him—and a great chunk of wall—away,
as when the eagle of Jove has clutched a hare
or snow-white swan, and soared off through the sky,
565 or when the wolf of Mars has stolen a lamb
from the fold, and left the dam to bleat and cry.
The Rutuli cheered, advanced, filled up the moat
with earth, and hurled brands at the battlements.
With a rock like half a mountain, Ilioneus
570 killed Lucetius (he'd piled brands at a gate),

Liger, Emathion; Asilas, Corynaeus
(the one a spearman, the other a wily archer);
Caeneus, Ortygius; Turnus, the victor Caeneus,
plus Promolus, Dioxippus, Clonius, Itys,
575   Sagaris, Idas (tall as a tower, he);
Capys, Privernus whom Themilla's dart
had grazed (he, like a fool, had dropped his shield
to grab at the wound): the arrow came on wings,
pinned hand to side, then passed within, to burst
580   the hidden pathways of man's life and breath.
The son of Arcens stood in shining armor
with cloak embroidered and bright with Spanish red,
a handsome lad (his father sent him to fight;
his home was in Mars' woods beside Symaethus,
585   and near Palicus' shrine, where prayers are heard).
Mezentius dropped his spear and seized a sling;
three times he whirled it whistling round his head
then let the pellet fly; the hot lead split
the poor lad's temples and stretched him on the ground.

590   For the first time, then, Ascanius, so men say,
shot arrows in anger (his only use before, to set
wild beasts to running): he killed Numanus the brave
(men called him "Remulus," too; he just had won
Turnus' young sister to share his marriage bed).
595   Numanus strode front-center to stand and shout
insults; his new-won princedom puffed him up
and made him strut like greatness on parade:
"Shame, Trojans! Twice besieged, twice trapped by walls!
Twice caught—or do you aim to fence out death?
600   Look who would fight to win new wives from us!
What god—what madness—sent you to Italy?
No blueblood princes here, no smooth-tongued liars!
We're a tough race! We take our newborn babes
to rivers and toughen them in the ice-cold wave.
605   For the hunt, our boys will beat the woods all night;
cavalry drill and archery are their games.

Our men love hardship and the frugal life:
they hoe their fields or shake a world with war.
We always wear the sword; a lance reversed
510   is our ox-goad. Old age is slow to come
and never weakens our spirit or slacks our strength:
our white heads don the helmet; what we need,
we take; for pleasure, we bring in fresh spoil.
But you! Your coats are scarlet trimmed with gold!
515   You love amusement, luxury, the dance,
sleeves to your wrists, a bonnet, ribbons to tie it.
Men of the East? No: women! Go climb your hill
of Dindymus! Hear the pretty flutes again!
Sweet bells and gongs! Your lady of Ida calls!
520   Go on! Leave war to men, and drop those swords!"

Such boasts, such insults, and such threats of doom
Ascanius could not bear. He strung his bow,
set shaft to sinew, drew his hands apart
and aimed—then made a humble prayer to Jove:
525   "Almighty Jove, bless this bold first attempt!
I'll bring each year an offering to your shrine:
a young bull for your altar, shining white
with gilded horns, head high beside his mother,
ready to fight, to gore, and paw the earth."
530   The father of heaven heard. From a clear sky
he thundered on the left. The death-bow twanged;
the arrow with eerie hiss sped from the string,
struck Remulus in the head and passed straight through
his temples. "Now mock and strut before the brave!
535   Thus 'twice-caught Trojans' answer the Rutuli!"
Ascanius shouted. The Trojans raised a cheer
and laughed aloud; their hearts rose toward the stars.

High in a zone of heaven, Apollo bent
to watch the Ausonian lines and Trojan camp:
540   Iulus had won! Apollo then addressed him:
"Blessed be your first brave act! Thus move toward heaven,
O son and father of gods! By right, all wars

fate brings to Assaracus' sons shall thus conclude:
Troy cannot hold you." He spoke, and took his way
645 down from high heaven, cleaving the air of life,
and sought Ascanius. First he changed his form
to Butes the old—squire, sometime, to Anchises
of Troy, and faithful watchman at his door;
to Ascanius now assigned. Apollo walked
650 with the old man's gait, like him in speech, complexion,
white hair, and load of fiercely rattling arms.
He found Iulus excited, and spoke thus:
"Son of Aeneas, enough, to kill Numanus
and meet no harm. Apollo grants you this
655 first glory, and takes no umbrage at your skill.
But no more fighting, son!" With that, Apollo,
waiting no answer, fled from mortal sight,
turning to thin air as men watched him go.
The Dardan princes knew him and his bow—
660 a god!—they sensed it when his quiver clanged.
So, by Apollo's stern command, they kept
Ascanius from the fight, themselves returned
to a struggle and risk that might well cost their lives.
Orders rang out all down the battlements;
665 men stretched the deadly bow and whirled the sling.
The ground was strewn with spears; helmets and shields
rang at the contacts; bitter fighting arose:
as in the rain-star season a downpour comes
from the west to lash the earth; as hail and storm
670 fall on the sea, when Jove, all rimed with ice,
flings flood and cold, and bursts the dams of heaven.

Pandarus and Bitias were Alcanor's sons,
born of the nymph Iaera in Jove's park,
tall as the pine-clad mountains of their home.
675 Confident of their strength, they opened the gate
they were to defend, and beckoned the enemy in.
Then, like two towers, they stood to left and right
with weapons ready and plumes like banners flying:

like twin oaks rising high upon the banks
680 of the clear, bright Po, or near that lovely spot,
Athesis: up toward heaven they lift their heads
untrimmed; their topmost branches nod and sway.
The Rutuli saw the opening and rushed in.
Then Quercens and Aquiculus, finely armed,
685 hot-headed Tmarus and Haemon, son of Mars,
either took all their men, turned tail, and ran,
or at the very gate laid down their lives.
Now hearts grew truly hostile; ill will rose.
The Trojans, now regrouped, swarmed to the spot
690 and charged more boldly—even beyond the gate.

Turnus, directing the fight some distance off,
killing and wounding, heard that the enemy
had opened their gates in strange new zeal for battle.
He dropped his plans; by monstrous ardor spurred,
695 he rushed to the Trojan gate and those proud brothers.
Antiphates met him first (a bastard, he,
born of a woman of Thebes to tall Sarpedon);
Turnus cast and killed him: Italian ash
flew through the air to strike his throat and sink
700 in his chest. The wound was a cavern belching blood
and froth; cold steel, fast in his lung, grew warm.
He next killed Meropes, Erymas, and Aphidnus,
then Bitias—hot-eyed, roaring his battle cry—
not with a spear (no spear could take his life):
705 a weighted pike came screaming, whirling in
like a lightning bolt; two layers of bulls' hide,
his faithful breastplate double-thick with gold
could not repel it. His great, tall frame collapsed;
earth gave a moan; his huge shield clanged above him.
710 So, sometimes, off the beach at Baiae, falls
a pier of masonry that men build large
and sink into the sea. It leans and leaves
a trail of ruin, strikes the bottom, and settles.
The waters hiss and swirl; black sand rolls up;

715 tall Prochyta echoes and shakes—Inarimë, too,
(the granite bed Jove made Typhoeus lie in).

Now Mars the war god gave the Latins courage
and strength; his goad struck sharp into their hearts.
Against the Trojans he sent black Rout and Terror.
720 Men met and clashed wherever battle offered;
the spirit of war fell on them.
When Pandarus saw his fallen brother's corpse,
saw how their fortunes stood, how things had gone,
with all his force he wrenched the gate around,
725 then leaned against it, leaving many a man
of his own to fight and die outside the walls.
Others came pushing past, whom he took in:
mad error! He missed Prince Turnus, who burst through
in a file of men, and locked him in the camp,
730 like a monstrous tiger loose among the sheep.
A strange light shone in his eye; his armor rang
with a terrible sound; his nodding helmet plume
was red as blood; his shield flashed lightning-bright.
The Trojans, seeing that hated face and frame,
735 broke ranks and ran, but Pandarus rose up
full height; in fury at his brother's death
he shouted, "Here is no royal dower-house,
Turnus, no village walls to hem you in!
This is an enemy camp; there's no way out!"
740 Turnus in perfect calm smiled and replied:
"Come on! If you've the heart for it, let's fight!
Tell Priam that here you found Achilles, too."
Pandarus seized a spear—a knotty stock
still rough with bark—and threw it with all his force;
745 the winds took it, but Juno, Saturn's child,
fended it off; it struck the gate and clung.
"This weapon you'll not escape, for my right hand
wields it; not of your kind this blow and wound,"
said Turnus, and raised his sword above his head.
750 The blade came down on Pandarus' skull, and split it

in two down to his jaws—a bloody mess.
His huge frame fell with a crash upon the ground.
His body and armor, drenched with blood and brains,
lay tumbled and dead; in equal halves his head
755 hung from his neck on this side and on that.

The Trojans in terror turned and ran away.
Turnus had won! If he had thought just then
to break the bars and let his men march in,
the war—and a nation, too—had that day ended.
760 But folly and blood-lust drove him madly on
against the enemy ranks.
First he took Phaleris; then with a ham-string slash,
Gyges. Grabbing their spears, he pressed behind
the fleeing Trojans (Juno gave him power).
765 Next he killed Halys, stabbed Phegeus through his shield,
then caught, off guard, men fighting atop the walls:
Alcander, Prytanis, Halius, and Noëmon.
Lynceus wheeled to attack and called his men.
Turnus leaned from the rampart; with his sword
770 he slashed: the single blow took Lynceus' head,
helmet and all, and whipped it away. And next
came Amycus, killer of beasts (no man more skilled
at dipping darts and arming the steel with poison),
then Clytius, Cretheus—he, the Muses' friend,
775 Cretheus, the Muses' darling: he loved song
and the lyre and ever to pluck its sounding strings,
to sing of battles, of horses, arms, and men.

At last the captains, Mnestheus and Sergestus,
heard of their losses, came, and saw their men
780 demoralized, and Turnus within the camp.
Mnestheus cried out, "Just where will you retreat?
Have you some other camp? Some other walls?
You are *soldiers?* And one lone man, boxed in
like that, could do such damage and escape—
785 send all those first-line fighters down to hell?

Bad days for Troy and for our ancient gods,
and for Aeneas! Shame, that you let them down!"
His words rekindled courage; the men closed ranks
and held. Turnus retreated, step by step,
790   back toward the river that blocked the camp's one side.
The Trojans shouted and pressed in close and closer,
a tight-knit crowd, like men with weapons poised
forcing a lion back: the frightened beast,
with hate in his eyes, retreats; he is too brave
795   and angry to turn his back, but men and spears
keep him from launching the charge he longs to make.
So Turnus retreated, step by doubtful step,
cautious and slow, while rage boiled in his heart.
Still he rushed twice against the advancing lines,
800   twice broke them and sent them pell-mell down the walls.
But then the whole camp formed a single mass,
and Juno Saturnia dared not give him strength
to resist. For Jove sent Iris down from heaven
with orders for his sister, none too kind,
805   if Turnus should fail to leave the Trojan camp.
And now the prince could not hold up his shield
nor make resistance, such the press of spears
thrown from all sides. His hollow helmet rang
about his head; rocks cracked the solid bronze;
810   his plumes were scattered; not even the knob could stop
the blows. Now Mnestheus and his men flashed in
with double volleys. All his flesh broke out
in sticky, streaming sweat; his breath was gone;
sick and exhausted, he shook in every limb.
815   At last he turned and in full armor leaped
into the river. Its swirling, yellow stream
took him, washed off the blood, and carried him,
on gentle waves, in joy, back to his men.

BOOK TEN

And now almighty Olympus opened doors:
the father of gods and king of men called council
high in his starry house, whence he could view
all earth, the Latin nation and Trojan camp.
5 To the gods in hall assembled then he spoke:
"You great of heaven, why have you now reversed
your will and moved to strife and cruelty?
I ruled that Troy and Italy must not fight!
Why this forbidden war? What fear has forced
10 either party to arms and clash of sword on sword?
The time for war will come (no need to seek it!)
when Carthage the cruel will split the Alps and flood
the very forts of Rome with doom and death:
then will be time to hate; then, to destroy!
15 Now cease, and in good will make terms of peace."

So Jove, briefly; but golden Venus spoke
not briefly in reply:
"O father, power eternal of men and worlds
(for to what else might we now make petition?)
20 see how the Rutuli prance, how Turnus rides
high horse and charges head-on, by success
inflated! Walls no more protect the Trojans:
inside the gates, up on the battlements,
the fight goes on; the moats are deep with blood.
25 Aeneas is off, unknowing. Shall never relief
from siege be granted? Enemies ring the walls
of newborn Troy; a second army comes;
from Grecian Arpi soon will march once more—

Diomede! All that's missing are my wounds:
30 doubtless I'll stop—your child!—a man-made spear!
If Trojans came to Italy by no leave
or grace of yours, they must atone, and you
need never help them. But if the spoken word
of god or ghost was their command, why now
35 may orders of yours be changed, or fate recast?
Why mention ships burned on Sicilian shores?
Why the king of storms and the howling winds
Aeolia loosed? Why Iris sent from heaven?
Now even ghosts are being raised (this trick
40 was yet untried); and, loosed on the upper world,
Allecto riots through Italian towns.
For empire I've no thought; that hope we held
in better days. Let whom you will be victor.
If there's no land your heartless wife will grant
45 to Trojans, father, I beg you by the flames
of ruined Troy: dismiss Ascanius
from arms, unhurt. Oh, let my grandson live!
Aeneas may toss upon some unknown sea
and follow whatever path Fortune may grant,
50 but let me save the boy from death and strife!
There's Amathus; I own Paphos and Cythera,
Idalium, too: here let him live his life
disarmed, unhonored. Let Carthage spread her **rule**
wide in Ausonia: none from there will block
55 her Tyrian towns. Why did my Trojans flee
the terrors of war, escape through Argive fire,
run every risk of endless land and sea
in search of Latium and a reborn Troy?
Better if they had settled the site of Troy—
60 a homeland's funeral ashes! Put them back
by Xanthus and Simois! Father, let my Trojans
relive their tragic fate!" Then Juno spoke
in regal wrath: "Why make me break my silence
and dress my sorrow in words for all to hear?
65 Aeneas! What man compelled him, or what **god**,

to take up arms against the Latin king?
Fate guided him to Italy (be it so!) ;
Cassandra's madness pushed him. Did I urge
that he leave camp and trust his life to winds,
70   handing a boy command of wall and field?
Or trouble Tuscan honor, and men at peace?
What god, what power of mine drove him to peril?
Where's Juno in this, or Iris from the clouds?
Foul, that Italians girdle a nascent Troy
75   with flames, that Turnus stand where his fathers stood—
Pilumnus' seed, divine Venilia's son!
What of the smoking torch Troy brought to Latium?
Their yoke for a land not theirs? Their plundering?
Decreeing matches, abducting promised brides?
80   Suing for peace from decks festooned with spears?
You, Venus, could save Aeneas from Argive hands,
drape clouds and empty airs before the man,
and turn his ships into as many nymphs:
if I help Turnus, that is sacrilege!
85   'Aeneas is off, unknowing': so let him be!
You own Paphos, Idalium, and Cythera:
Why trouble rough hearts and cities alive with war?
'Phrygia falters!'—because *I* ask her ruin?
I? Or the one who tossed a wretched Troy
90   to the Greeks? What cause made Europe and Asia spring
to arms? What sneak-thief broke the bonds of peace?
I captained a Dardan whoresman into Sparta?
I armed the hosts? Used Cupid to warm up wars?
Then was the time for worry: you come too late,
95   with ill-based pleas and meaningless reproof."

So Juno pleaded, and all the heavenly host
shouted assent, like the first gusts that howl
caught in a woods: under the trees they whirl
and whine, warning sailors of winds to come.
100   Then spoke the father almighty, king supreme
of worlds (and the halls of heaven on high were stilled,

the earth shook to her base, steep air fell still,
breezes died down, and Ocean calmed his waves) :
"Now hear my words and nail them to your hearts.
105 Since there could be no pact between Italian
and Trojan, and since your ill will finds no end,
what fortune today, what hopes each man may have—
Trojan, Rutulan—I'll hold all the same,
whether Fate led Italy to besiege the camp,
110 or Trojan blunder and ill-conceived advice.
Nor are the Rutuli free: both sides must reap
as they have sown. Jove is the same to all.
Fate will find ways." By Styx, his brother's stream,
its swollen, sucking waters, and pitch-black shores,
115 he sealed his oath, and all Olympus trembled.
The council ended. Jove from his golden throne
rose and by gods escorted left the hall.

Meanwhile the Rutuli, pressing at every gate,
were slaughtering men and ringing the walls with fire.
120 The troops of Aeneas, besieged, locked in, pinned down,
could not escape. Discouraged, men stood their posts
on tower and wall—a thin and luckless line—
Asius, the son of Imbrasus, Thymoetes,
Assaracus (two by that name), Castor, Thymbris:
125 these at the front. Behind them, Clarus, Thaemon—
Sarpedon's brothers, come from Lycian hills.
Now Acmon heaved with all his strength and hurled
a rock—fair half a mountain: he was equal
to his father Clytius and his brother, Mnestheus.
130 Defending the wall, men fought with spears, with stones,
with firefall, and with arrows nocked to strings.
Amid them all, that boy whom Venus loved
most justly—prince of Troy, with head uncovered—
shone like the gem that splits the tawny gold
135 of collar or crown, or like the ivory
that craftsmen set to gleam in terebinth
or boxwood; on his fair white neck, his hair

hung flowing, clasped by a circlet of soft gold.
The embattled great that day saw Ismarus
140   shooting to wound with arrows poison-tipped:
prince of Maeonia, he, whose fertile fields,
turned by the plow, Pactolus the golden washes.
Mnestheus was there (exalted, proud, for he
had earlier driven Turnus from the walls)
145   and Capys (Latin Capua bears his name).

Thus had these fighters met in heartless war;
Aeneas at midnight hour cut through the waves.
Leaving Evander, he'd gone to the Tuscan camp,
approached the king, told him descent and name,
150   what he could offer, what he would need, what troops
Mezentius and Turnus the hothead had assembled;
he spoke of the lot of man—how far one dared
trust it—and made his plea. At once, King Tarchon
accepted alliance; the Tuscan folk, in bond
155   to a foreign leader, as fate had decreed,
were free to man their fleet. Aeneas led
in a ship whose figurehead showed Phrygian lions
under Mount Ida—where Troy once found sweet refuge.
Here sat Aeneas the great in silent thought
160   for the turns that war may take. At his left side,
Pallas now checked the stars—road map of night—
now asked of Aeneas' trials by land and sea.

Muses, now open Helicon! Start the song
of men who came from Tuscany to join
165   Aeneas, who manned their ships and sailed the seas.

Massicus in his "Tigris" led the line;
his thousand men had mustered from the walls
of Clusium and Cosae—bowmen, they,
with quiver and deadly arrows at their backs.
170   Next, Abas scowling at his corps, for all
their polish (a gilt Apollo rode his bows).

Populonia sent six hundred men to him,
all seasoned troops, and Ilva sent three hundred—
that island where men mine the noblest steel.

175 Third was Asilas, prophet of gods and men,
who read beast's entrails and the stars of heaven,
the speech of birds, the tale the lightning tells;
he led a phalanx of a thousand lances
enlisted at Pisa (colonized by Elis,

180 but Tuscan now). Astyr the fair came next
(Astyr the horseman, with his rainbow shield).
He had three hundred men, all volunteers,
from Caerë and the plains of Minio,
from moldering Pyrgi and fog-bound Gravisca.

185 I'll not forget that brave Ligurian lord,*
Cupavo, with his modest corps of men.
The wings of a swan rose high upon his head
(Love was to blame) —mark of his father's form:
Cycnus, men say, loved Phaethon. At his death

190 he sang a dirge beneath the poplar trees
(Phaethon's sisters) : sad lines to ease his loss.
There, as he sang, his white hair turned to plumes;
he left the world and rose on song to heaven.
His son had manned a ship with soldiers young

195 as himself: the "Centaur." Her great figurehead,
holding a boulder high above the waves,
menaced the water; her long keel plowed the deep.

Ocnus, too, led men from his native shores.
Son of Manto the seer and Tuscan Tiber,

200 he founded Mantua in his mother's name—
Mantua, child of the great, not of one race:
she has three bloodlines, with four peoples each;
she heads them all, her power is Tuscan-born.
From here five hundred marched against Mezentius.

* Following Ladewig in omitting the name variously given as *Cinyra,
Cinere, Cumare,* etc.

205 They rode a ship with Mincius at her bows,
son of Benacus, draped in gray-green reeds.
Aulestes, heavy, with a hundred oars
flailed at the flood and whipped the wave to foam.
He rode a Triton, huge, grotesque, whose horn
210 frighted the deeps, whose trunk was like a man's,
but shaggy; his lower parts were like a fish.
The water muttered at his beast-man's breast.
So came the captains and their thirty ships
to rescue Troy; their bows cut through the sea.

215 Now day had dropped from heaven; the gentle moon
rode her night-speeding car just past Olympus;
Aeneas (his cares could never let him rest)
still governed the tiller and kept the sails in trim.
Midway on course, he saw his friends, the Nymphs,
220 dancing before his eyes—the ones Cybebe *
had given sea powers and changed from ships to nymphs.
Beside him they swam along, cleaving the waves,
one for each ship once moored beside the piers.
They knew their lord and ringed him with their dance.
225 The one most skilled at speech, Cymodocë,
swam up astern. Seizing the rail, she rose
from the water (her left hand gently stroked the wave).
He did not see her. She spoke, "My lord Aeneas,
are you awake? Wake up! Let all sheets run!
230 We are the pines from Ida's sacred crest,
now nymphs of the sea, your ships. But when that liar,
the Rutulan, tried to sink us with steel and flame,
in sorrow we broke our ties and sought for you
at sea. This guise our mother in mercy gave us,
235 and made us goddesses living beneath the waves.
Your boy Ascanius is pinned down by wall
and moat, by spears and Latins hot for war:
Arcadian and picked Tuscan horse have moved
as ordered. Turnus will send his squadrons in

* I.e., Cybele.

240   to block them from the camp: such is his plan.
       Up, then, and with the dawn's light call your men
       to stations! Take the shield the fire-god gave
       (it cannot be pierced; its rim is bound with gold) :
       tomorrow, unless you think my words are vain,
245   you'll see great bloody heaps of Latin dead."
       She spoke, and with her right hand pushed the ship
       (she knew what force to use) ; it sped away
       fast as a spear or as a wind-quick arrow.
       The others then put on speed. Anchises' son
250   was puzzled, and yet the presage gave him heart.
       He looked toward heaven and spoke a word in prayer:
       "God-mother of Ida, who hold Dindymus dear,
       and tower-girt towns and harness-broken lions,
       lead me to battle now, bless and fulfill
255   this prophecy. Lady, march beside my men!"
       He said no more. Meanwhile the day rolled round;
       light came to fullness and drove out the night.
       Aeneas ordered his men to battle groups:
       "Be brave as your swords are bright! Prepare to fight!"

260   Now he could see the Trojans and his camp;
       he rose on his quarterdeck and lifted high
       his glowing shield. The Trojans on their walls
       raised shouts to heaven; fresh hope enflamed their hearts.
       Spears flew, as when beneath the black raincloud
265   the cranes of Strymon sound their call and stream
       whooping across the sky before the storm.
       Turnus and his Italian captains stood
       amazed, until they saw the vessels veering
       toward shore, and all the sea afloat with ships.
270   Aeneas' helmet glowed; his plumes poured out
       flames; the gold on his shield spat floods of fire:
       like falling stars that sometimes on clear nights
       burn bloody and baleful, or like the Dog Star, born
       afire, who brings to sick mankind the drought
275   and fevers: his luckless light turns heaven grim.

Still Turnus, bold and confident, advanced
to seize the beach and beat the invaders off.
He turned to address his men and lift their hearts:
"This is the hour you prayed for! Break their lines!
280 Yours is the victory, men! Think everyone
of wife, of hearth and home! Recall the deeds
that made your fathers great! On! To the shore:
the first foothold is fearful and unsteady!
Luck blesses the brave and bold!"
285 He spoke, debating which men to take with him
and which he could trust to keep the camp besieged.

Meanwhile Aeneas was disembarking men
from the tall ships. Most waited for the ebb
of breakers and leaped into the shallow wash;
290 some slid down oars. Tarchon surveyed the shore
for spots where the backwash showed no break or sign
of reefs, where seas rolled in unbroken, smooth,
then put the helm hard down and hailed his men:
"With a will, now, men! You can! Heave on those oars!
295 Full speed ahead to ram! Now split that land:
you hate it! Force keel and all into the breach!
On such a mission I'll gladly wreck the ships:
just make that beachhead!" Soon as Tarchon spoke
his orders, the men rose to their oars
300 and drove the foaming ships toward Latin soil
till rams lay on dry land and every keel
was safely beached—except for Tarchon's ship.
She crashed on a humpbacked reef, and as she hung,
half in, half out of water, flailing the waves,
305 she split and spilled her people in the sea
to cope with a floating tangle of broken oars
and planks, while undertow dragged at their heels.

But Turnus had not hung back; with all his men
he hurried to hold the beach against the Trojans.
310 Bugles blew. Aeneas led off. He charged
some armed peasants and routed them (good sign!) .

He killed Theron—their tallest man; he'd charged
Aeneas, who plunged his sword through brazen mail
and gold-sewn tunic to lay his flank wide open.

315   Next he felled Lichas—cut from a just dead mother—
sacred to Phoebus (but to what end escaped
that childhood brush with death?). Soon after, Cisseus
and Gyas the giant: fighting with clubs, they'd killed
whole columns. (But clubs could not avail them now,

320   nor strong right arms, nor that their sire, Melampus,
had stood by Hercules through all his labors
on earth.) Now Pharus shouted empty threats:
Aeneas rammed a spear between his teeth.
Clytius, downy-bearded, blond, and young,

325   was trailed—a love new found—by luckless Cydon
(darling of all the boys), whom Trojan hands
would certainly have felled—a poor, sad thing—
but for his seven brothers, Phorcus' sons:
they interposed their tight-knit line, and threw

330   a spear apiece. Some struck Aeneas' shield
or helmet, and dropped; some grazed his flesh, but Venus
turned them aside. He hailed his friend Achates:
"Hand me my spears! Not one must miss its mark
of all that came to rest in Grecian flesh

335   on Trojan fields!" He seized a heavy lance
and threw it; it whipped its way through Maeon's shield
all brazen, to gore his breastplate and his ribs.
His brother Alcanor caught him as he fell,
but then at once the flying spear passed through

340   Alcanor's arm; the bloody point slashed on
and left the dead arm dangling from the shoulder.
Numitor ripped the spear from Maeon's body
and cast at Aeneas, but failed to pierce his flesh:
he only grazed the thigh of tall Achates.

345   Here now came Clausus of Cures, young and strong:
with a long spear-cast he wounded Dryopes
in the throat. He yelled; the heavy point pressed on

into the gullet to steal both voice and breath.
He fell on his face; thick blood poured from his mouth.
50   Three boys from Thrace, sons of the lordly North,
three sons of Idas, levied in Ismara—
these, too, Clausus dispatched. Up ran Halaesus
and his Auruncans; Messapus, Neptune's son,
drove his proud horses in. One force advanced
55   and then the other: at Italy's very door
the fight raged on. As when discordant winds
raise battle in heaven with equal will and strength:
cloud never yields to cloud, nor sea to sea;
the issue is long in doubt, both sides hold hard—
60   just so the Trojan lines, the lines of Latins
clashed: foot clung to foot, man pressed on man.

At another point, where sprawling floods had rolled
and driven boulders and trees torn from the banks,
Arcadian horse had tried to fight on foot.
65   Turnus now had them scrambling to fall back
(the rough terrain had forced them to dismount).
Pallas saw them; one thing remained to do:
plead with them, curse them, fire their hearts again.
"Retreating, men? *You?* You were always brave!
70   You fought for King Evander—fought and won!
You are my hope of glory great as his!
Take to your heels? No! Take the sword! Slash through
the enemy lines there where the press is thickest!
Forward with me! This is our country's call!
75   No gods oppress us; the foes we fight are men,
mortal, like us, same hearts, same hands as ours.
See! A vast ocean blocks us; no land's left
for retreat; shall we plunge in and swim for Troy?"
He spoke, and charged where enemy troops were massed.

80   Suborned by heartless fate, Lagus was first
to meet him. As Lagus tugged at a heavy stone,
Pallas hurled and struck him, and drove a spear

where spine keeps rib from rib; he tried to free it,
but it stuck fast in bone. Hisbo ran up
385 to catch him off guard, but failed; in his wild rush
of fury at Lagus' bloody death, young Pallas
caught him and sank a sword's length in his lung,
then went for Sthenius and—of Rhoetus' line—
Anchemolus, who raped his father's wife.
390 The sons of Daucus, too, died on this field:
Larides and Thymber, twins so like that all
mistook them, even their parents—with a smile.
But Pallas made them cruelly different now;
Evander's blade decapitated Thymber,
395 but severed Larides' hand, which groped for him;
its fingers twitched, still trying to swing the sword.

Inspired by Pallas' words and heroism—
hurt, too, and shamed—his men took arms and charged.
Now Rhoeteus drove past, panicked. Pallas' spear
400 struck him—and Ilus gained brief lease on life,
for Pallas had heaved and hurled his spear at him,
but Rhoeteus caught it as he passed between them
in flight from Teuthras and his brother Tyres.
He rolled from his car and, dying, kicked the ground.
405 As in the summer, when hoped-for winds arise,
a shepherd fires the woods at scattered points:
the flames rush through the gaps; soon one long line
of sharp-tongued fire spreads far across the plain;
he is the king: his flames pass in review.
410 So, seeing the courage of many joined in one,
Pallas rejoiced. But Halaesus, hot for war,
charged his opponents, braced and ready to fight.
He cut down Ladon, Demodocus, and Pheres.
Strymonius tried to choke him, but his sword
415 whipped off a hand; he smashed the face of Thoas
with a rock, to spatter bone and blood and brains.
Halaesus' father, a prophet, had hidden him
in the woods, but when his old eyes closed in death,

the Fates reclaimed the boy and ruled him forfeit
420 to Arcadian spears. Now Pallas attacked him, praying:
"Grant to the spear, Lord Tiber, that I throw now,
good luck and a path through hard Halaesus' heart!
Your oak shall have the arms I strip from him."
The god heard. As Halaesus covered Imaon,
425 he bared his luckless breast to Pallas' spear.

The hero died; his men shrank back. But Lausus,
strong as an army, checked them: Abas charged
(a focus of battle, a bulwark) ; Lausus killed him.
Sons of Arcadia fell, Etruscans fell,
430 and Trojans—souls that Greeks could not destroy.
The columns clashed, fair matched in might and men.
The rear ranks crowded the front; so close the press
no hand could move a weapon. On this side, Pallas,
on that, Lausus pushed on—two of like years,
435 handsome young men, but Fate denied them both
return to home. Yet even so, the king
of tall Olympus did not let them meet:
death was reserved for them at greater hands.

Now Turnus' sister warned him: "Lausus needs
440 your help!" His chariot swiftly cut the lines;
reaching the front, he cried, "Now men! Fall back!
I'll take on Pallas alone; his life is forfeit
to me! I wish his father were here to watch!"
At this, his men withdrew and cleared the field.
445 Such self-assurance! Pallas stood open-mouthed
as the men fell back. He cast a fighter's glance
from top to toe over that hulking frame,
then stepping forward, hailed the warlord thus:
"I shall win glory, either for battle spoils,
450 or a hero's death. My father respects both lots.
Leave off your threats." He marched out to mid-field
while blood flowed cold into Arcadian hearts.
Turnus leaped to the ground, prepared to fight

on foot: as a lion from his mountain lair,
455 spying a bull that paws the distant plain,
charges—so Turnus looked as he advanced.
When Pallas thought him within range of spear
he made first move—for luck and pluck might bless
inferior strength—and sent a prayer toward heaven:
460 "A welcome guest, you shared my father's board,
Alcides; help me take this giant step.
Let Turnus fall, and let his dying eye
see me victorious, stripping his bloodstained arms."
Alcides heard the boy; beneath his heart
465 he buried a groan, and shed a useless tear.
Then Jove addressed his son with kindly words:
"Each has his day. Man's life is brief, and none
can purchase more. But fame lives on, if men
live, as men should, by courage. By Troy's walls
470 the gods lost many a son—yes, with them died
Sarpedon, my own son. And Fate will summon
Turnus where life has drawn his finish line."
So speaking, he looked away from Latin lands.

But Pallas with all his force threw out a spear,
475 and from its scabbard ripped his shining sword.
The spear arched toward the spot where breastplate covers
shoulder; it nicked the border of the shield
and passing marked its path on Turnus' flesh.

Here Turnus raised his iron-pointed shaft,
480 took careful aim, and threw toward Pallas, shouting:
"See if this spear of mine can pierce more deep!"
Now through the shield—those plates of steel and bronze,
those layers of bull's hide lapped and lapped again—
right at the center the spearpoint whipped its way,
485 piercing through corselet, through to Pallas' heart.
He tore the blood-warmed weapon from the wound,
but blood and life passed down one path together.
He fell on the wounds (his armor crashed about him);

blood poured from his mouth; he bit the earth, and died.
490 Over him Turnus stood and shouted:
"Now hear, Arcadians! Tell Evander this:
I send him Pallas dead; this much he earned.
The honor, the small comforts of the grave
I freely grant. His welcome to Aeneas
495 has cost him dear." With his left foot he held
the body and ripped its heavy sword-belt off,
with its carven tale of crime: one wedding night
bloodied by bridegrooms butchered in their beds *
(chased work by Clonus, all inlaid with gold);
500 a Turnus triumphant took it now for spoils.
Man knows nothing of fate and future time,
or how, when blessings flow, to check his pride!
The hour will come when Turnus would give much **gold**
for Pallas unharmed, and curse the day he took
505 those spoils! Now Pallas' men with groans and tears
laid him upon his shield and brought him back.
To your father now in grief and glory, go!
One day brought you to war and took you off,
yet still you left dead Rutulans piled high!

510 No shallow report of trouble, but sure word,
sped to Aeneas—how slender the gap between
Trojans and death; retreating, they called for help.
He mowed down all he met, his fiery blade
cut a broad swathe as he sought Turnus boasting
515 of new-shed blood. Pallas, Evander, all
passed his mind's eye, the table where first he found
welcome, the hands he grasped. The four young **sons**
of Sulmo, as many again that Ufens raised,
he took alive for offering to the dead:
520 their captive blood would drench the funeral flames.
At Magus next he aimed his deadly spear;
he dodged: the humming shaft flew overhead.

* On their wedding night, the daughters of Danaus murdered their husbands, the sons of Aegyptus.

He ran and fell at Aeneas' knees, and spoke:
"By your father's ghost, by your hopes for young Iulus,
525   I beg you, save my life for son, for father.
I have a palace; I have deep buried wealth:
thousands in minted silver, gold in bars
and nuggets. Trojan victory does not ride
with me; my single life bears no such weight."
530   No more. In answer then Aeneas spoke:
"The silver and gold, the thousands that you tell,
save for your sons. Turnus annulled all deals
like yours by prior act when he killed Pallas.
So says Iulus, so says my father's ghost."
535   As Magus babbled, Aeneas pressed his head
backward, and buried a blade deep in his throat.
Next came Haemonides, Apollo's priest.
He wore on his head a sacred band of wool;
his garb shone all of white, his standard, white.
540   Aeneas met him, chased him, tripped, bestrode him,
loomed huge above him, killed him, while Serestus
stripped off his arms to be a gift for Mars.

The ranks now rallied, led by Vulcan's son,
Caeculus, and that Marsian hill man, Umbro.
545   Aeneas attacked; his blade cut off the arm
of Anxur, whose shield fell with it to the ground
(Anxur had made some boast, as if mere talk
had power—perhaps usurped a place in heaven
and promised himself long life and hoar old age).
550   Tarquitus now pranced up in bright new armor
(son of Faunus and Dryope, forest bred).
He blocked Aeneas, who tensed to throw his spear
but on its point impaled cuirass and shield.
The boy cried out, but midway in his plea
555   Aeneas lopped off his head and rolled the trunk,
still living, aside, and spoke in warrior's words:
"Lie there, now, terror of war! No loving mother
shall lay you in earth or in your father's tomb.

Lie there for buzzards, or sink beneath the sea
560 to roll while hungry fish rasp at your wounds."
Antaeus next, and Luca (front-line men),
Numa the brave, and Camers the fair, he killed
(the son of Volcens, richest of all the lords
of Italy; silent Amyclae was his seat).
565 Just like Aegaeon, called the hundred-armed
and hundred-handed (fifty mouths and hearts
breathed flame and fury; against Jove's thunderbolts
rang fifty shields, and fifty swords were bared):
so raged Aeneas, victor in all the field
570 when once his blade drew blood. Niphaeus' team
came driving against him, but Aeneas rushed
toward them with giant strides and frightful yells.
The horses, soon as they saw him, shied and reared;
they spilled their driver and galloped toward the shore.

575 Now Lucagus charged the lines with his matched team
of greys; his brother Liger held the reins
while Lucagus whirled his blade for the attack.
Aeneas could scarcely let such fury pass;
he rushed to make his stand with spear held high.
580 Then Liger spoke to him:
"These horses are not Diomede's, nor this car
Achilles', nor these plains Troy; here mark the land
where life and warfare end." Such madman's talk
flew loud from Liger; but the prince of Troy
585 made no talk in reply: he whirled a spear.
Now Lucagus, leaning forward, used his sword
to whip up the team; with left foot to the front
he was ready to fight: the spear passed through his shield
at the lower edge and pierced him in the groin.
590 Knocked from the car, he rolled in the dirt and died.
Aeneas the good addressed him mockingly:
"Lucagus, where's your chariot? Was your team
too slow? Did hostile goblins make them bolt?
Why, no! You jumped and left them!" With these words

595   he seized the horses. Liger now slid down
       from the car and stretched out useless, luckless hands:
       "In your parents' name who got you great, my lord
       of Troy, have mercy, I beg you! Let me live!"
       he babbled. Aeneas spoke: "Not such your words
600   of moments ago. Die! Never desert a brother!"
       His blade laid bare the breast, life's hiding-hole.
       Such deaths about the field the Dardan lord
       dealt out, in fury like a stream in spate
       or cyclone, till he broke the siege and let
605   Ascanius and his men burst from the camp.

       Meanwhile Jove, condescending, spoke to Juno:
       "Sister of mine, both sister and wife beloved,
       you did not err; it's Venus, as you thought,
       who bolsters Trojan power, not strong right arms
610   that live to fight, nor brave, adventurous hearts."
       Juno softly replied: "My lord, my husband,
       why harass the sick at heart, who fear your anger?
       If my love meant as much as once it did,
       and as it should, you would not now forbid me,
615   almighty, to rescue Turnus from the fight
       and bring him home unscathed to his old father.
       Now let a patriot die to pay Troy's price!
       Yet where did his line begin? With you and me,
       down through Pilumnus, on to him; his hand
620   has often piled your temples high with gifts."

       To her Olympus' heavenly king replied:
       "If you would ask for Turnus brief reprieve
       from death, and will accept my ruling so,
       save Turnus; let him escape impending fate;
625   that much is allowed. But if your prayer conceals
       some broader plea—some thought to end the war
       or change its course, you feed an empty hope."
       With tears then, Juno: "What if your heart should grant
       what voice denies and Turnus yet keep his life?

630 Now he must die, though innocent, or my name
    is Truthless. Let me rather be the victim
    of foolish fears! Take kinder course! You can!"

    So speaking, she hurtled down from heaven's height,
    riding an icy wind and wrapped in rain;
635 she made for the Trojan lines and Latin camp.
    Then out of mist she made a foolish guy
    to look like Aeneas (a strange and eerie thing);
    she dressed it in Trojan armor; shield and crest
    she shaped like his; she gave it gibbering speech
640 (mere maundering noise), and made it walk like him:
    like shapes of the dead that flit about (men say)
    or like the dreams that muddle us when we sleep.
    In front of the lines the grinning phantom pranced,
    jabbing at Turnus and daring the man to fight.
645 Turnus attacked: he hurled his whistling spear;
    the creature turned its back and ran away.
    What? Aeneas retreating? So Turnus thought;
    deluded, his heart drank in a foolish hope:
    "Running, Aeneas? Don't leave your promised bride!
650 My hand will give the soil you sailed to find!"
    he shouted, and flashing his naked blade, pursued
    the guy, not knowing his joys rode on the wind.

    So happened, a ship moored to a tall stone pier
    stood with her plank and boarding ladders out
655 (she'd carried Osinius, king of Clusium).
    Here fled the fearful phantom of Aeneas,
    and hurried to hide; Turnus was at its heels
    leaping the bollards and dashing up the plank.
    Scarce had he reached the deck when Juno broke
660 the hawser and rushed the ship through rolling waves.*
    The phantom then no longer sought to hide
    but flew to the tops and vanished in a cloud.

    * Lines 661–664 have been rearranged in the following order: 663, 664,
    661, 662.

(Meanwhile Aeneas challenged an absent foe;
all mortal flesh he met, he sent to death.)

665   A storm was blowing Turnus across the sea;
not knowing how he'd been saved, he stared astern
and cried aloud and raised both hands toward heaven:
"Father almighty, have you adjudged me guilty
in such degree? Imposed such penalties?

670   I'm sailing—where? Away? How then return?
Laurentum—camp: Shall I see them once more?
What of the men who marched with me to war?
Sacrilege, shame, that I left them so to die!
I see them milling and falling, and I hear

675   their groans! Oh, where might earth gape deep enough
for me? No, quicker: winds, show mercy now!
to cliffs, to reefs (see Turnus on his knees!)
carry this craft, or drive it on sandy shoals,
where Rutulans and disgrace may never find me."

680   While yet he prayed, his resolution wavered:
should he (mad thought) for such dishonor flesh
his dagger, and drive the raw blade through his ribs,
or leap out in mid-sea and swim for shore
and harbor, to face the arms of Troy once more?

685   Three times he tried both ways; Queen Juno thrice
stopped him, and for her love restrained her prince.
By favor of wind and wave the ship sailed on
and came to shore at Daunus' ancient home.

Meanwhile Jove sent Mezentius out aflame

690   for battle; he charged the cheering Trojan lines.
The Tuscans grouped and rushed him; all their hate
and a thousand spears were aimed at that lone man.
But he (like a rock that runs far out to sea,
in the path of winds and bare to the ocean's rage;

695   though storms may howl and breaking waves may crash,
it stands unmoved) —he stretched young Hebrus out
on the ground, then Latagus and Palmus, too:
Latagus, with a rock like half a mountain,

he smashed in the face; Palmus, the quick to run,
700 he left to flop, hamstrung, and gave his arms
to Lausus, and plumes to fasten to his casque.
He killed Euanthes and the friend of Paris,
Mimas, the son of Amycus and Theano,
born on that night when, pregnant with a torch,
705 the queen of Troy bore Paris (Paris lies
in the homeland, Mimas in strange Latin earth).
Just like the boar that snapping hounds drive down
from mountains after years of lurking high
on Vesulus or beside Laurentine swamps,
710 fattened on sedge: into the net he comes
and halts and snorts; his shoulder bristles rise,
and none has courage to jab him or come near,
but all stand back and shout and hurl their spears;
just so Mezentius to his vengeful foes:
715 none had the heart to draw his sword and charge;
all stood aloof and yelled and threw at him.
He circled forward, step by fearless step,
grinding his teeth each time he stopped a spear.

Acron had come from Corythus—a Greek
720 midst wedding rites compelled to leave the land.
Across the field Mezentius saw him fighting
in purple and plumes, gift of his promised bride.
Like a hungry lion ranging a high plateau,
mad and starving, if he should chance to spy
725 a nimble goat or stag with budding horns,
his great jaws gape, his ruff stands up, he clings
and lies to a feast of guts while bloody muck
drips from his maw,
just so Mezentius charged the massing foe.
730 Down went the luckless Acron, drumming earth
with dying heels; blood drenched the splintered spear.
Orodes turned and ran; Mezentius deigned
no killing by unseen spear cast from behind,
but raced ahead and met him face to face

735 to win by honest fighting, not by stealth.
Straddling the man, he tugged to free his spear;
"There lies Orodes, a fighter none should scorn,"
shouted his men and sang the victory song.
Orodes, dying: "You've won, but there's a price
740 to pay, for joy is short. A fate like mine
eyes you already: you'll grip this same sod soon."
Mezentius smiled but spoke with indignation:
"Now die! For me, the father and king of heaven
see to it!" With that, he drew the spear point out.
745 Over the man cold peace and steel-clad sleep
fell heavy; eternal night locked up his eyes.

Now Caedicus killed Alcathoüs; and Sacrator,
Hydaspes; Rapo, Orses and Parthenius;
Messapus, Clonius and young Erichaetes—
750 the one as he lay fallen from his horse,
the other, on foot. On foot came Agis, too,
whom Valerus killed (brave as his bold grandsire) ;
Thronius fell to Salius, Salius then
to Nealces—famous alike for spear and bow.

755 Now Mars had made the burden of grief and death
equal; victor and vanquished killed and died
alike; none marked retreat on either side.
The gods in heaven pitied the senseless wrath
of both—that mortal men should suffer so!
760 Venus stood watching here, and Juno, there;
death-pale Tisiphone raged all through the ranks.
Mezentius, brandishing a gigantic spear,
marched onward, lowering—huge as is Orion
when he strides through the ocean's deepest pools,
765 and cuts the waves, but stands out shoulder-high;
or from the hills brings down an ancient ash:
he treads the earth; his head hides in the clouds.
Such was Mezentius, and so vast his weapons.

Far down the line, Aeneas saw him coming,
770 and hurried toward him. He stopped, and without fear
he watched Aeneas come, stood massive, firm,
and judged with a glance how far a spear might fly;
"My hand, my spear (my gods), be with me now
as I weigh and throw. I promise my son as trophy
775 dressed in the spoil stripped from that robber baron
Aeneas." He spoke, and threw his whistling spear
far; it rebounded from Aeneas' shield
and pierced Antores just above the groin
(Antores, friend of Hercules; sent from Argos,
780 he'd stayed with Evander, and settled in Italy).
He fell by a wound meant for another, and died
with eyes on heaven, and thoughts of well-loved Argos.
Aeneas then threw his spear; it pierced the shield
concave, of triple bronze, and on through linen
785 and leather—three layers—then at the groin it stopped,
but its force was spent. Still, there was Tuscan blood!
Aeneas saw it and smiled; he ripped the sword
from his flank and made for a terrified Mezentius.
Lausus, for love of his dear father, cried
790 aloud at the sight and tears poured down his face.

Here death was cruel, for all your bravery,
young soldier! If men will trust so old a tale
of greatness, then I shall tell it, as you deserve.

Mezentius retreated; helpless and encumbered,
795 he dragged the spear still dangling from his shield.
His son burst from the ranks and joined the fight.
Aeneas rose full height and swung his sword
to strike, but Lausus parried the blow and blocked
the attack. His men rushed forward with a shout;
800 as father protected by his son fell back,
they circled Aeneas and with a shower of spears
diverted and held him pinned behind his shield.

As when the stormclouds pour down rain and hail
in streams, and every plowman flees the field,
805   and every farmer; travelers hide in holes
in riverbanks or under arching rocks
(the earth streams rain), that when the sun returns
they may resume their day—just so Aeneas
in a spate of spears lived out the cloud of war
810   to its thundering end, then called out, "Lausus! Lausus!
You'll die! Why charge me, and dare beyond your powers
Loyalty tempts you to folly!" Still, on he came
with a leap and a yell. Now savage battle fury
surged up in Aeneas; the Parcae gathered in
815   Lausus' last threads. The Trojan drove his sword
down to the hilt through the young soldier's heart.
The blade passed through his shield (too light for the bold)
and through the tunic his mother had sewn with gold;
blood filled its folds; his life fled through the air,
820   sad to the home of ghosts, and left his flesh.
But when the son of Anchises saw his face
as he lay dying—his face so strange and pale—
he cried aloud for pity, stretched out his hand,
as the shape of a father's love rose in his mind:
825   "What now, poor boy, what shall Aeneas give,
for a heart so great, a hero's heart like yours?
You loved that armor: keep it. You I release
to join your sires in death—if that concern you.
Let this be comfort for your tragic death:
830   you fell by Aeneas' hand." When Lausus' men
hung back, he haled them on, and raised the corpse
from the earth and blood that stained its smooth, soft hair

Meanwhile, Mezentius by the Tiber's wave
was washing his wound of blood; he leaned for rest
835   against a tree. At a space his brazen helmet
hung from a branch; his armor crushed the grass.
His picked men stood nearby. He retched and gasped,
and, easing his neck, let beard flow over breast.

He begged for word of Lausus, and sent his men
840 to recall him, with orders from a heartsick father.
But men came carrying Lausus on his shield,
bewailing a great man dead of a great man's wound;
far off Mezentius heard, and knew the worst.
He made his gray head foul with dust, and raised
845 both hands to heaven, and clung fast to the corpse.
"Son, was I gripped by such a lust for life
that I let you meet the enemy's hand for me—
flesh of my flesh? Your father, saved by your wound?
Alive, by your death? Now at this last I feel
850 the force of my failure; now the cut goes deep!
The charge they brought against me stained your name,
when ill will drove me from my fathers' throne.
'Twas I stood debtor to my homeland's hate:
would I'd pled guilty, and died by any death!
855 Now I still live, still have not left the light,
yet I shall leave." Then on his wounded thigh
he raised himself; despite the crippling pain,
he stood and called for his horse. This was his pride,
his comfort; on him he'd ridden to victory
860 in every war. He addressed that drooping head:
"Rhaebus, we have lived long, if mortal things
be 'long.' Today we two will bring the head
and bloodstained spoils of Aeneas home, avenging
the pangs of Lausus, or, if force fails us there,
865 we'll die together; you, brave old friend, I know,
will bear no stranger's bit, no Trojan rider."
Eased onto Rhaebus' back, he found the seat
he knew so well, and filled both hands with darts;
a horsehair plume hung over his brazen helmet.
870 He cantered off to the field; vast waves of shame,
anger, and sorrow surged up in his heart.*

Three times he called a challenge to Aeneas,
who heard and knew and said a prayer of joy:

* Line 872, which is identical with XII. 668, is omitted by most editors.

875 "So be it, father of gods! So, Lord Apollo!
Let battle begin!"
He advanced and took his stand with weapon poised.
Mezentius then: "Savage! What—kill the son,
then scare the father? That was my one weak spot!
880 I fear no death nor bow to any god.
Stop, for I come to die, but first I bring
these gifts." He spoke, and hurled a whirling dart—
a second—a third; they struck (this, while he loped
in a wide ring) but the golden shield-boss checked them.
885 Three times he rode to the left, hurling his darts,
circling Aeneas; three times the Trojan prince
turned round, while forests of darts grew from his shield.
The duel dragged on, with endless darts to pluck—
the match unequal, trying, a weary round.
890 With an eye for risks, Aeneas broke free and planted
a spear in the forehead of that fighter horse.
The animal reared straight up and beat the air
with his hoofs, throwing his rider, then collapsed
in a heap on him, head down, his shoulder thrown.
895 Trojans and Latins alike filled heaven with shouts.
Aeneas dashed forward, drawing sword from sheath,
and calling, "Mezentius the bold, where are you now?
Where is your fighting force?" The Tuscan then
looked up and gasped, as consciousness returned:
900 "Why these vindictive yells and threats of death?
Killing's no crime, when soldiers take the field:
not I, nor Lausus, made such pact with you.
If fallen enemies may, I ask one favor:
let me be buried. My Tuscans wall me round
905 with hate, I know: pray, hold their fury off
and grant me to share a tombstone with my son."
So speaking, he watched the sword sink in his throat;
blood welled up over his armor—and then he died.

BOOK ELEVEN

Meanwhile the Dawn rose up and left the sea.
Aeneas knew deep concern—the press of time—
the need to bury his men—dark thoughts of death.
But first for victory he must thank the gods.
5 He trimmed the branches from a huge oak tree,
set it upright, and dressed it in shining armor,
the spoils of Lord Mezentius, to your glory,
great god of war! He hung up the soldier's plumes
blood-soaked, his broken darts, his breastplate pierced
10 in twice six spots; on the left he looped the shield,
and draped from the top the ivory-hilted sword.
His generals stood in close-packed ranks behind him;
to their applause he spoke these heartening words:

"Most of our work is done, men; have no fear
15 for the rest. These spoils are thanks for victory;
here, by my hands, proud Prince Mezentius stands.
We march now on the king, on Latin walls.
Make ready! With courage and hope arm for the fight!
Let none hang back unschooled, when heaven shall **send**
20 signal to raise our standards and advance.
Then lead out your men! Fear must not slow our pace!
Commit now our loyal friends, unburied here,
to earth; this honor alone lives in the grave.
These noble dead who shed their blood that here
25 we might bring forth a nation: pay them now
last honors. First to Evander's town dispatch

Pallas—a soldier and every inch a man,
he sank in darkness down to bitter death."

He spoke, and with a tear walked toward his tent
30 where Pallas' body lay; Acoetes stood
on guard beside it (old now, he once had been
Evander's squire, but Fate had been less kind
when for his love he'd marched beside the son).
His people, and Trojans too, were crowding round,
35 and the women of Troy, their hair let down in mourning.
Soon as Aeneas passed the entrance way,
their cries of grief rose toward the stars; they beat
their breasts; loud waves of wailing filled the house.
There lay poor Pallas, cushioned, pale as snow.
40 When Aeneas saw his face, his smooth breast gashed
by Italian spear, he spoke, and tears welled up:
"I'm sorry, son! Fate smiled to start this day,
but turned adverse: you could not see me throned,
nor ride victorious to your father's house.
45 Not these the promises I gave your father
when I marched out, so lovingly dispatched
to power and glory. In fear, he warned me then
my battle would be with brave and heartless men.
And even now, the prisoner of vain hopes,
50 he may be praying and piling god-gifts high
for this dead boy, whose debts to heaven are paid,
whose death march now our useless tears adorn.
Father, behold your son, so cruelly dead!
Is this the return, the triumph, of our dreams?
55 Is this my solemn word? Still, you shall see,
Evander, no shameful wound, nor pray to die
because your son survived. What bulwark here,
Ausonia, have you lost—and you, Iulus!"

With this sad eulogy, he bade them lift
60 the pitiful corpse, and from his army chose

a thousand men to march as honor guard
and share a father's tears—small comfort, sure,
for grief so great, but owed a stricken father.
Quick hands now wove a stretcher to carry the dead.
65 They plaited withes of arbute, wands of oak,
built a soft bed and shaded it with branches.
Upon this peasant's couch they laid the prince,
like a blossom plucked off by a maiden's hand—
soft violet or fainting fleur-de-lis—
70 still bright and fresh, with beauty unimpaired,
but no more fed and strengthened by the earth.
Aeneas brought two matching coats, all stiff
with purple and gold—the work of Dido's hands,
made for him long before, with smiling care,
75 the pattern picked out in fine thread of gold.
He dressed the boy in one of these—a last
sad honor—and draped that head soon to be burned.
Spoils too he gathered, won from the Rutuli
in battle, and ranged them in a long parade,
80 and horses, armor stripped from the enemy,
and pinioned prisoners, victims to appease
the ghosts (their slaughtered blood would drench the pyre).
He ordered his captains all to carry poles
dressed in enemy arms, with names nailed on.
85 Acoetes, old and luckless, joined the march
(now he would bruise his breast, now scratch his face,
now throw himself full-length upon the ground).
Next came the chariots, red with Rutulan blood,
and then the war horse Aethon, bare of trappings
90 (he walked weeping, while great tears wet his face).
Men carried Pallas' spear and helmet (Turnus
had seized all else); then came the long, sad files
with arms reversed: Arcadians, Trojans, Tuscans.
They all marched on; Aeneas watched them pass,
95 then paused and sighed and spoke these final words:
"The war goes on; Fate calls me to new tears

and terrors. Pallas the great, forever hail!
Farewell forever!" That was all. He turned
and hastened back to camp and palisade.

100   And now from Latium came ambassadors,
crowned with the olive branch, to ask indulgence:
"Our dead lie scattered afield just as they fell;
allow us to lay them under mounds of earth.
No quarrel with the conquered and the reft of life!
105   Spare them, your hosts once, kin of your bride to be!"
Such prayer could not be scorned; Aeneas gave
gracious assent, and spoke these further words:
"What unkind fortune, Latins, tangled you
in war like this, and made you shun our love?
110   You ask a truce for the lifeless—those who died
in action? I'd give it to the living, too!
Nor had I come, but Fate assigned this place.
On the people I wage no war; your king resigned
my friendship, leaning instead on Turnus' arms.
115   Far fairer, had Turnus here marched out to die!
If he would end the war by force, and drive
us Trojans out, he should have faced my sword:
Let him have lived whom God or right arm saved.
Go now; lay your poor friends upon the pyre."
120   Aeneas had spoken. The envoys stood dumfounded,
glancing from man to man, and said no word.

Then Drances, elder statesman—one who vexed
Turnus forever with charges and ill will—
replied: "O vast of glory, vaster still
125   in battle, my lord: how best exalt your name?
Praise you for justice, first? Or might in arms?
Gratefully we shall bear your message home,
and set you beside our king, if Fortune find
a way. Let Turnus seek a separate peace!
130   We shall rejoice to raise your fated walls,
and bear on our backs the masonry of Troy."

Then with one voice the company cheered his words.
Twelve days of truce were set; they went their ways
in peace, unharmed, through woods and hills—Trojan
135 and Latin together. Tall trees rang to the ax;
the ash was felled, and pines that touch the stars;
with wedges men split oak and scented cedar,
and wagons groaned beneath their loads of elm.

Report now flew ahead with tragic news
140 that filled Evander's heart and home and town
(she'd told till now how Pallas had *won* in Latium).
Arcadians rushed to the gates; in ancient style
they seized the death torch: long, long lines of flame
shone down the road, dividing field from field.
145 The Trojan columns met and joined their ranks
in mourning, and as the mothers saw them come
near home, they fired the town with cries of grief.
No force could hold Evander; out he came
straight to their midst. Stretcher and corpse were lowered;
150 he fell on Pallas, and clung and wept and moaned,
till sorrow at last unlocked the path of speech:
"Not this, Pallas, the promise you made your father.
Oh, had you willed more cautious trust in Mars!
I know how much fresh glory in arms can mean,
155 how sweet the honor won in first encounters.
Oh, tragic initiation, so close to home!
Oh, bloody primer of war! My prayers, my vows—
not one god heard them! Dearest, purest wife,
blessed in your death, nor saved to know this sorrow!
160 I lived—yes, lived beyond my time: 'The father
survives'! Oh, had I followed my Trojan friends,
to fall by Rutulan sword! I'd lost my life,
and the catafalque had carried me, not Pallas.
I must not blame you, Trojans, nor our pact,
165 our hand of friendship. This blow had to come
to my old age. But if untimely death
awaited my son, he killed his thousands first,

and led Troy into Latium: this was good.
And for cortege, deemed I had no other worthy
170   than this: Aeneas the good, his Phrygian knights,
the generals and the troops of Tuscany.
They carry trophies—those he sent to death.
And Turnus had been a trophy hung with arms,
if Pallas had been his match in years and strength
175   and skill. But why do I keep you from the fight?
March on! Mark this and tell it to your king:
'With Pallas lost, I loathe my life; I live
solely for your right arm, that now owes Turnus
to father and son. This debt remains unpaid
180   by you and fate. For life, I ask no joy
(nor dare I), but only in death to bless my son.' "

And now to wretched man the Dawn brought light
and life—another day of work and grief.
On the curving beach, Tarchon and Lord Aeneas
185   built pyres; here, in the fashion of their fathers,
each brought his dead. They tossed the pitch-pine torch;
the smoke rolled up and darkness hid high heaven.
Thrice in full armor they paraded round
the burning pyres; thrice round the funeral fires
190   the cavalry rode, keening the grim death-cry.
Tears sprinkled the earth and sprinkled armor, too;
to heaven rose crash of trumpet and cries of men.
Others tossed on the flames the spoils they'd torn
from Latin dead: helmets and fine steel blades,
195   harness, and whirling wheels; some, well known things:
shields of their dead, their unproductive arms.
Whole herds of cows were slaughtered there to Death;
from every field men drove off sheep and swine
to kill for the flames. All up and down the shore
200   they watched their comrades burn, then by the coals
kept ceaseless guard until the dewy night
turned heaven full circle, tricked with glowing stars.

No less, across the field, the Latins mourned
and built their endless pyres. Some of their dead
205 they buried deep in the earth, some they bore off
to nearby farms or sent back to the city.
The rest, a great and tangled pile of slain,
they burned unwept, uncounted; field on field,
with fire on fire, shone brighter than the next.
210 The third day drove chill darkness from the sky:
weeping, they raked up piles of bones and ashes
hot on the pyres, and mounded them with earth.
Now in the homes of Latinus the wealthy's town
the sobs were loudest, and longest the wails of grief.
215 Here brides and mothers, and here the cherished hearts
of sisters grieved; here sons bereft of fathers
cursed the foul war, and Turnus, and his wedding:
"Let *him* don arms! Let *him* take sword and fight
who claims the homage of Italy, and her throne!"
220 Savagely Drances backed them; Turnus alone,
just Turnus, he swore, was called to take the field!
Others defended Turnus with many a claim
and plea; above him loomed the queen's great name,
while glory, fame, and merit raised him high.

225 Midst this debate, while anger burned and surged,
enter: long faces—envoys just returned
from Diomede with his answers: all their effort
had gone for nothing; gifts, gold, and fervent prayer
had had no force; Latium must seek for help
230 elsewhere, or beg the prince of Troy for peace.
At such grim news Latinus himself lost heart:
"Aeneas was blessed by Fate; God was his strength.
Proof was the fury of heaven, and those fresh graves."
He issued his command: his generals
235 and princes must meet in conclave in his halls.
They gathered, streaming to the royal house
through crowded streets. There sat the aged king,

commander in chief, Latinus, stern, unsmiling.
The envoys just returned from Diomede
240 he bade repeat their message—each response,
word after word. A hush fell on the hall.
Then Venulus, thus enjoined, made his report:

"Friends, we saw Diomede, saw the Argive camp;
we traveled the stages, passed all obstacles,
245 and touched the hand that leveled the land of Troy.
His town, Argyripa (named for his father's people),
he's building on land he won in Apulia.
Once we had entered and gained the right to speak,
we offered our gifts, told him our names, our nation,
250 who was attacking us, why we had come to Arpi.
He listened, then answered with a quiet smile:

" 'You are a people blessed, the realm of Saturn,
the Old Italians: what has troubled your peace?
What led you to hostile acts you never knew?
255 All we whose blades despoiled the plains of Troy
(forget war's waste of wealth beneath those walls,
those dead by Simois downed) throughout the world
paid frightful price and penalty for our crimes.
Priam himself must pity us! Pallas' star
260 and Cape Caphereus took revenge: they know!
Winds drove us, after the war, to different shores:
Menelaus, up to the Pillars of Proteus, far
from home; Ulysses, to Aetna, Cyclops-land.
Neoptolemus lost a throne, Idomeneus
265 a home; the Locri settled on Libyan shores.
Our Mycenaean general,* lord of Greeks,
died at his doorway by his wife's vile hand:
behind the conquered East, a whoresman squatted.
Gods ill-disposed kept me from hearth and home,
270 from the wife I loved, from beautiful Calydon.
And portents, too, pursued me (terror to see!):

* Agamemnon.

my men were lost, took wing, fled to the sky;
river birds now (what tragic fate for men
like mine!) they fill the bluffs with mournful cries.
275 But then, I knew such things must be, the day
I lost my mind and with my sword attacked
divinity—wounded the holy hand of Venus.
I tell you, no! Tempt me to no such fight!
The crash of a castle ended war 'twixt Troy
280 and me; my grim old memories bring no joy.
Those gifts you brought me from your native shores
give to Aeneas. I met him, blade to blade,
and hand to hand. Trust one who knows, how tall
he stands to a shield, how speeds his whirlwind spear.
285 If Ida's land had raised two more like him,
Dardanus then had marched on Inachus,
and fate, reversed, had filled Greek towns with tears.
Those dragging years of terror by Trojan walls—
our laggard victory—Aeneas, Hector:
290 they two were cause that slowed our step ten years,
both brilliant, brave, and skilled in warlike arts—
Aeneas the better *man*. Join hands in peace,
however you may; don't challenge sword with sword.'
Your Majesty, you've heard the full reply
295 of Diomede, and his view of this great war."

The envoys ceased. A mutter of hate and fear
ran through the scowling Italian ranks, as when
surf waters, blocked by boulders, swirl and roar,
and nearby shores echo the growling waves.
300 As soon as tempers cooled and fears fell silent,
the king, with a word to God, spoke from his throne:

"This, Latins, is life or death. We should have met
long since to settle it, not sit now perforce
in conclave, with the enemy at our walls.
305 This war is cursed! We fight a race of gods
and men unconquered, tireless of battle,

who, though defeated, never drop the sword.
You hoped that Diomede would join our arms?
Forget it! A man may hope, but we're close pressed.
310 Our state in shattered ruins lies around us.
Your eyes can see, your hands can touch it all.
I blame no man: your courage was all that courage
can be; our people fought with all their strength.
Now, though with doubt at heart, I will present
315 my views. I will be brief. Please hear me out.
I've ancient holdings by the Tuscan stream;
they stretch to the west, then south toward Sicily:
Rutulan and Auruncan farmland, rough
and hard to plow; the poorest is pasture land.
320 All this, and a stretch of pine-clad mountainside,
shall go for Trojan friendship. We will make
fair terms of peace and bid them share our throne—
settle, if such their wish, and build their towns.
But if they've heart to capture other lands
325 and other men, and they could leave our soil,
we'll build them ships—twice ten, of native oak.
Or if they've strength for more, all sorts of lumber
lie near the shore: let them provide keel size
and number; we'll give labor and chandlery.
330 Further, I move that, to present our terms,
a hundred envoys plenipotentiary
shall go, with wands of peace held in their hands,
with gifts, and minted gold, and ivory,
my royal chair and robe, signs of my power.
335 Take thought together and help our weary state."

Then Drances rose, whom Turnus' haughty looks
and sneers and barbed remarks had stung to fury
("a man of means"—"good speaker"—"something less
than fiery fighter"—"most wise counselor"—
340 "skilled at subversion"—"proud of his descent
on mother's side—on father's, who can say?");
Drances buried them under angry words:

"My lord, there's no man here but sees your point;
there's nothing that I need say. Our people know
345 our nation's fate; they mutter but dare not speak.
Let him allow free speech and cease his bluster
whose unblessed auspices, whose boorish ways
(and I'll speak out, for all his threats of death!)
have killed our greatest men. We've seen our land
350 flattened by grief, while he attacked the Trojans
by running away, and shook a shaft at heaven.
You mentioned generous gifts and grants you'd make
to the Trojans: add one more, Your Majesty,
just one (and let no wild man beat you down!) —
355 your daughter. Give her the prince that she deserves
for spouse, and make eternal bond of peace.
But if a terror so great has gripped our hearts,
let's fall on our knees and beg our prince for mercy:
Step down! For king and country yield your rights!
360 Why hurl your people into dangers clear
and constant—you, the cause of Latium's grief!
War cannot save us: peace is our demand,
Turnus, and that sole guarantee of peace.
See me, your first beggar! (You think you hate me—
365 if so, what then?) Have mercy on your people.
You've lost: step down. We have been routed and seen
enough of death, defeat, and lands stripped bare.
Or is your motive glory? Is your will
that stubborn? And *must* you marry a kingly crown?
370 Be brave, then! Offer Aeneas that fearless heart!
To get our Turnus his royal bride—we're cheap;
spread us across the field—mere common herd
that costs no grave or tear? No! If you've got
your father's fighting strength: look! There he stands,
375 your challenger!"

Such talk put Turnus in a towering rage.
He roared; the words came bursting from his breast:
"You always flood us, Drances, with your talk,

when warfare cries for action. Call the Senate,
380 you're first on hand. But fill no halls with words—
loud, windy words, so safe while walls hold off
the invader, and moats are not yet filled with blood!
On that day, thunder and rant (as is your way)
and call me coward, when your hand has built
385 windrows of Trojan dead, and dotted our land
with trophies. We might hold a trial of strength
and courage—we should scarce have far to seek
for enemies: they stand all around our walls.
Well—shall we go? What? Hanging back? For you,
390 Mars will ever be god of the windy tongue
and runaway feet.
          I've lost? In justice, who, you scum, can say
I've lost, and still see Tiber swelled to flood
by Trojan blood, Evander's line and house
395 in ruins, and his Arcadians stripped of arms?
Not so thought Bitias nor tall Pandarus,
not so the thousand whom I sent to death,
locked and hemmed in that day by hostile walls.
'War cannot save us!' Save such talk for Troy
400 and for yourself, you fool. Go on, spread fear
and panic! Praise the prowess of a tribe
twice conquered, and talk down our Latin arms!
Myrmidon chiefs now shiver at Trojan power
(and Diomede, and Achilles of Larissa)—
405 and Aufidus runs backward from the sea!
See him pretend he fears to face my wrath:
the hypocrite uses fear to barb his slander.
Your life you'll never lose by hand of mine
(no fear!): let it keep domicile in your breast!
410 Now, Sir, I return to you and your proposals.
If you see no more hope for us in arms,
if we're deserted, and with one retreat
we've lost a war, and fortune cannot change,
then sue for peace; hold out a helpless hand.
415 Oh, for some vestige of our native valor!

That man I envy—call him blessed in toil
and great in heart—who to avoid such scenes
fell, and in death agony bit the earth.
But if we have resources and fresh troops—
420 help and to spare from Italy's towns and tribes—
and if the Trojans paid high price in blood
to win (they have their dead; the storm's alike
for all), why this disgrace, this giving up
at the gate, this panic before the bugle call?
425 Time, effort, and change of pace have often brought
turns for the better, and Luck has laughed and shown
her other face, to set men straight once more.
No help from Arpi, then, or our Greek friend;
we've still Messapus and Tolumnius, still
430 our many allies, and no mean fame attends
our levies from Latin and Laurentine land.
The noble Volscians, too, have sent Camilla
leading her cavalry squadrons bright with bronze.
But if I'm called as champion, and this meets
435 approval, and I alone impede the good
of all—not so has Victory shunned my hand
that, with so much at stake, I'd fail the challenge.
I'll go gladly, though he were great Achilles
and wore, like him, armor made by the hand
440 of Vulcan. I pledge my life here for my king
and you—I, Turnus, soldier second to none
since time began. Aeneas calls? Good! Let him!
No Drances pay my pledge, if gods disown me,
nor to his glory redeem it by his valor."

445 While thus they argued matters of grave import,
Aeneas broke camp and moved his forces up.
The news spread tumult through the royal house
and quickly filled the city with wild fears:
"The Trojan lines were marching from the Tiber,
450 and Tuscan forces swarming over the plains!"
At once men panicked, and the people's hearts

were stricken and sharply goaded to fight back.
The frightened and the young cried out, "To arms!"
The old men wept and grumbled. Shouts arose,
455 and quarrels; the argument turned into bedlam,
as when in some tall grove a flock of birds
has settled, or by the fish-filled Po the swans
send loud, hoarse calls across the noisy ponds.
Seizing his chance, "Oh, no, dear friends!" cried Turnus.
460 Call your meeting to order; sit praising peace!
An army is marching against us!" That was all.
He leaped to his feet and hurried from the hall.
"Volusus! Call out the Volscian infantry,
the Rutulan, too. Messapus, you and Coras
465 and his brother, deploy our cavalry on the field.
Some guard the roads and gates and man the towers.
The rest prepare to attack, and follow me!"

All through the city men hurried to the walls.
Latinus himself left council room and plans
470 for another day: the hour was grim and fearful.
He blamed himself for failing to make Aeneas
prince in the city, his son-in-law and heir.
At the gates men dug trenches and brought up stakes
and stones; the bugle blew the bloody call
475 to arms. A motley gallery girt the walls:
women and children; all heeded the fatal hour.
Then to the temple of Pallas, to her hill,
up marched the queen and all her Latin ladies
with gifts, the maid Lavinia by her side—
480 cause of their sorrow—her eyes cast shyly down.
In they all came. The temple smoked with incense.
Their tearful prayers came pouring through the door:
"Ruler of arms and war, Tritonian maid,
reach down and break that Phrygian pirate's spear,
485 then tumble him, throw him to earth beneath your gates!"
Turnus made furious haste to arm for battle.
He put on his corselet bright with brazen mail,

rough as fish scales, and clothed his legs in gold;
his head he left bare, but buckled on his sword.
490 He ran down from the fort all glitter and gold,
head high, heart high, intent on battle to come—
just like a horse that bursts his stable bars
and canters free: he owns the open field.
He flashes to pastures where the mares are feeding,
495 or off to a stream he knows, to sink full-length
in the water. With neck arched high, he prances tall
and whinnies; his mane flies wild about his withers.

Now up rode royal Camilla with her files
of Volscians; just at High Gate she leaped down
500 from her horse, and all her cohort followed her,
slipping from mounts to earth. Camilla spoke:
"Turnus, if merit give boldness to the brave
then I am bold. I'll meet Aeneas' men
and ride alone against the Tuscan horse.
505 Let me and my horsemen risk the first encounter:
you keep to the rear, afoot, and guard the walls."
The girl meant terror! Turnus stared and spoke:
"You honor Italy, Lady! What return,
what thanks could I offer? Since your courage stands
510 high over all, share my command with me.
Aeneas—so runs the story, and so my spies
report—has blundered, sending his cavalry
to thunder across the field, while he climbs through
a lonely mountain pass and flanks the city.
515 I'm setting a trap: I'll follow a forest trail
and man the outlet of the pass, both sides.
You gather forces to meet the Tuscan horse:
your people, Messapus, his crack Latin troops,
Tiburtus and his men. You're in command."
520 He spoke; then to Messapus and the rest
he gave like battle orders, and marched out.

There is a winding, rugged valley, apt
for trap and ambush; foliage dense and gloomy

darkens its slopes. A narrow trail leads to it;
525   the approach is treacherous, and the outlet pinched.
Above it are hills like watchtowers; at their crest
lies level land, unknown, safe spot to hide
and launch a sally to the right or left,
or stand on the heights and roll great boulders down.
530   Here Turnus came by routes and ways he knew,
seized the spot and dug in among scrub trees.

Meanwhile on heaven's heights Diana called
Opis the swift—one of her company
of holy maids—and spoke sad words to her:
535   "Camilla is marching off to heartless war,
dear girl; those are my arms she wears—in vain,
though she is my dearest. This is no sudden love
I feel; no strange new sweetness stirs my heart.
Ill will and arrogance drove Metabus,
540   her father, from throne and ancient home, Privernum.
Through war and riot he carried the infant child
to share his exile, naming her 'Camilla'
('Casmilla,' her mother's name, but slightly changed).
Bearing her in his arms, he sought the woods
545   and long, lone hills; sharp weapons dogged his heels
while round him Volscians marched and countermarched.
Halfway to safety, the Amasenus foamed
bank-full in flood, so vast a rain had burst
the clouds. Poised for the plunge he stopped in fear
550   and love for the child (dear burden!). Everything
raced through his mind, and left him with this plan:
In one huge hand he carried a massive spear
(he was a fighter!), all knots and seasoned oak;
bundling the baby in sheets and strips of bark
555   he tied her handily midway of the shaft
then poised it in one great hand and said a prayer:
'Sweet virgin, Leto's daughter, lady of woods,
my daughter shall be your maid; she grips your spear
in this first flight to safety. Make her yours,

560 Lady, I pray; the wild winds have her now.' "
He spoke, drew back his arm, and sent the spear
spinning. The waters roared; across the flood
poor little Camilla rode the screaming shaft.
But now patrols pressed closer. Metabus
565 plunged in the stream and crossed, then pulled the spear
and baby from the turf—Diana's gift.
No city within its walls would grant him home
or refuge; his fierce pride forbade surrender:
in lonely hills he lived a shepherd's life.
570 Midst thorn and thicket he fed the little girl
at the teats of grazing mares, and on wild milk
squeezed on her tender lips from ferine udders.
Soon as the baby began to set her feet
to walking, he armed her hands with pointed darts,
575 hung bow and arrows from her tiny shoulders.
In place of golden coronet and long robe
she wore a hood and cape of tiger skin.
With tender hand she hurled a child-size spear
and whirled a plaited sling around her head
580 to bring down cranes of Strymon or white swans.
In Tuscan towns the mothers dreamed of her
as daughter-in-law—in vain: she loved Diana
alone; content with spear and maidenhood,
she remained her maid. Would she had not been caught
585 in such campaign, nor sought to trouble Troy!
She would have joined our ranks—one whom I loved.
But come! Since she's hard-pressed by bitter fate,
Opis, slip down from heaven to Latium land
where men are fighting a grim, ill-omened war.
590 Here, take my quiver! Shake out the shaft of vengeance!
She's holy to me! Whoever harms her flesh—
Italian, Trojan—shall shed his blood to pay!
She'll not be stripped! I'll bear off body and arms
in a cloud, and bury my poor child in her home."
595 With that, the nymph dropped down through weightless air,
her form wrapped up in thunderclap and cloud.

Meanwhile the Trojan army neared the walls,
the Tuscan lords, and all the cavalry,
in squadrons counted off. Across the plain
600 horses snorted and pranced; they plunged and reared
against tight reins; the field bristled with steel,
a mass of spears flashing, and swords raised high.
Against them hurried Messapus and his Latins;
Coras, his brother, Camilla and her men
605 took to the field; with arms drawn back, they held
their spears braced forward, vibrant for the charge.
The clatter of horse and marching men flared high.
Both sides marched on, until within spear's throw
they halted; then came the charge, the shout, the spur
610 put to wild horses: spears flew on every side
thick as the snow—cloud that clothed the sky.
Tyrrhenus and brave Aconteus leveled spears
each at the other, and charged; there came a crash
and death—the first: their horses met head-on
615 in crush and crumple. Then was Aconteus thrown
like a lightning bolt or catapulted stone.
He fell head first; his life fled with the wind.

At once men panicked; the Latins whirled about
hung shield on back and galloped toward the walls.
620 The Trojans pursued; Asilas led their lines.
Now they approached the gates. The Latins wheeled
again, and yelled, and reined their mounts around.
And now Trojans retreated, gave rein, and fled,
just as the sea swirls in and rushes out:
625 it rolls toward land, and foaming combers dash
high over rocks, deep onto the streaming sands.
Now it runs back; rocks roll in its sucking tide
but stop as it drains away and leaves the shore.
Twice Tuscans drove the Latins to their walls,
630 and twice, repulsed, they covered their backs and ran.
They met on the third attack; lines passed through lines
all over the field; each soldier picked his man.

Then came the screams of the dying; blood ran deep
over arms and flesh. Trapped among mangled corpses
635 horses, half-dead, floundered; the battle raged.
Orsilochus shrank from Remulus, but attacked
his horse: the spear point lodged behind his ear.
The creature reared at the blow; maddened with pain
he rose straight up, chest high, with flailing hooves.
640 Orsilochus fell to the ground. Catillus killed
Iollas and Herminius, great of heart
and strength and skill—his head unhelmeted,
his shoulders bare. He had no fear of wounds,
he towered so tall. The vibrant spear passed through
645 those broad shoulders and doubled him up with pain.
Black blood flowed everywhere, as men dealt death
and sought it—the death of honor on the field.

Amid the slaughter an Amazon rode high—
Camilla, the archer, one breast bared for battle.
650 Now from her hand whipped clouds of flying darts,
now, never resting, she seized her battle ax;
her gilt bow twanged, she shot Diana's shafts.
Even when driven to turn her back and run,
with bow reversed, she sent her arrows flying.
655 Beside her rode her fighter-girls: Larina,
Tulla, and, swinging her brazen ax, Tarpeia—
daughters of Italy, chosen by Camilla
as honor guard, her aides in peace and war;
like Amazons who in their rainbow arms
660 pound off to war by Thermodon in Thrace:
Hippolyta leads them, or, in battle car,
Penthesilea; loud come their female cries
as they ride by, proud with their half-moon shields.

Who was her first victim, and who her last?
665 How many did that hard maid hurl down to die?
Euneus first: he rushed her; when his breast
showed bare, she threw and whipped the long spear home.

Vomiting streams of blood, he fell, and bit
the gory ground; clamped to his wound, he died.
670 Liris was next; thrown from his fallen horse
he was grabbing the reins, when Pagasus ran up
unarmed to give his injured friend a hand;
both fell, one on the other. Amastrus next:
she chased him, threw her spear, and brought him down.
675 Tereus, Harpalycus, Demophoon, and Chromis:
for every shaft Camilla whirled and threw
a Trojan soldier died. Up rode the hunter
Ornytus with outlandish horse and arms:
a bull's hide draped still raw on his broad back
680 made him a soldier; on his head, the skull
of a giant wolf, white fangs and all, yawned wide;
he carried a crude harpoon. Straight through the ranks
of horse he rode, head high above them all.
She caught him (no task: his men had turned and run),
685 stabbed him, and spoke in words of hate and scorn:
"You thought this, Tuscan, a boar hunt in the woods?
The words your people spoke: a woman's hand
today has proved them false. Still, you may boast
in hell that by Camilla's blade you died!"

690 Orsilochus next, and Butes—tallest men
of Troy: Butes had turned his back; she stabbed
where between helmet and cuirass the neck
showed white (there, on the left, the shield hung low).
She let Orsilochus chase her; circling wide
695 she slipped inside their circle—and chased *him.*
Tall in her stirrups, she raised her battle ax;
he screamed; he begged: through helmet and through skull
she struck him—twice. Hot brain poured down his face.
In terror at this unexpected sight,
700 the son of Aunus the mountaineer stopped short
(a Ligurian, and at skulking not the worst).
Here was a fight! He saw no way to run
nor to distract the princess: on she came!

A trick! He must try a trick, some clever ruse!
705 He spoke: "What glory: a woman mounted safe
on a war horse! Now: no riding away—dismount,
fight fairly, face to face; meet me on foot!
You'll see whose windy boasting plays him false."
Camilla, seared by fury, gave her horse
710 to a friend and stood afoot, armed like the other
with simple sword and shield—and unafraid.
Her enemy, sure of his ruse, reined round at once
(in flick of an eye) and galloped away in flight
urging his animal on with steel-tipped spur.
715 "Ligurian idiot! Proud of your foolish trick!
Your slippery native wiles will do no good,
no fraud deliver you safe to liar Aunus!"
So said Camilla; on feet as fast as fire
she passed the horse, faced round, and seized the reins,
720 then lunged, and made her enemy pay with blood:
easily as a sacred goshawk swoops
from a cliff and drives a dove high in the clouds,
catches it, grips it, tears it with curved talons;
then bloody feathers come floating from the sky.

725 Not without eyes for the fight, the sire of gods
and men sat high on his throne atop Olympus.
He roused Tarchon the Tuscan to savage strife
and stirred his blood-lust with ungentle spur.
Out where his men were dying and falling back
730 rode Tarchon; cursing, shouting, he urged them on,
calling their names, re-forming their battle lines:
"What scared you, Tuscans—ever-shameless cowards!
What vast disinclination touched your hearts?
A woman has run you ragged and turned you back!
735 Why do we bear the steel—these useless blades?
For love, the nightly battle of the bed,
you're never slow, for flute and wine and dance.
Wait for the feast, the cup, the well-stocked board
(there lie your hearts), till priests cry, 'All is fair!'

740 and sizzling meats draw you to temple parks."
So speaking, he rode straight toward the enemy lines,
intending to die. He charged at Venulus,
grabbed him, hugged him, dragged him from his horse,
slung him across the saddle, and dashed away.

745 A yell went up, and every Latin turned
to look; like fire across the field flew Tarchon
carrying arms and a man. He broke the tip
from his lance, and probed for unprotected spots
where he might strike to kill. The other struggled

750 to keep the hand from his throat: force met with force.
As when an eagle flies off with a snake
he's caught and gripped with toe and clinging talons;
the injured creature turns and twists and coils,
raises his rough and scaly crest, and hisses,

755 struggling, straining; the golden bird fights back
with slashing beak—and never a wing beat missed:
so Tarchon, fiercely proud, bore the Tiburtine
off and away. Taking their warlord's lead,
the Tuscans charged. Arruns (today he'd die)

760 took spear, and using all his arts, sneaked round
Camilla, to find where luck was likeliest.
Wherever that blood-mad virgin charged the ranks,
Arruns followed and—noiseless—tracked her down;
when she ran back triumphant from a kill

765 the soldier reined about and slipped behind her.
Houndlike, he circled her, darting in now here,
now there, to attack, spear poised—an ugly sight.

Chloreus rode past—priest, once, of Cybele,
splendid to see in flashing Phrygian armor.

770 He rode a foaming horse caparisoned
in mail (like some big bird of bronze and gold),
and wore a cape—outlandish blue and red.
The bow slung on his back was gilded horn
of Lycia; he shot Cretan arrows. Gold

775 his helmet, saffron his priestly gown—its folds

of flapping linen caught by a golden clasp;
tunic and trousers tricked with Persian lace.
Camilla singled him out from all the field
(to nail that finery to some temple door,
780   or dress herself—for hunting—in golden spoils).
Blind and incautious she trailed him through the host
with a woman's burning love to win that wealth.
Arruns, in hiding, saw his chance had come;
he aimed a spear, and prayed the gods above:
785   "God of gods, Apollo, lord of the mountain,
our prayer goes first to you; for you we build
the pitch-pine blaze, and then in faith and love
walk through the fire and tread the glowing coals:
grant that my spear may wipe away our shame,
790   father almighty! I do not ask for spoils
or trophy of her defeat: my fame shall rest
on other deeds. Let but this monster fall
by wound of mine: I'll go unhonored home."

Apollo heard the prayer and granted part
795   in love, part scattered to the winging winds:
that Arruns should strike Camilla with sudden death,
he granted, but not that he should see again
the hills of home: that prayer rode on the storm.
The spear left Arruns' hand and whined away
800   as every Volscian turned both heart and eye
sharp on the princess. She was without thought
for whines in the air or weapons from the sky
until the spear point struck her naked breast
and sank and clung and drank her virgin blood.
805   Her fighter-girls came running to support
their fallen lady. Arruns ran in terror,
glad, yet abashed; he had no faith in spears—
no more!—nor dared to meet a virgin's dart.
Just as a wolf, before pursuit can find him,
810   runs far from trails, deep in the mountain peaks,
when he has killed a shepherd or fine, fat steer,

and, conscious of rashness, thrusts his trembling tail
for warmth under his belly, and seeks the woods:
so Arruns in terror shrank from human sight,
815   content to lose himself midst rank and file.
Camilla, dying, tugged at the spear; its point
deep-driven, stuck in her ribs, steel blade in bone.
She fainted from loss of blood; her eyes fell cold
in death, the flush of life fled from her face.
820   With her last breath she called her loyal friend
Acca, whom she most trusted, who alone
shared her concerns, and spoke these words to her:
"Dear Acca, I've done my best; this painful wound
will finish me soon—the world turns dark around me.
825   Now hurry, and take my final word to Turnus:
he must command; he, hold the Trojans off.
And now, good-bye." So speaking, she dropped the reins
and with one final struggle fell all cold,
as little by little she left the flesh. Her head,
830   prisoned by death, drooped, and her arms dropped free;
sobbing, protesting, her life fled to the shades.
Then came a shout that rose and spread and struck
the golden stars: "Camilla is dead! Fight on!"
In countercharge, the Trojan forces massed
835   with Tuscans and Evander's cavalry.

Diana's sentinel, Opis, long had sat
high on a mountain and calmly watched the fight.
Now 'midst the frenzied, yelling soldiery
she saw Camilla die her tragic death.
840   She uttered a cry of heartfelt grief, and spoke:
"Too cruel, poor girl, too cruel the price you paid
for daring to challenge the sons of Troy in war.
Cloistered in lonely woods, you served Diana;
you wore the quiver we wear—to no avail.
845   Yet still your lady has not left you shamed
here at the end of life, nor shall your death
pass in the world unsung and unavenged.

Whoever the man that stained your flesh with blood,
he'll die: he must." The tomb of King Dercennus
850 stood at the mountain's base—a huge earth mound
(oaks shaded the old Laurentine's resting place);
here Opis the beautiful swiftly swooped and stopped,
searching for Arruns from the barrow's top.
She saw him—all glittering arms and foolish pride—
855 "Why slip away?" she cried. "Turn back! Come here,
here, to your death, earned when you killed Camilla.
You—even you!—die by Diana's bow!"
She spoke, and from her golden quiver shook
a feathered shaft. She nocked it to her bow,
860 took aim and drew until the bow tips curved
and met; her hands with equal effort touched,
the left, the arrow point, the right, her breast.
Even as Arruns heard the whistling shaft
sing through the air, the point stood in his flesh.
865 His fellows left him gasping, groaning, dying,
forgotten, lost on the dusty battlefield.
Opis took wing and flew to tall Olympus.

Camilla was dead! Her nimble horsemen fled;
the Rutuli panicked and fled; Atinas fled.
870 Confused commanders, leaderless rank and file,
wheeled and raced for the city walls and safety.
On came the Trojans, dealing death. No soul
could face their spears or stand against their march.
No: nerveless shoulders carried bows unstrung,
875 and four-foot hoofbeats drummed a crumbling field.
On toward the walls a thick black cloud of dust
rolled; on the watchtowers mothers beat their breasts
and voiced their grieving to the stars of heaven.
The rout came bursting through the open gates
880 with enemy troops pursuing, pushing in.
It was a mob that ran from death, but died
by the gate, the walls, the safety of their homes;
transfixed, they breathed their last. Some slammed the gates

and blocked escape and refuge for their friends
885 despite their pleading. There they were butchered down
defending the gates or charging against the spears.
Locked out—poor souls!—while parents watched and wept,
some in the press and crush rolled headlong down
into the moat; some, blind and frenzied, rushed
890 like rams at the gates, at heartless bolt and bar.
From the walls at battle's peak, the very women
(Camilla had shown what love of country meant)
threw weapons with hands that shook: tough oaken staves,
and poles fire-hardened—a masquerade for steel.
895 They leaned out, bold defenders, eager to die.

Meanwhile in the woods heartrending news poured down
on Turnus; terror struck him at Acca's words:
"The Volscians routed and Camilla dead;
the enemy—blessed by Mars—advancing, killing,
900 sweeping the field; the city in panic now."
Half mad (this, too, by Jove's unkind command),
he abandoned the hill post, left the rough terrain.
Scarce out of sight he'd marched, and reached the plain,
when Lord Aeneas entered the open pass,
905 climbed the ridge, and escaped the lightless woods.
So both rushed toward the walls; with all their men
they rode, nor were they many steps apart.
Just as Aeneas caught a first far glimpse
of dust clouds, battlefield, and Latin lines,
910 Turnus beheld Aeneas, savage in arms,
and heard the tramp of feet and snort of horses.
They would have tested mettle and fought right then
but that the Sun, red over the Spanish Main,
dipped his spent team, and brought on night for day.
915 Outside the town they tented and walled their camp.

BOOK TWELVE

When Turnus saw the Latins broken, crushed,
ill starred, and calling him to make good his promise,
with every eye on him, he flared in fury
and gained new courage. As in the Punic land
5   the lion, gashed at the heart by huntsman's spear,
stirs then at last to fight: exultantly
he shakes his shaggy mane, and calmly breaks
his killer's lance, and roars with bloody mouth:
just so the fiery blood-lust rose in Turnus.
10 He turned and spoke in violence to the king:
"Turnus is ready! the coward sons of Troy
shall not retract one word, renounce one clause.
I'll meet them. Set up an altar; make the pact:
either I send that Dardan down to hell—
15 turn-tail of Asia!—Latins, sit and watch!—
and my lone sword refute the charge we share,
or call us conquered; Lavinia be his bride!"

Latinus forced down anger and replied:
"Prince of our soldiers, as you are the best
20 and bravest of all, so must I be most strict
and cautious as I judge and weigh events.
You have your father's throne; your hand has taken
many a town; I too have wealth to give you.
Other young girls live in your land and mine—
25 princesses, too. Now let me speak cold truth,
frankly and openly; hear me with your heart.
To join my daughter to any erstwhile suitor
was sacrilege: so spoke both god and priest.

263

For love of you, for kinship, I succumbed,
30 and for my poor wife's tears I broke the law,
tore bride from groom, and took up tainted arms.
Since then, Turnus, you've been the first to see
and suffer what has ensued—the war, the peril.
Twice we have fought and lost; these walls immure
35 our final hopes. Our blood still warms the flow
of Tiber, and broad fields whiten with our bones.
Why argue the point again? What is this madness?
If, when Turnus is dead, I'll call these men
our friends, why not stop fighting while he lives?
40 What will your Rutulan kinsmen say, and what
all Italy, if I send you (God forbid!)
to die—you who still seek my daughter's hand?
Think of war's thousand turns; think of your father,
burdened with years and sorrow, far from you
45 in Ardea." Words were useless to move Turnus
the hothead; remedy raised his fever's pitch.
As soon as speech would come he turned and spoke:
"You care for me, sir? Lay that care aside,
I beg you. Let me barter death for fame.
50 My hand too throws the spear; no crippled steel
flies from it. When I wound a man he bleeds.
Venus is too far off to wrap herself
and her runaway son in foolish female fog."

But Amata was frightened at this new battle risk;
55 weeping and near to death, she seized her prince:
"See, Turnus, my tears! Think how your heart esteems
your queen! You are the hope, the sole repose
of my old age; your king's prestige and throne,
all our enfeebled house lean on you now.
60 I beg you, raise no hand against these Trojans!
Your struggle will have a like result for you
and me; together we'll leave a life we loathe.
No manacled mother shall see Aeneas married."
Lavinia at these words burst into tears

65 that flooded over her burning cheeks, all red
with a fiery blush that flamed across her face.
If one should stain an Indian ivory
with bloody red, or 'midst white blooming lilies
a rose should blush: such hues her cheeks displayed.
70 Turnus fixed passionate eyes upon her face.
Aflame with war-lust, he addressed the queen:
"Mother, I go to the battle of heartless Mars.
Please do not send me off with tears and talk
of doom: I am not free to stave off death.
75 Idmon, be envoy! Bring to my lord of Troy
words he'll not like. When first tomorrow's Dawn
rides rose-red up the sky on crimson wheels,
let there be truce: no Trojan take up arms,
no Latin. His blood and mine shall end this war,
80 and on that field we'll seek Lavinia's hand."

He spoke, then hastened back into his house,
called for his horses, smiled at their eager champing—
they were Pilumnus' pride, the Wind Maid's gift,
whiter than snow and swifter than the breeze.
85 The grooms came rushing round; with hollowed hands
they slapped the horses' chests, and combed their manes.
Turnus pulled on his corselet, rough with scales
of gold and bronze; then ready to hand he slung
his sword and shield, and fitted his red-plumed casque
90 (the sword, his father's, the god of fire had forged
for Daunus, and dipped it white-hot in the Styx).
In center hall against a massive pier
stood a stout spear (spoil of Auruncan Actor);
Turnus now seized it, shook it till it hummed,
95 and shouted: "Spear that never failed to heed
my summons, now is the hour. Actor once,
now Turnus holds you. Grant me to throw him down,
to tear his corselet from him, rip it off—
our Phrygian laddy!—and foul his pretty curls
100 crimped with hot iron and dripping with perfume."

Such madness seized him; from his flaming face
hot fury flashed; his eyes shot sparks of fire.
Just like the bull that bellows to start a fight—
a fearful roar; he spends his rage in butting,
105   ramming a treetrunk, flailing at the winds,
charging, and pawing sand, preluding battle.

No less the warrior, wearing his mother's arms,
Aeneas prepared for fighting and battle frenzy,
glad for the pact that meant the end of war.
110   Recounting his destiny, he calmed his friends
and his worried son, and sent men with replies
for King Latinus, to name the terms of peace.

The morrow's dawn had barely touched the hills
with light—the time when from the deep sea rise
115   sunhorses with wide nostrils breathing light.
Under the city walls the Rutulans
and Trojans were pacing off the dueling field
and building between their lines altars of turf
to gods they shared. Some brought up fire and water;
120   they wore the stole and wreathed their heads with leaves.
Out marched the Latin army; lines of lancers
poured through the open gates. The Trojans too,
and Tuscans in various armor, all rushed out
ordered and weaponed as if the cruel call
125   to charge had sounded. Midst their thousands rode
generals, quick and proud in purple and gold:
Mnestheus, son of Assaracus, brave Asilas,
Messapus, tamer of horses, Neptune's son.
The bugles blew retreat; each side drew back,
130   drove spears in the ground, and stacked their shields against
    them.
Then came the women, the helpless mob, the old,
eager, hurrying out to tower and roof
for places, or to the gangways over the gates.

But Juno, from the hilltop now called "Alban"
135 (unhonored then, a slope unsung, unnamed),
was glancing over field and battle lines,
Italian and Trojan, and toward Latinus' city.
Abruptly then she spoke to Turnus' sister,
goddess to goddess, for she was lady of lake
140 and stream (granted this sacred post by Jove,
the king of heaven, for ravaged maidenhood) :
"Blest maid of rivers, dearest to my heart,
you know that I have loved you more than all
the Latin girls who've shared Jove's thankless bed,
145 and gladly found a place for you in heaven.
Now hear, Juturna, and grieve—but no reproaches!
Where Fortune and the Fates allowed the Latins
success, I sheltered Turnus and your walls.
But now your prince battles with ill-matched fate;
150 the day of doom, the force of wrath draw near.
This pact, this battle, my eyes cannot observe.
He is your brother: be bold! Help if you dare;
stand by in honor. Good luck may follow bad!"

With that, Juturna flooded her eyes with tears;
155 three times and four she struck her lovely breast.
"No time for tears!" Saturnian Juno cried.
"Hurry! Save Turnus from death, if way there be;
if not, start warfare! Shatter their promised pact!
Courage: I stand with you!" Exhorting thus,
160 she left her frightened, wounded, worried, sad.

Meanwhile Latinus in all his royal splendor
rode out in four-horse chariot; round his brow
shone twice-six golden rays, a glittering crown,
mark of his sire, the Sun. Two snow-white horses
165 drew Turnus, who bore two spears tipped with broad steel.
Then Lord Aeneas, sire of the Roman race,
his shield a blazing sun, his arms like stars,
with him Ascanius, great Rome's second hope—

they strode from the camp. A priest in pure white robes
170 brought young of a bristled pig, an unshorn ewe,
and drove cattle close up to the altar fires.
The company turned and faced the rising sun,
sprinkled salt meal, and marked the victims' heads
with knives, then poured libation on the altars.

175 Aeneas the good then drew his sword and prayed:
"Be witness, Sun; O Italy, hear my cry
(you gave me reason and strength to bear these toils);
father almighty, and consort daughter of Saturn
(be kinder, lady, I pray); O godhead Mars,
180 father, lord of the wring and wrench of war!
Hear me, rivers and springs, dominions, powers
of high heaven and of the deep blue sea!
Agreed: If victory here shall pass to Turnus
the vanquished shall fall back to Evander's town,
185 Iulus vacate, the sons of Aeneas raise
no arms to protest, nor harass this land hereafter.
But if our arms shall win the victory-nod
(as I rather think—and may God prove me right!),
I'll not demand that Italy bow to Troy.
190 I want no crown. Both peoples join in bond
equal, unconquered, friends and allies forever.
My gift be god and cult. Latinus—father-in-law—
shall keep his arms and wonted power. My men
shall build my city; Lavinia shall name it."

195 So first Aeneas. Latinus followed then,
his eyes on heaven, his right hand toward the stars:
"Agreed, Aeneas, I swear, by earth, sea, stars,
by Leto's double birth and twiform Janus,
the mighty hell-gods, and dread Pluto's shrine;
200 hear, father, who seal our pacts with lightning flash.
I touch the altars; be witness, fires and gods:
Italians will never break this bond of peace

whatever the outcome, and no power persuade
me to evasion—not if the deluge wash
205 earth into ocean, and heaven down to hell.
Even as this staff (so happened, he held a staff)
shall never sprout twigs and leaves, or cast a shade,
once men in the woods have cut it from its root,
and steel has made it motherless, leafless, armless—
210 sometime a tree, but now the smith has sheathed it
in bronze, a scepter for Latin aldermen."
Such oaths they took to ratify their pact
while princes watched. They blessed the victims then,
slaughtered them over the flames, ripped entrails out
215 alive, and piled the altars with plates of gifts.

To the Rutuli, the duel had long since seemed
unfair; their hearts were filled with deeper doubt
the closer they saw the ill-matched pair approach—
still more when Turnus stepped forth wordlessly
220 with downcast eye to reverence the altar
(his cheeks were sunken, his young man's flesh was pale).
Juturna heard the mutterings increase
and saw the soldiers' hearts beset with fear.
Disguised as Camers, she stepped between the ranks
225 (Camers, scion of kings; his father's fame
was great, and he himself a brilliant fighter) —
with well-laid plan, she stepped between the ranks;
she spread vague rumors, and uttered words like these:
"Shame, men, to make a single soul stand bulwark
230 for a whole host! Count us; assess our strength:
are we not match for all their force—Trojans,
Arcadians, Tuscans (the death band: they hate Turnus)?
Each two of us could scarce find one to fight!
Turnus has pledged his life; he'll rise in glory
235 up to the gods and live on the lips of men;
we who sit passive here will lose our country
and bend the knee perforce to haughty lords."

Her speech inflamed the hearts of fighting men
more, and still more as angry murmurs crept
240   through Latin and Laurentine ranks—now changed.
They'd hoped for rest, security, and peace,
but now they called for arms and wished the truce
revoked; their sympathies went out to Turnus.
To this Juturna added a stronger sign
245   in heaven, a portent forceful past all else
to frighten and deceive the Latin mind.
The sky turned red; Jove's bird flew golden against it
in chase of shore birds and a noisy flock
of winged fowl, then swooping to the waves
250   he seized in cruel talons a lordly swan.
The Latins watched transfixed, as all the birds
wheeled from their flight with screams (wonder to see).
They darkened the sky with wings; formed in a cloud
they pressed their enemy till sheer force and weight
255   subdued him; from his claws he dropped his prey
into the river, then soared off through the clouds.

At this portent the Rutuli raised loud cheers.
They dressed their lines; the augur Tolumnius spoke:
"This was the sign I prayed for, time and again!
260   I know God's word! I'll lead! I'll lead! Take arms,
you sorry fools, whom some damned foreigner frightens
with war, like feeble birds, and sweeps your shores
clean with the sword. He'll turn and run, hoist sail,
take to the sea! Together, now! Close ranks!
265   They've taken your prince: defend him! Forward! Fight!"

He spoke and, dashing forward, hurled a spear
at the enemy; through the air the speeding shaft
whistled. At once a great shout rose; the troops
milled madly, discipline faltered, fury flared.
270   The spear flew on. By chance, nine handsome brothers
stood in its path (one faithful Tuscan wife
had borne them all to Arcadian Gylippus).

It struck one brother at the waist, just where
the baldric's buckle and stitching chafe the flesh—
275 a well-built lad, with armor polished bright;
the spear passed through and hurled him to the ground.
His brothers, aflame with grief, leaped into line.
Some drew the sword, some snatched up spears to throw;
they charged, blindly. Against them rushed a column
280 of Latins; in answering waves, dense-packed, came Trojans,
Arcadians, Tuscans, in bright-painted armor.
All had one aim: to battle with the steel.
They ripped the altars apart; across the sky
wild storms of weapons passed, and steel-clad rain;
285 chalice and fire went flying; Latinus ran,
arms full of conquered gods, his pact a shambles.

Men harnessed team and chariot, others leaped
to the saddle; they all drew swords, the lines advanced.
Messapus, eager to tear up the treaty, rode
290 full-tilt at Aulestes, prince of the Tuscan blood,
in all his purples: frightened, he backed his horse,
poor fool, straight into an altar, and was thrown
head over heels. Messapus, hot for a kill,
rushed up and, as Aulestes begged for mercy,
295 leaned from the saddle, dispatched him, and cried out:
"That does it! Here's better offering for our gods!"
The Latins ran in to strip the bleeding corpse.
Corynaeus advanced and seized an altar brand
still burning; as Ebysus charged and lunged at him
300 he thrust the flame in his face; his long beard smoked,
flared up, and stank. Corynaeus then pressed in,
with left hand seized his panicked opponent's hair,
kneed him and leaned and forced him to the ground,
then sank a blade in his side. Podalirius
305 brandished a naked sword above the shepherd
Alsus, who'd run to the front to meet the spears.
Up came the shepherd's ax to split through chin
and brow, and flood his enemy's arms with blood.

A peace as hard as iron pressed his eyelids
310 down, and eternal night closed on his eyes.

Aeneas the good stretched out his unarmed hand,
tore off his helmet, and shouted to his men:
"Why this charge? What sudden quarrel arose?
Halt, men! Calm down! We've made a pact; the terms
315 are settled; lawfully, I alone may fight.
Leave this to me! No fear: my hand will prove
the treaty sound. Our oaths made Turnus mine!"
While yet he spoke, amid his very words,
an arrow whistled in and struck the man.
320 Who shot it, what breeze had blown it, no one knew.
Who gave the Rutuli such renown: some god?
mere chance? The stroke was glory, the credit lost:
no man dared boast the wounding of Aeneas.
Aeneas dropped out of line; his captains paled.
325 Turnus saw it; fresh hope flared up at once.
He called for team and weapons; in prancing pride
he sprang to his car and gathered the reins to hand.
His headlong rush sent many brave men to death,
and mangled many; he crushed firm-standing files,
330 but showered spears on those that broke and ran.
As Mars the bloody beside the ice-cold Hebrus
comes galloping, clanging on his shield the call
to war; his maddened horses sweep the plain
faster than West or South Wind; farthest Thrace
335 groans at their hoof beats. Fear, with face of corpse,
Blood-Lust, and Treason ride at the war god's side:
so Turnus straight through the battle wildly lashed
his smoking, sweat-soaked team: they trampled the dead
to shapeless rags; their speeding wheels splashed blood
340 like rain, and kneaded a muck of blood and sand.
A cast of his spear killed Sthenelus; hand to hand
he slaughtered Pholus and Thamyrus; spears again
took Glaucus and Lades, sons of Imbrasus, twins

he'd raised in Lycia, and armed them both alike
345 for the fight afoot or the wind-swift cavalry charge.

At another spot Eumedes rode to battle
(grown great in war, the son of once-great Dolon,
named for his grandsire, soldier like his father,
who dared to ask, as price for slipping out
350 to spy on Greeks, the chariot of Achilles;
daring he was, but Diomede paid him price
far different: Achilles' horses lost their charm).
Turnus spied him across the open field
and with a long-range spear-cast struck him down,
355 then pulled his team to a halt, leaped from his car,
strode to the dying man and placed a foot
on his neck, then from his right hand wrenched the sword,
plunged the shining blade in his throat, and spoke:
"Here, Trojan, the land you wanted to win by war;
360 stretch out and measure the Westland! Such the prize,
the home they win, who try me with the sword!"
He hurled a spear and made Asbytes join him,
Thersilochus, too, and Chloreus, Sybaris, Dares,
and then—thrown from his horses's back—Thymoetes.
365 As when the blast of Boreas howls across
the Aegean, and rolls the breakers toward the beach
(where lies the wind, there run the clouds of heaven):
so Turnus slashed his way, and men fell back,
whole companies crumpled and ran; speed bore him on,
370 the wind of his chariot's rush whipped at his plumes.
At this frenzied, screaming onset, Phegeus rebelled.
He leaped for the chariot, seized the reins, and wrenched
the heads of the racing, foam-flecked horses round.
He hung there, dragging; Turnus drove a lance
375 at his unprotected flank. It broke the links
of his corselet, scratched the flesh, and tasted blood.
But Phegeus threw up his shield, whirled, and advanced
against his opponent, drawing his sword to fight.

Turnus lashed at his team; the car leaped forward,
380 struck Phegeus, and laid him flat. Turnus ran up,
slashed at the space 'twixt helmet and cuirass,
lopped off his head and left him on the sand.

While Turnus was winning, and dealing death afield,
Aeneas was brought by Mnestheus and Achates
385 (Ascanius with them) into the camp; he bled
and with a long lance propped his limping steps.
He cursed and struggled to pull the arrow free.
It broke; he called for the speediest way to help:
slice the wound with a sword, cut deep, and bare
390 the hidden point—and send him back to fight.
Now Iapyx son of Iasus came, whom Phoebus
held dearest of all; to him one time the god
had offered his arts and powers in love and joy—
his music, prophetic gifts, and speeding arrows.
395 But he, to prolong his dying father's life,
preferred to learn the powers of herbs, and arts
of healing—to follow a mute, inglorious craft.
There stood Aeneas, propped by his spear and cursing
bitterly, but unmoved by the press of men
400 and Iulus' worries and tears. Old Iapyx
rolled up his robe like Apollo, and tucked it in.
He laid on a healing hand, he rubbed in salves
of Phoebus himself, in vain; in vain he worked
with fingers and tugged with forceps at the point.
405 Luck would not guide him nor his god Apollo
help him. Out on the field blood-chilling fears
increased and death drew closer. Now they saw
dust hang in the sky; the cavalry charged, and arrows
rained on the camp. The noise of battle rose
410 to heaven as young men fought and bled and died.

Now Venus, shocked that her son should suffer so,
plucked dittany on the slopes of Cretan Ida
(its stalk and leaves are hairy; it wears a crest

of purple flowers: an herb the wild goats know
415   and crop when arrows cling fast in their flesh).
This Venus brought and, wrapping herself in mist
and darkness, dipped it into the polished jug
of water—a covert cure—then added drops
of ambrosia and sweet-smelling panacea.
420   With this infusion Iapyx washed the wound
unwittingly; all at once the pain was gone—
completely!—and from the wound no blood welled up.
A touch of the hand—no more: the arrowhead
dropped out, and former vigor was renewed.
425   "Don't stand there! Hurry! Bring the man his arms!"
Iapyx shouted, renewing their will to fight.
"No human power, no skill was teacher here;
you were not saved, Aeneas, by hand of mine.
A greater—a god—directs you to greater deeds!"
430   Eager for battle, Aeneas encased both legs
in gold, chafed at delay, and shook his spear.
With shield at his side and corselet on his back
he gathered Ascanius in his full embrace,
took through his helmet the top of a kiss, and spoke:
435   "Learn courage, my son, from me, and true endurance;
learn luck from others. My right arm will defend you
in war today, and lead you to wealth and power.
Remember this when riper years have come
and, searching your line for glory, be inspired
440   by Aeneas, your father, and by your uncle, Hector."

So speaking, he strode from camp, a towering man;
his huge lance shook in his hand. Antheus and Mnestheus
formed their columns and marched out, trailed by the host
who rushed to abandon camp. Dark, roiling dust
445   rose on a field that shook to tramping feet.
Turnus on his embankment saw them come:
the Ausonians saw: their blood ran cold, their bones
shook to the marrow. Juturna, sooner than they,
heard the noise and knew it—shivered, and ran.

450 Over open land Aeneas advanced his men.
As when in a break of weather the rain clouds move
from sea toward land (far off, the farmer knows
what is to come, and quakes: the storm will flatten
orchard and grain in one wide swathe of death);
455 first, winds come racing, roaring toward the shore:
so marched the lord of Troy toward enemy lines,
leading his men; pressed into tight-packed ranks
they massed beside him. Thymbraeus killed Osiris,
and Mnestheus, Arcetius; Epulo fell to Achates,
460 Ufens to Gyas. Tolumnius, priest, fell too,
who first hurled spear against the enemy lines.
The shouting rose to heaven, as Rutulans now
turned tail and ran; the dust rolled up behind them.
Aeneas would kill no man whose back was turned
465 nor even engage the men who took firm stand
and offered to fight. He hunted Turnus alone
in the dust of battle, him only he called to fight.

Here was terror that struck Juturna's heart!
Metiscus, Turnus' driver, stood to his reins:
470 she pushed him out and left him far behind,
then took his place and managed the rippling lines,
assuming Metiscus' voice and form and arms.
As when in the great halls of some wealthy lord
a swift, black swallow wings through the colonnades
475 searching for mites to feed her shrill-voiced young:
now in the empty yards, by ponds and pools
her voice is heard: just so Juturna drove
through the enemy, dashing and darting everywhere.
Now here, now there, she showed her brother triumphant,
480 but flew from the clash and would not let him fight.
Aeneas too ran toward him, twisting, turning,
dogging his tracks, shouting his name, and sending
the columns flying. Each time he sighted his man
and raced to catch the galloping, wing-foot team,
485 Juturna wrenched the chariot from his path.

What should he do? Frustrated and distraught,
he felt caught in a shifting tide of care.
And now Messapus, whose left hand chanced to hold
two vibrant, steel-tipped spears, came running up
490 and with sure aim threw one, and made it spin.
Aeneas halted and shrinking within his guard
dropped on one knee; the speeding shaft broke off
his helmet's peak and tore the plume to shreds.
Then truly his rage boiled up: chicanery—
495 a chariot dashing and shying in wild retreat—
this drove him to act. He prayed Jove to remember
defilement of pact and oath, then savagely
charged at the enemy, fighting, winning, killing
whomever he met; his rage poured out unchecked.

500 And now what god could tell it—the bitterness,
the bloodshed, and the dying? Across the field
now Turnus and now Aeneas harried the great
and killed them: was it the will of God, that men
soon to be brothers in peace should so contend?
505 Aeneas met Sucro the Rutulan, first to stand
and fight and halt the headlong Trojan rush—
but not for long: straight through his side and ribs
(cage of the heart) Aeneas drove raw steel.
Turnus, on foot, killed Amycus and Diores,
510 his brother—both men unhorsed—the one with thrust
of spear, the other with sword; he lopped their heads
and hung them to dribble his chariot with their blood.
Aeneas killed three at once—Cethegus the brave,
Talos, and Tanais; then Onites the sad
515 (his father, Echion; his mother, Peridia);
Turnus, two Lycian brothers (Apollo's men),
and young Menoetes, hater in vain of war
(Arcadian, he: by Lerna's fish-filled streams
he labored, a poor man, but he owed the great
520 no service; his father sowed on rented land).
Like fires started at widely scattered spots

in bone-dry woods and stands of crackling bay,
or like swift flash-floods pouring from the hills,
foaming and roaring and rushing toward the plain,
525   each leaving its track of ruin: so sped the two,
Aeneas and Turnus, from fight to fight; now, now,
their fury welled up; now courage that would not yield
burst free: with every ounce of strength, they killed.

Murranus was boasting his ancient family line
530   ("Father, grandfather, blood royal, Latins all!") ;
Aeneas whirled a boulder huge as a hill
and knocked him flat beneath his chariot's pole:
the wheels rolled over him; galloping horses' hooves
trampled him, for his team forgot their master.
535   Now Hyllus charged like a hothead, wildly yelling;
Turnus ran up and cast at his gilded brow:
the spear pierced metal and stopped, fast in the brain.
Nor could your right hand, Cretheus, bravest of Greeks,
save you from Turnus, nor home-gods guard Cupencus
540   from Aeneas: he turned to face the steel; poor man,
his bronze shield blunted the blow but did not save him.
The Laurentine plains saw you too, Aeolus,
fall on the field, to lie there huge in death:
you died, whom hordes of Argives, whom Achilles,
545   destroyer of Priam's throne, could never kill.
Your death-goal here, your home stood tall on Ida,
tall in Lyrnesus, your tomb on Latin soil.
The whole host turned to battle: all the Latins
and all the Trojans, Mnestheus, Serestus the fierce,
550   Messapus, tamer of horses, and brave Asilas,
Evander's Arcadians and the Tuscan lancers—
each took a stand and fought with all his might:
no stopping, no resting: battle, far and wide.

Now to Aeneas his lovely mother sent
555   the thought of marching straight to the city walls,
confounding the Latins by surprise attack.

Searching for Turnus all through the battle lines
and casting glances about, he'd marked the city
untouched by all the fighting, unharmed, at ease.
560 At once a bolder stratagem stirred his mind:
he called Sergestus, Mnestheus, brave Serestus—
his generals—climbed a mound, where all his troops
came crowding round (no time to lay down spears
and shields), and, stationed high above them, spoke:
565 "Hear this! Obey at once! Jove stands with us!
This change is sudden, but let no man hang back!
That city, Latinus' throne, the cause of war,
must do us homage and wear our yoke today;
else, burn it; level its towers with the ground!
570 Am I to wait till Turnus condescends,
though beaten once, to fight another day?
Here, friends, the head, the source, of fiendish war.
Bring fire! Let flame redress our broken truce!"
He spoke, and all in rivalry of courage
575 pressed toward the walls in one vast, wedge-shaped mass.
As if by magic, ladders and brands appeared.
Some turned off toward the gates and killed the sentries;
some whirled the spear and darkened the sky with weapons.
Far to the front, Aeneas raised a hand
580 up toward the walls, and loudly blamed Latinus:
"God witness: I renewed the strife perforce;
the Latins turned hostile twice, twice broke a truce!"
Among the frightened townsmen, quarrels arose.
Some shouted, "Open the city! Unbar the gates
585 to the Trojans! Force our king to mount the walls!"
Others, "To arms! Fight on! Defend our homes!"
As when a shepherd has traced a hive of bees
to a hole in a rock and filled it with bitter smoke;
inside their waxen castle, frightened, confused
590 they dash about and buzz to whet their fury.
The pitchy stench rolls through their house; the rock
hums dark and hollow, smoke rises through the air.

A further blow now struck the weary Latins
and shook the city to its base with grief.
595 The queen looked out and saw the Trojans coming,
the walls attacked, flames flying toward the roofs,
yet never a line of defense—no troops, no Turnus.
The poor soul thought her prince had lost his life
in battle; a sudden pang deranged her mind.
600 She called herself disaster's source and cause,
and babbled on in madness, grief, and pain.
Determined to die, she ripped her purple robe
and hung from the ceiling a noose of ugly death.
The women of Latium heard the tragic news;
605 Lavinia started to tear her flower-like hair
and petaled cheeks; after her, all the rest
went wild: the halls re-echoed to their screams;
the sad news spread from there through all the city.
People lost heart; Latinus tore his robes,
610 crushed by his consort's death and the city's fall;
with dust and filth he fouled his white old head.
He blamed himself for failing to make Aeneas
a prince ere this, his son-in-law and heir.

Meanwhile, at field's far edge, a fighting Turnus
615 pursued the stragglers, but his pace had slowed
and at every overtaking he felt less joy.
And now a breeze brought shouts and cries to him
frightened with unknown fears; he listened and heard
the sound of a city in turmoil, terror, and grief.
620 "What's that? What blow could cause such consternation?
What noise comes from the city so fast, so far?"
He spoke, drew rein, and stopped; fear gripped his heart.
And now his sister (as his charioteer,
Metiscus, she still governed car and team)
625 turned and addressed him: "Turnus, hold this course
against the Trojans; victory here lies clear.
Others stand ready to defend our homes.
Aeneas is fighting Italians, driving hard:

let us loose savage death on Trojans, too.
630 You'll win no fewer fights, gain no less honor."
Turnus replied:
"Sister—I knew, the moment you schemed to break
the truce, and came to join me in this war;
now, too, disguise is useless. Who in heaven
635 sent you, a goddess, down to bear such toils?
Or was it to watch your luckless brother die?
See me! What turn of fate could save me now?
With my own eyes I saw Murranus, heard him
calling me—and no dearer friend is left me.
640 He fell; one vast wound cut his vast frame down.
Ufens is dead: he could not bear the sight
of my disgrace. The Trojans own his corpse.
And now—the final blow!—to stand and see
our homes destroyed, and not prove Drances wrong?
645 Shall I turn tail—this land see Turnus run?
Is it so bad to die? Ghosts of the dead,
be kind to me, since heaven has turned away.
I come to you a soul untainted, clear
of the wrong done here; I shall not shame my fathers."

650 Just then on a lathered horse Saces rode up
(he'd burst through enemy lines, his face all blood
from an arrow). He fell to the ground at Turnus' feet:
"Turnus, have mercy! You are our only hope!
Aeneas, whose sword is lightning, will throw down
655 and crumble our fort—the crown of Italy.
Already the brands are flying. Every eye
in Latium looks toward you: Latinus maunders
of 'sons-in-law' and 'pacts' and 'where to turn?'
The queen, your loyal partisan, is dead
660 by her own hand; fear drove her from the light.
Alone at the gates Messapus and Atinas
hold firm our lines: to right and left their lancers
stand man by man; an acre of naked blades
bristles, while you ride empty fields of grass!"

665   Bewilderment of images struck the mind
       of Turnus; he stood and stared; vast waves of shame,
       madness, and sorrow surged up in his heart,
       and love guilt-ridden, and courage that knew no doubt.
       When darkness of mind dispersed and light returned,
670   deeply troubled, he wrenched a fevered eye
       away from his chariot, back toward the city walls.

       There he saw fire—a timbered structure wrapped
       in billowing, swirling, heaven-bent flames—his tower,
       the tower he'd built himself, each nail and beam,
675   with wheels at the base and gangways at the top.
       "Death, sister, has won—yes, Death. Don't stop me now.
       I follow where God and heartless Fortune call.
       I'll battle Aeneas, I'll bear the bitter pangs,
       I'll die. You'll never see me shamed again.
680   Madness? Let me be mad this one last time!"
       So speaking he leaped at once down to the ground,
       and dashing past hostile weapons left his sister
       in tears, and charged full-tilt through battle lines.
       As when from a mountain peak a boulder rolls
685   headlong, torn out by tempest or washed away
       by rain, or loosened by age and lapse of years.
       Over it goes, a mount gone driving mad;
       it leaps from the ground, sends trees and beasts and men
       spinning: so scattered the battle lines, as Turnus
690   dashed for the city walls, where earth was drenched
       with blood, and whistling weapons filled the air.
       He raised a hand in signal and shouted loud:
       "Halt, Rutulans! Hold there, Latins! Ground your arms!
       The hazards are mine; I only may atone
695   for all, for breach of truce. My sword decides!"
       They all fell back and left an empty space.

       But Lord Aeneas had heard the name of Turnus.
       He turned from walls, from battlements turned away,
       brushed caution aside, broke off all other tasks,

700 and shouted and leaped and terribly drummed his shield:
huge as Athos or Eryx, huge as the mount
of rustling, glittering oaks, that lifts his snows
in joy toward heaven—our lord, the Apennine.
And now Italians, Rutulans, Trojans—all
705 turned eager eyes toward them; the men who held
the walls, the men who struck them with the ram—
all laid down arms. Latinus himself was awed
that these great champions, born a world apart,
had now met face to face to fight a duel.
710 They two, when the field lay smooth and clear to see,
ran forward and, from a distance, hurled their spears,
then charged to the fight with shield and clanging bronze.
Earth groaned as they matched blow for blow—a hail
of sword thrusts, a melee of luck and skill.
715 In Sila forest or high on Mount Taburnus
sometimes two bulls in furious contest charge,
head down: their trainers, terrified, leap back,
the steers stand awed and mute, the heifers mumble—
("Who'll be king of the grove; who'll lead the herd?").
720 They two charge murderously one at the other,
lock horns and heave, while floods of blood drench necks
and shoulders, and the woods roar back their roars.
Just so Aeneas of Troy and Italy's prince
met shield to shield; the great crash filled the air.
725 Jove raised his scales, and leveling the pans
placed in the two the lots of those two men:
which would be sentenced? which weight dip toward death?

Now Turnus, thinking it safe, rose to full height,
and swinging his flashing blade high overhead,
730 struck. Both Trojans and Latins yelled in terror,
and tensed, watching. But see! The traitor sword
broke, and failed the attacker in mid-blow—
but flight would save him. Fast as the wind he ran
when he saw that unknown hilt and unarmed hand.
735 Men say that, hastening to begin the battle

he'd leaped to his team, forgetting his father's sword;
confused, he'd seized his man Metiscus' weapon.
So long as the Trojans turned their backs and scattered,
this served, but meeting Vulcan's arms—a god's—
740   this mere man's blade shattered like brittle ice;
its broken fragments spangled the dark brown sand.
In a panic, Turnus ran, seeking escape;
circling wildly, he weaved to left and right.
All round, the tight-packed Trojans hemmed him in;
745   here a morass, and there high walls, confined him.

Aeneas, too, pursued him, though his knees,
slowed by the arrow, sometimes refused the race;
he kept close on the frightened hero's heels.
As when a hound has cornered a stag hemmed in
750   by a river, or trapped by fear of scarlet flags:
he runs at the frightened animal, barks and snarls.
The stag, wary of traps and riverbanks
runs off, runs back, a thousand ways; the hound
sticks to him, jaws agape—he has him; almost
755   he has him! His jaws snap shut—on empty air.
Then comes a torrent of barking; bank and pool
re-echo, and heaven's vault rings with the noise.
So Turnus ran, and running called his men,
each one by name, demanding the sword he knew.
760   Aeneas warned them—Instant death to any
who dared approach!—and held them terrified
with threats to level their city despite his wound.
Five times they circled left and five times right,
running, attacking; this was no foolish game
765   for prizes: Turnus' lifeblood was at stake.

So happened, a bitter olive here had stood
sacred to Faunus, for sailors a place of prayer
(saved from the sea, they'd nailed thank offerings there
for Laurentine Pan, and hung their promised clothes).

770　The Trojans, with never a thought if it were holy,
　　　had taken it out to clear the field for fighting.
　　　Here, when Aeneas had thrown his spear, it stopped,
　　　and here stood fast, prisoned by tough tree roots.
　　　He leaned against it and tried to wrestle the point
775　free: a weapon might serve to catch the man
　　　where running had failed. Turnus, in panic, prayed:
　　　"Faunus, have mercy! Beloved Earth, hold fast
　　　that spear, if I have ever done you honor
　　　and Trojans have fought over and defiled you."
780　The prayer was not in vain: God heard his cry.
　　　Aeneas hung back, battling the stubborn stump,
　　　but all his effort could not break the clench
　　　of oak-hard wood. And while he leaned and heaved,
　　　Juturna, guised once more as charioteer,
785　ran out to her brother and handed him his sword.
　　　Venus, in outrage at such shamelessness,
　　　strode in and from the root's grip wrenched the spear.
　　　Both men, with arms regained, took heart again;
　　　one sure of his sword, one boldened by his lance,
790　they squared off for the battle, breathing hard.

　　　To Juno (from a golden cloud she watched
　　　the fight) now spoke the lord of high Olympus:
　　　"When will it end, dear wife? What's left to do?
　　　You know Aeneas is godhead; you confess
795　him heaven-bound and destined for the stars.
　　　What aim, what hope, in cold mist still enfolds you?
　　　You thought it right that man should wound a god?
　　　That Turnus (Juturna's hand was yours!) recover
　　　the sword he lost and, conquered, gain new strength?
800　Cease now: it's time! I beg you, bear with me!
　　　No more unspoken anguish! No more floods
　　　of bitter care course toward me from your lips!
　　　The end has come. You had fair leave to trouble
　　　the Trojans by land and sea, to rouse foul war,

805   to blacken a house, turn wedding song to dirge—
       all further, I forbid." So Jove proclaimed;
       then Saturn's daughter humbly smiled and spoke:

       "My lord, it was because I knew your will
       that, spite of myself, I left the world and Turnus.
810   Else you would never see me alone in heaven
       bear foul and fair; I'd stand flame-wrapped in line
       of battle, and wave the Trojans on to fight.
       I urged Juturna (yes, I!) to help her brother,
       and dare still bolder things to save his life,
815   but never to throw the spear or draw the bow:
       I swear by the wells of Styx, that hear no prayers—
       the single oath that binds the heavenly gods.
       Now I yield and withdraw; I hate this war.
       One favor I beg (no law of fate forbids it!)
820   for Latium, for the honor of your people:
       when they make peace and bless the marriage bonds
       (so be it!) and join in justice and in law,
       the Latins must not change their ancient name
       to 'Trojans,' or turn citizens of Troy;
825   bid no man change his language or his dress.
       Always a Latium! Forever, her Alban kings!
       Italian hearts make mighty the sons of Rome!
       Troy died: let 'Troy' and 'Trojan' rest in peace."

       The great creator smiled and answered her:
830   "You *are* Jove's sister, Saturn's second child,
       such floods of fury surge within your heart!
       But come! Your wrath is needless: softly, now!
       I grant your wish and gladly yield to you.
       Italians shall keep their fathers' ways and speech,
835   yes, and their name; except in blood commingled,
       Trojans shall sink from sight. I'll teach our Latins
       new rite of worship; one tongue shall serve for all.
       From Italy's mingled blood one folk shall rise,
       surpassing god and man in righteousness,

840 no nation more devout in prayer to you."
Juno assented; in joy, she changed design
and left her cloud, departing from the sky.

This done, the father turned to other thought:
how sever Juturna from her brother's service?
845 Men tell of twin death-dealers, called the Dirae—
daughters of Night—they and their hellish sister,
Megaera, born in a storm, all three at once,
winged like the wind and girdled with coiling snakes.
Near to the throne of Jove, the king of wrath,
850 they show themselves, and whet men's fevered fears,
whenever the monarch marshals ghastly death
by plague or war, and makes the guilty tremble.
One of these two Jove sent swift down from heaven
to be an omen athwart Juturna's path.
855 She flew off, spiraling swiftly toward the earth.
Like an arrow sent from a bowstring through the clouds
(the Parthian arms it with wild, bitter poison—
or Cretan, perhaps—and shoots the cureless shaft):
it whistles through the murk, and none observes it:
860 so sped the daughter of Night down toward the earth.
She sighted the Trojan lines, the ranks of Turnus,
then changed at once into the tiny bird
that sometimes perches by night atop the tombs
or lonely towers and sings her bad-luck song—
865 so formed, the fiend flew at the face of Turnus—
flew in, flew back—and drummed against his shield.
A strange torpor and fright unstrung his limbs;
his hair stood up in fright; his voice stuck fast.

From far, Juturna knew those whistling wings—
870 the Dira! She let her hair fall loose and tore it,
scratched foul weals on her face, and beat her breast:
"How, Turnus, can your sister help you now?
What's left of my resolve? What arts of mine
could save your life? Can I block off this fiend?

875   I'll leave the battlefield. Fright not the frightened,
       you birds of hell! I know those wing beats well:
       they sound like death! I know who sent you, too:
       great, generous Jove—pay for my maidenhood?
       Why did he give me endless life, and steal
880   my right to die? I'd end my sorrows now,
       and walk at my brother's side down through the dark.
       Immortal—*I*? What joy can life afford me
       without you, brother? Somewhere, let Earth gape wide
       and deep: let a goddess join the ghosts in hell!"
885   She covered her head then with her grey-green gown
       and, sobbing, sank her godhead in the stream.

       And now Aeneas pressed in; he flashed his spear
       (huge as a tree) and spoke with savage heart:
       "Why this delay? Why, Turnus, do you hang back?
890   We're running no race; we'll fight now, hand to hand.
       Change form as you will! Marshal all your powers
       of courage and skill; pray for wings to ascend
       the stars, or hide in the dungeons of the earth!"
       Turnus, proudly: "I fear no fiery words,
895   soldier! I fear the gods and Jove estranged."
       Saying no more, he searched and found a stone,
       a huge old boulder, lying on the field,
       placed there to settle the boundary of two farms.
       That stone twelve chosen men could scarcely lift,
900   sinewed as are the sons of Earth today;
       he strained, and raised, and whirled it at his foe,
       rising full height and running to make his cast.
       But running, moving, he did not know himself—
       raising his arms and throwing that monstrous stone:
905   his knees trembled; his blood ran freezing cold.
       The very boulder, spinning through empty space,
       failed of the distance and did not strike its blow.
       Just as in dreams, when weariness and sleep
       press night on our eyes, we seem to try to run
910   eagerly, vainly, and in mid-trial we fail

and fall—our tongue is useless, every muscle
forgets its force; no word, no sound, will come;
so Turnus: no matter how bravely he attacked,
the Dira denied success. His heart was filled
915 with wavering thoughts: he saw his men, his city—
he halted in fear—he shook at death's approach—
no way to escape—no power to press attack—
his chariot gone—no sister holding the reins.

He wavered; Aeneas flashed the fatal spear,
920 sighting, gauging his chance, then with full force
made the long throw. Rocks hurled from siege machine
whine never so loud, nor from the lightning leaps
such crackling. Like the black tornado sped
the lance freighted with death; finding the gap
925 'twixt corselet and the shield's last sevenfold orb,
it shrieked its way through Turnus' thigh. He fell,
that huge man, crumpling as his knees gave way.
The Rutuli rose with a groan; the hills around
moaned in answer; tall trees sent back their cry.
930 Turnus spoke, with the suppliant's outstretched hand
and humble glance: "I earned it. I have no plea.
Take what you've won. If a poor father's pain
can touch you, hear me: You had a sire, Anchises—
as old as mine: have mercy on white-haired Daunus.
935 Return me—or if you will, my lifeless corpse—
to my home. You've won; all Italy saw me beaten
and on my knees; Lavinia is your wife.
Press your ill will no further." Aeneas checked
a savage blow; his eye wavered, he halted;
940 his hesitation had grown with every word.
Just then at shoulder-peak he saw the baldric,
proclaimed by clasp and shining studs the belt
of Pallas, the lad whom Turnus fought and killed:
he wore it—spoils of the fallen, an ill-starred prize.
945 Aeneas, seeing the trophy, felt fierce pangs
revive; a flame of fury and dreadful rage

flared up; "Shall you escape, dressed in the spoils
of those I loved? No! Pallas wounds you here;
he spills your blood as price and expiation!"

950   So saying, with savage thrust he sank the blade
in Turnus' heart: his limbs fell cold in death;
his life, with a curse and a moan, fled down to hell.

GLOSSARY OF PROPER NAMES

GLOSSARY OF PROPER NAMES

The Glossary includes names of persons and places important to the understanding of the *Aeneid*. Omitted are: (1) names that are only names (e.g., Aletes, "a Trojan"); (2) names presumably known to anyone likely to read the poem (e.g., Italy, Greece, Athens, Rome, the Mediterranean) ; (3) names sufficiently identified for the purposes of the poem by the poem itself (e.g., Sinon, in Book II; Mezentius, in Books VII and X) .

ABAS. The name is used in the *Aeneid* three times: (1) one of the captains of Aeneas' company, whose ship was lost in the storm in Bk. 1; (2) a Greek warrior, killed at Troy, whose armor Aeneas erects as a trophy in Bk. III; (3) a Tuscan general who joins forces with Aeneas in Bk. X.

ACESTES. A Trojan who settled in Sicily; in the *Aeneid,* ruler of the western part of that island.

ACHATES. A Trojan, Aeneas' "faithful friend."

ACHERON. A river in the Underworld.

ACHILLES. A great Greek warrior, the central figure of Homer's *Iliad,* and the slayer of Hector.

ACRISIUS. A king of Argos. *See* DANAË.

ACTIUM. A promontory at the extreme northwestern corner of Greece. In 31 B.C. the emperor Augustus defeated the forces of Antony and Cleopatra there in a decisive sea battle.

ADRASTUS. A king of Argos.

AEAEA. The island of Circe, the witch goddess of Homer's *Odyssey.* By tradition the island was just off the coast of Latium near what was later the promontory of Circeii.

AENEADAE. A settlement founded by Aeneas on the coast of Thrace.

AENEAS. Son of the goddess Venus and of Anchises, a prince of Troy. After the destruction of Troy, Aeneas assumed leadership of the survivors, and as such he is the central figure of the *Aeneid.*

AEOLIA. An island north of Sicily, legendary home of the winds, and ruled by Aeolus.

AEOLUS. (1) A god, legendary ruler of the winds; (2) in Bk. XII, a Trojan, member of Aeneas' company.

AETNA. A volcano in Sicily.

AGAMEMNON. King of Mycenae, commander in chief of the Greek armies at Troy; brother of Menelaus.

AGRIPPA. M. Vipsanius Agrippa, soldier and engineer, friend and adviser of Augustus.

AJAX. The "lesser" Ajax, son of Oileus. (The "great" Ajax, son of Telamon, committed suicide before the destruction of Troy.) His crime was the rape of the princess and prophetess, Cassandra, for which Minerva punished him.

AKRAGAS. A city on the southwestern coast of Sicily, called Agrigentum in Latin.

ALBA LONGA. The city founded in Italy by Ascanius.

ALCIDES. Another name for Hercules (q.v.).

ALL-HALLOW'S VALE. Latin *Amsancti valles*, the Italian-Roman entrance to the Underworld.

ALPHEUS. One of the largest rivers in southwestern Greece.

AMASENUS. A small stream in Latium.

AMATA. Queen of Latium, wife of King Latinus, mother of the princess Lavinia.

AMAZONS. Legendary female warriors, whose home was in Cappadocia in Asia Minor. In Bk. VI they are said to come from Thrace.

AMPHITRYON. Husband of Alcmena, the mother of Hercules. Although Hercules was, strictly speaking, the son of Jupiter, he is often called the son of Amphitryon.

ANCHISES. Prince of Troy, father of Aeneas by the goddess Venus.

ANCUS. Ancus Martius, the fourth king of Rome.

ANDROGEOS. (1) In Bk. II, a Greek who fought at Troy; (2) in Bk. VI, the son of King Minos of Crete. The Athenians murdered Androgeos after his victory in the Panathenaic games. As expiation the Athenians were required each year to send seven boys and seven girls to Crete as a sacrifice to the Minotaur.

ANDROMACHE. Wife of Hector. In Bk. III, she has remarried, and is the wife of Helenus (q.v.), another Trojan.

ANNA. Sister of Dido.

ANTANDER. A coastal town not far from Troy.

ANTENOR. A Trojan leader who reached Italy before Aeneas and there, according to legend, became the founder of Patavium (modern Padua).

ANTONY. M. Antonius (Mark Antony), an associate and

later the only serious rival of Augustus, who defeated him at Actium (*q.v.*).

ANUBIS. An Egyptian deity, regularly represented as a dog. He often stands as the symbol of an outlandish religion, such as the Egyptian was popularly supposed to be.

APOLLO. God of archery, of healing, and—particularly in the *Aeneid*—of prophecy. Under the name Phoebus, he is also god of the sun.

ARAXES. A river in Armenia, bridged by Augustus.

ARCADIA. Arcady, a mountainous section of the Peloponnesus, in southern Greece.

ARCHER GOD. An epithet of the god Apollo.

ARCTURUS. The brightest star in the constellation Boötes, which is near the Great Bear. Its rising and setting were thought to be accompanied by bad weather.

ARETHUSA. A stream (and its attendant goddess) of southern Greece. According to legend, it flowed under the sea to Sicily, where it reappeared as a spring of fresh water near Syracuse.

ARGILETUM. *See* ARGUS (2).

ARGIVE. "From Argos": a generic name for the Greeks who fought at Troy.

ARGOS. A city in the north of the Peloponnesus, often spoken of as the home of Agamemnon.

ARGUS. (1) In Bk. VII, the many-eyed guardian set by Juno over Io. He was killed by Mercury at Jupiter's orders. (2) In Bk. VIII, the legendary stranger who was murdered near the holy wood of Argiletum and from whose name "Argiletum" ("murder of Argus") is supposedly derived. Actually, Argiletum means "clay pit," from *argilis,* "white clay."

ARISBA. A town near Troy.

ARPI. A city in Apulia, in southeastern Italy. According to legend, it was founded by the great Greek warrior, Diomede (*q.v.*).

ASCANIUS. The son of Aeneas and his Trojan wife Creusa.

ASSARACUS. Son of Tros, father of Capys, grandfather of Anchises.

ASTYANAX. Son of Hector and Andromache, thrown to his death from the walls of Troy by the Greeks.

ATHENA. *See* MINERVA.

ATHOS. A mountain at the tip of of the promontory of Acte, in the Thracian Gulf, northeast of Greece.

ATLAS. A mountain in the northwestern corner of Africa, by legend the pillar of the universe. It is often represented as a white-haired and bearded giant, carrying the heavens on his shoulders.

ATRIDES. "Son of Atreus"; i.e.,

Agamemnon or Menelaus, or, as a plural, the two of them.

AUGUSTUS. C. Octavius, grandnephew of Julius Caesar, adopted by him, and thereafter known as C. Julius Caesar Octavianus (Octavian). He is generally regarded as the founder of the Roman imperial throne and the first emperor of the Roman Empire. He was given the title "Augustus" by the Senate in 27 B.C. and reigned until his death in A.D. 14.

AURORA. *See* TITHONUS.

AURUNCANS. One of the early peoples of Italy. They lived in the region around the Bay of Naples.

AUSONIA. One of a number of names used by Vergil for Italy. Strictly speaking, it means the land inhabited by the Ausones, an ancient people who lived in southern Italy.

AVERNUS. A lake near Cumae, just north of the Bay of Naples. According to tradition, the name means "the birdless" (Greek *aornos*); it is supposed to have been so called because the vapors it exhaled killed the birds that tried to fly across it. It was one of the legendary entrances to the Underworld.

BACCHUS. Another name for Dionysus, the Greek god of the vine and of wine. The most prominent aspect of his worship was the wildly orgiastic festival celebrated yearly in the mountains by women and girls called Bacchantes or Thyiades.

BACTRIA. A region around the Oxus River, roughly midway between the Caspian Sea and the northwestern corner of India.

BAIAE. A resort on the Bay of Naples, just across from Puteoli (modern Pozzuoli). It was the favorite sea resort of the Romans and was noted for its gaiety and freedom from restraint.

BARCA. A city in Libya, center of a wild nomadic tribe much feared by Dido.

BEBRYX. Also called Amycus, a king of Phrygia, famous chiefly for having been defeated in a boxing match by the god Pollux.

BELLONA. The Roman goddess of war.

BENACUS. A lake in northern Italy, northwest of modern Verona; now called Lago di Garda.

BRIAREUS. A giant with a hundred hands, also known as Aegaeon. In Bk. X, he is represented as one of a company that attempted to dethrone Jupiter but was defeated.

BRUTUS. L. Junius Brutus, the traditional liberator of Rome. He is supposed to have driven out the last of the kings of Rome, Tarquin the Proud, near the end of the 6th century B.C.

BUTHROTUM. A city on the coast of Epirus, northwest of Greece proper. According to legend, Helenus, prince of Troy, settled here with his wife Andromache, Hector's widow.

CAENEUS. (1) In Bk. VI, the "boy name" of the nymph Caenis. As Vergil tells the story, Neptune changed her into a boy, and then back into a girl. (2) In Bk. IX, the name of a Trojan warrior killed by Turnus.

CAERE. A city in Etruria. In the *Aeneid* it is a center of religious worship.

CAESAR. In the *Aeneid*, Augustus (*q.v.*), not Julius Caesar.

CAIETA. Aeneas' old nurse. The spot where she died, a promontory in southern Latium, was given her name.

CALCHAS. The prophet-priest who accompanied the Greeks to Troy.

CALYDON. The home of Diomede, just off the northwestern end of the Gulf of Corinth.

CAMERINA. A city on the southeastern coast of Sicily. An oracle forbade the moving of the town to any other site.

CAMILLA. A Volscian princess, half elfin child, half warrior, now light and ethereal, now bloodthirsty and cruel.

CAPITOL ROCK. The Capitoline Hill in Rome.

CARINAE. A section of Rome, in historical times occupied by the homes of the great.

CARTHAGE. A city in North Africa, strategically located just across from the western tip of Sicily. In historical times it was a great naval and military power, Rome's rival for the domination of the Mediterranean world. Carthage was defeated only after three bloody and costly wars that began in 264 B.C. and ended in 146 with the destruction of the city by Scipio the Younger. Carthage was a Phoenician colony, settled by people from Tyre. The legendary account of her founding is given in *Aeneid* I. 335–368.

CASSANDRA. Princess of Troy, daughter of Priam. A virgin, she promised to give her love to Apollo in return for receiving the gift of prophesy from him; but once he had granted it, she refused to fulfill her part of the agreement. Apollo could not take back his gift, but he rendered it useless by ruling that no one would ever believe her.

CASTLE HILL. The *arx,* the fort or citadel located on a hill in the center of the city of Troy.

CATILINE. A Roman aristocrat who in 63 B.C. attempted to seize power in Rome by a *coup d'état.* Cicero, then consul, put down the plot and executed the conspirators; his achievement is celebrated—and perhaps somewhat overexalted—in his four orations *Against Catiline.* Sallust, in his *Catiline,* gives a soberer but perhaps no more trustworthy account of the event.

CATO. Cato the Younger, a contemporary of Cicero and Caesar; his reputation for rigid righteousness was blown up into a romantic legend after his death. He was the grandson of Cato the Elder, a no less stern but far more sensible statesman of the early part of the 2nd century B.C.

CAULON. A colony founded by Greeks on the "instep" of the Italian peninsula.

CELAENO. The chief of the Harpies (*q.v.*) .

CERAUNIA. Also called Acroceraunia, a promontory just across from the "heel" of Italy. Between these two points navigation was difficult, and the reefs of Acroceraunia were particularly hazardous to ships sailing from Italy to Greece.

CHAONIA. The northern part of Epirus, lying along the Adriatic Sea.

CHARON. The ferryman of the Underworld, who transports the shades of the dead across the river Styx.

CHARYBDIS. A dangerous whirlpool on the Sicilian side of the narrow strait separating the northeastern corner of Sicily from the southwestern "toe" of the Italian peninsula (Straits of Messana) . In legend, the whirlpool is represented as a huge female monster that sucked ships down her gullet.

CHIMAERA. A mythical creature mentioned by Homer (*Iliad* VI 179–182): "her foreparts, a lion's, her tail, a serpent's, her middle, a she-goat's, and she breathed out a deadly powerful flaming fire." In *Aeneid* VI, she is one of the guardians at the entrance to the Underworld. In Bk. V, one of the ships bears her name.

CIRCE. A witch goddess (*Odyssey* X) who trapped men by her spells and turned them into animals. Ulysses, by means of a magic herb, was able to withstand her powers. By tradition, she occupied the island of Aeaea (*q.v.*) .

CITHAERON. A mountain in Boeotia, near the city of Thebes. It was sacred to Bacchus.

CLEOPATRA. *See* GYPSY QUEEN.

CLOELIA. Livy (II.13.6–7) tells her story: She was a Roman maiden who was taken prisoner and held as a hostage by Lars Porsenna, king of the Etruscans, but she managed to break her bonds and swim back across the Tiber to Rome.

CNOSSUS. The capital city of Minos, king of Crete, and site of the famous labyrinth.

COCLES. Horatius Cocles ("the one-eyed"). Livy tells his story (II.10): He singlehandedly held the bridge across the Tiber against the Etruscans until his companions could destroy it; then, in full armor, he jumped into the river and swam to safety.

COCYTUS. A river in the Underworld.

CORYTHUS. Strictly speaking, an Etruscan city (modern Cortona); so it appears in Bks. VII and X. In Bk. III, however, Vergil seems to use it as a synonym for Italy.

CREUSA. First wife of Aeneas, daughter of Priam, mother of Ascanius.

CUMAE. A Greek settlement on the western coast of Italy, just north of the Bay of Naples. It was by tradition the site of one of the entrances to the Underworld and the home of the Sibyl (*q.v.*).

CUPAVO. *See* CYCNUS.

CUPID. The Latin name for Eros, the god of love. Son of Venus, he appears in the *Aeneid* as a mischievous small boy.

CURES. A small town in the Sabine district, chiefly famous as the home of Numa Pompilius, second king of Rome, and of Titus Tatius, king of the Sabines, during whose reign the famed "Rape of the Sabine Women" occurred.

CYBELE. The "great mother of the gods." Native to Asia Minor, she was brought to Rome in 205–204 B.C., during the second Punic War. Her rites, orgiastic in character, were celebrated by eunuch priests. She is usually depicted as wearing the "mural crown," a headdress shaped like the walls of a city.

CYCLOPES. A race of one-eyed giants whose home was near Mt. Aetna in Sicily. *See also* POLYPHEMUS.

CYCNUS. In the *Aeneid,* King of Liguria and father of the Ligurian warrior Cupavo (Bk. X). According to myth, Cycnus fell in love with the youth Phaethon, and at his death was transformed into a swan.

CYLLENE. A mountain in Arcadia, traditionally the birthplace of the god Mercury.

CYMODOCE. A sea nymph, one of the daughters of Nereus. In *Aeneid* X, she appears as the leader of the band of sea nymphs.

CYMOTHOE. A sea nymph, one of the daughters of Nereus.

CYNTHUS. A mountain on the island of Delos, traditionally the birthplace of Apollo and Diana.

CYTHERA. An island off the southernmost tip of the Peloponnesus, famed as one of the chief centers for the worship of Venus.

DAEDALUS. An engineer and architect who designed and built the labyrinth at Cnossus (*q.v.*) but was best known for the wings he constructed for himself and his son Icarus. Despite his father's warnings, Icarus flew too close to the sun; the heat melted the wax that held his wings together, and he fell into the sea and was drowned.

DANAË. Daughter of Acrisius, king of Argos. She was locked in a tower to preserve her chastity, but Jupiter turned himself into a shower of gold, which fell through a hole in the roof, and violated her. Acrisius set Danaë and her baby son Perseus adrift in a chest on the sea. Vergil has her reaching land in Italy and there founding the chief city of the Rutuli.

DARDANUS. Son of Jupiter and the Arcadian Electra, he founded the city of Dardania in the Troad and was the ancestor of the Trojan royal line. The Trojans are often called Dardans or Dardanians after him.

DAUNUS. Legendary king of Apulia, father of Turnus.

DECIUS. Decius Mus, seeing that his army was being defeated, offered his own life as a sacrifice for victory and rode unarmed at the head of his troops onto the spears of the enemy (Livy VIII. 10 and X, 28).

DEIPHOBUS. One of the sons of Priam. After the death of Paris, he married Helen, who betrayed him to the Greeks when Troy was captured.

DELIAN SEER. Apollo. *See* DELOS.

DELOS. An island in the Aegean Sea, traditionally the birthplace of Apollo and Diana.

DEMOLEOS. A Greek killed by Aeneas at Troy.

DIANA. The Latin name for Artemis, goddess of wild nature, hunting, and the moon. *See also* HECATE.

DICTE. A mountain in Crete. In a cave on this mountain the infant Jupiter was hidden from his father, Saturn, who sought to destroy him.

DIDO. Queen of Carthage, leader of a band of Phoenicians from Tyre. *See* CARTHAGE.

DINDYMUS. A mountain in Asia Minor, seat of the worship of the goddess Cybele (*q.v.*).

DIOMEDE (DIOMEDES). Son of Tydeus, and one of the greatest of the Greek warriors at Troy. He figures prominently in the *Iliad* V, where he fights with Ares (Mars) and wounds Aphrodite (Venus). After the destruction of Troy he was forbidden to return to his home in Aetolia, and settled in Apulia (southern Italy) where he founded the city of Arpi (Argyripa).

DIRAE. The Latin name for the Erinyes, the Furies (*q.v.*).

DODONA. A town in Epirus, famous for its oracular oak tree, sacred to Jupiter.

DOG STAR. *See* SIRIUS.

DONUSA. A very small island in the Aegean Sea, just east of Naxos.

DORIAN. The name of one of the early Hellenic peoples, commonly used as a synonym for "Greek."

DREPANUM. A city at the western tip of Sicily.

DRUSUS. M. Livius Drusus Salinator defeated Hannibal's brother, Hasdrubal, at the Metaurus River in Umbria in 207 B.C.

DULICHIUM. An island off the western coast of Greece, southeast of Ithaca, the home of Ulysses.

ECHION. The legendary founder of Thebes.

ELIS. The northwestern section of the Peloponnesus; also the name of its capital city.

ELYSIUM. The section of the Underworld set apart for the souls of the good and great.

ENCELADUS. One of the giants who tried to dethrone Jupiter and who were punished by being buried under Mt. Aetna.

EPIRUS. A region lying along the shore of the Adriatic Sea, northwest of Greece. It forms part of modern Albania and Yugoslavia.

ERIDANUS. Either the River Po or—more likely—the mystic "river of the West" that supposedly flowed through the Garden of the Gods. Vergil has transferred it to Elysium.

ERIPHYLE. Wife of Amphiaraus, king of Argos. Her son, Alcmaeon killed her because she allowed herself to be bribed into persuading Amphiaraus to join the expedition of the "Seven against Thebes," although through his prophetic powers Amphiaraus knew that if he did so he would be killed.

ERYMANTHUS. A mountain range in Arcadia. As one of his labors, Hercules had to capture and kill a huge boar that lived there.

ERYX. (1) A legendary king of Sicily, son of Venus, and famous as a boxer; (2) a mountain, a city, and a nearby district, at the western tip of Sicily.

ETRUSCANS (TUSCANS). A people who settled in Italy north of Latium, in the section now known as Tuscany. According to Herodotus, they came originally from Asia Minor, but their provenance is still in doubt, as is the origin of much of their culture and the nature of their language. Romans commonly thought of them as coarse and cruel—with what justification, no one knows.

EUROTAS. A river in the southern part of the Peloponnesus. On its banks stood the city of Sparta.

EURYALUS. The younger of the two friends (the older named Nisus) who figure prominently in Bks. V and IX of the *Aeneid.*

EURYSTHEUS. King of Tiryns (or Mycenae). According to legend, it was he who at the command of Juno imposed the familiar "Twelve Labors" on Hercules.

EVADNE. Wife of Capaneus, one of the "Seven against Thebes." Capaneus was killed, and Evadne in sorrow threw herself on his funeral pyre.

EVANDER. An Arcadian Greek who with a band of fellow exiles settled on the banks of the Tiber on the future site of the city of Rome. He called his settlement Pallanteum.

FABII. A famous Roman family, prominent as statesmen and soldiers throughout the Republic. Most distinguished of them all was Q. Fabius Maximus, called "the Delayer" (*Cunctator*), who, after the Roman armies had been roundly defeated by Hannibal, saved Rome by using guerilla tactics against the Carthaginians.

FABRICIUS. A Roman hero in the war against Pyrrhus of Epirus (282–279 B.C.). He is constantly cited as a model of honor, dignity and incorruptibility.

FAITH (goddess). *Fides,* Roman personification of the moral qualities of honor, faithfulness, and trustworthiness.

FAUNUS. Legendary son of Picus, grandson of Saturn, and father of Latinus, king of Latium. A patron of agriculture and animal husbandry, after his death he became the god of wood and field. He was eventually identified with the Greek god Pan.

FURIES. Known to the Greeks as the Erinyes and to the Romans as the Dirae, the Furies were goddesses or "spirits" whose function was the punishment of bloodshed, especially within families. They commonly drove men mad.

GAETULIANS. A people of northwestern Africa, living in the section now called Morocco. They were savage nomads.

GANYMEDE. A Trojan prince, son of Tros (or, according to other sources, of Laomedon). His beauty caused Jupiter to fall in love with him and take him to Olympus to be his cupbearer, an act that aroused the bitter enmity of Juno.

GAULS. A Celtic people inhabiting northern Italy, France, and much of Switzerland and Belgium. In the 4th century they attacked and captured Rome; but the Romans, with the help of the Greeks settled at Massilia (Marseilles), drove them back and regained their supremacy.

GELA. A river and a city on the southeastern coast of Sicily.

GERYON. A king in Spain, rich in cattle. According to legend, he was a three-bodied giant. Hercules, as one of his labors, killed him and drove off his oxen.

GETIC. Pertaining to the Getae, a Thracian tribe living on the lower Danube.

GIANTS. Mythical creatures, the "sons of Earth," who attacked the gods and attempted to de-

throne them, but were defeated.

GLAUCUS. (1) In Bk. V, a sea god, leader of a band of nymphs; (2) in VI. 36, the father of Deiphobe, priestess of Apollo and Diana at Cumae; (3) in VI. 483, commander of the Lycians, allies of the Trojans; he figures prominently in the *Iliad* VI.

GORGONHEAD. The Gorgon was a female creature with snakes for hair; her glance turned men to stone. She was killed and beheaded by the hero Perseus, and her head was fastened to Athena's shield.

GREAT MOTHER. *See* CYBELE.

GYPSY QUEEN. Cleopatra, last of the Ptolemies, queen of Egypt, a brilliant and reputedly beautiful woman, whose story is too familiar to need repeating. She is called a "gypsy" here because of the supposed derivation of "gypsy" from "Egyptian," and because of the derogatory nature of the reference.

HARPALYCE. A princess of Thrace, famed as a huntress and charioteer.

HARPIES. Mythical creatures with the bodies of birds and human (female) heads. In the *Aeneid,* they are half birds of prey, half carrion-eaters. Their leader, Celaeno, had prophetic powers.

HEBRUS. (1) In Bk. I, a fast-flowing river in Thrace; (2) in Bk. X, a Trojan warrior killed by Mezentius.

HECATE. The "witch goddess," associated with magic-making. Because of the association of the moon with magic, she is often identified with the moon goddess Diana.

HECTOR. Prince of Troy, eldest son of Priam, chief Trojan warrior, and opponent of Achilles in Homer's *Iliad*. His defeat and death marked the end of effective resistance to the Greek armies.

HECUBA. Queen of Troy, wife of Priam.

HELEN. Wife of Menelaus, king of Sparta, and, according to legend, the most beautiful woman in all Western history. Venus awarded Helen to Paris as compensation for his naming her most beautiful of the three goddesses, Juno, Venus, and Diana. Paris stole Helen from Menelaus; this incident was the immediate cause of the Trojan War. *See also* LEDA.

HELENUS. Prince of Troy, son of Priam. After the death of Hector, he married Hector's wife, Andromache. In Bk. III of the *Aeneid,* they have settled in Epirus.

HELICON. A mountain in Boeotia, north and west of Attica, the legendary home of the Muses.

HELORUS. A river and its swampy mouth, on the eastern coast of Sicily.

HELYMUS. A Sicilian, one of the people of Acestes (*q.v.*) .

HERCULES (ALCIDES). Son of Jupiter by a mortal woman, Alcmena, wife of Amphitryon, king of Thebes. Juno, jealous of Alcmena, tried to kill the baby Hercules by sending serpents to devour him, but Hercules strangled the serpents, thus beginning his earthly career as the strong man of antiquity. A huge muscular man, sometimes a bit dull, but universally good-humored and kind, he is perhaps best portrayed by Euripides in his *Alcestis.* His famous "labors," imposed on him by Eurystheus at Juno's command, involved mostly the killing of monsters and the performing of supposedly impossible tasks, such as cleaning the Augean stables and stealing the girdle of Hippolyta, queen of the Amazons. In the *Aeneid,* only one of his exploits is of primary importance: In Bk. VIII, as he is returning from Spain after killing Geryon and stealing his cattle, he kills the monster

Cacus and thus earns the eternal gratitude of the Arcadians who live on the future site of Rome. His destruction of Troy —because King Laomedon (*q.v.*) had cheated him of a promised reward—is mentioned in passing in Bk. VIII.

HESPERIA. One of the names used by Vergil for Italy. It means "Westland."

HESPERIDES. The "daughters of the West," maidens who lived on an island beyond Mt. Atlas and guarded the tree of the golden apples.

HIPPOLYTUS. Son of Theseus, king of Athens, he was falsely accused by Theseus' second wife, Phaedra, of attempting to seduce her. When his horses were stampeded by a bull sent by Neptune, he was thrown from his chariot and killed. The story is told with vast human insight by Euripides in his tragedy *Hippolytus*.

HOMOLE. A mountain in Thessaly, the home of the Centaurs.

HYADES. *See* RAIN-STARS.

HYDRA. (1) In Bk. VI, a fifty-headed monster in the Underworld; (2) in Bk. VII, a snake with seven heads, killed by Hercules as one of his labors.

IARBAS. A North African king. He asked Dido to marry him but was scornfully rejected.

IASIUS. Son of Jupiter and Electra, brother of Dardanus (*q.v.*).

ICARUS. *See* DAEDALUS.

IDA. (1) The mountain near Troy from which Ganymede (*q.v.*) was taken up to heaven; (2) the mountain in Crete where Jupiter was cared for by the Curetes, a band of dancing priests. *See also* DICTE.

IDAEUS. A Trojan warrior, charioteer of Priam.

IDALIA (IDALIUM). A city built on a mountain in Cyprus, one of the favorite haunts of Venus.

IDOMENEUS. A Cretan warrior, leader of the Cretan contingent against Troy. Like a number of others (e.g., Diomede, *q.v.*) he is represented in the *Aeneid* as having settled in Italy after the sack of Troy.

ILIA. A Vestal Virgin. Violated by Mars, she became the mother of Romulus and Remus. She was also called Rhea Silvia.

ILIONEUS. One of Aeneas' trusted lieutenants.

ILIUM. A name frequently used for Troy (*q.v.*).

INACHUS. A king of Argos.

INFERNAL KING. A translation of *infernus rex;* Pluto is meant.

IO. Daughter of Inachus (*q.v.*). Jupiter fell in love with her and changed her into a heifer in order to conceal his activities. However, Juno discovered the ruse, and set Argus, the hundred-eyed god, to watch her.

IRIS. Goddess of the rainbow; along with Mercury, one of the message-bearers of the gods.

ISLE OF OLIVES. A translation of *Olearum* (Olearos), an island near Naxos in the Aegean Sea.

ISMARA. A mountain, and the city near it, on the southern coast of Thrace.

ITALUS. A legendary king of Italy, from whom the peninsula supposedly takes its name.

ITHACA. An island off the western coast of Greece, the home of Ulysses.

IULUS. Ascanius. *See also* JULIUS.

IXION. Son of Phlegyas, father of Pirithous, king of the Lapiths in Thessaly, a violent and barbarous man. Among other colorful crimes, he seduced Juno and became the father of the Centaurs. For this he was thrown into the Underworld and fastened to an eternally revolving wheel.

JANUS. The god of doorways and of the beginnings of things, e.g., of the year. He is represented with two faces.

JOVE. Another name for Jupiter (*q.v.*) .

JULIUS. The name of the family, supposedly decended from Aeneas through Iulus (Ascanius) , to which Julius Caesar belonged and into which he adopted his grandnephew Octavian, later called Augustus.

JUNO. The Latin name for Hera, queen of the gods. Juno is both wife and sister to Jupiter (*q.v.*) . In the *Aeneid* she functions as the divine opposition to Aeneas and his mission.

JUPITER. The Latin name for Zeus, king of the gods. In the *Aeneid* he functions as administrator, judge, director, and final arbiter of disputes, whether between mortals or immortals.

JUTURNA. A water nymph, sister of Turnus.

LACINIA. A name for Juno, derived from Lacinium, a promontory in southern Italy where a temple of Juno was located.

LADY OF IDA. Cybele (*q.v.*) .

LAERTES. The father of Ulysses.

LAODAMIA. Wife of Protesilaus, the first of the Greeks to be killed at Troy. Rather than live without him, she committed suicide.

LAOMEDON. King of Troy, father of Priam. After promising to reward the god Neptune if he would help him build the walls of Troy, Laomedon cheated him, whereupon Neptune sent a monster to terrorize Troy. Laomedon then hired Hercules to dispose of the monster, and similarly cheated him of his promised reward.

LAPITHS. A barbarous and violent people of Thessaly, best known for their battle with the Centaurs at the wedding of Pirithous, king of the Lapiths.

LAR, LARES. Together with the Penates, the Lares are the gods of hearth and home, of which they are the divine symbol.

LATINUS. Son of Faunus (*q.v.*), grandson of Picus, king of Latium, father of Lavinia.

LATIUM. The section of west-central Italy where the Latins lived. Rome lies just within its northern border.

LATONA. Another name for Leto (*q.v.*).

LATONIA. "Daughter of Latona," i.e., Diana.

LAURENTUM. The capital city of Latium.

LAVINIA. Princess of Latium, daughter of King Latinus and Queen Amata. She was first betrothed to Turnus, but the engagement was broken when an oracle declared that she must not marry a native Italian. Subsequently, she became the wife of Aeneas.

LAVINIUM. A city in Latium, near the seacoast. It was founded by Aeneas and named in honor of his wife, Lavinia.

LEDA. Wife of Tyndarus. Made pregnant by Jupiter, who took the form of a swan, she bore two eggs. From one of these sprang Helen and Pollux, from the other, Castor and Clytemnestra. Helen is sometimes called Tyndaris ("daughter of Tyndarus") after her supposed father.

LERNA. A swamp near the city of Argos. It was the home of the seven-headed serpent, the Hydra, whom Hercules killed as one of his labors.

LETHE. A river in the Underworld. Those who drank its waters lost their memory of all past events in their lives.

LETO. The mother of Apollo and Diana.

LEUCATA. A promontory on the island of Leucas, just off the northwestern corner of Greece.

LIBURNIA. A section lying along the northeastern shore of the Adriatic. It was famous for its ships, which were small but fast and easily maneuvered.

LIBYA. A section of the North African coast lying west of the Nile.

LILYBAEUM. A promontory at the extreme western tip of Sicily.

LOCRIANS. A people of northern Greece, who founded the city of Naryx (Narycium) on the underside of the "toe" of the Italian peninsula.

LUCIFER. The Morning Star.

LUPERCI. Priests of a Latin fertility cult, perhaps that of Faunus. When they celebrated their rites they wore nothing but wolf skins.

LYCIA. A section at the south-western corner of the peninsula of Asia Minor. It was grain-raising country, and its men were famous as archers. There was an oracle of Apollo there.

MAIA. The mother of the god Mercury.

MALEA. A promontory at the extreme southeastern tip of the Peloponnesus.

MANLIUS. A Roman hero of the early days of the Republic. It was he who in 390 B.C. was warned by the honking of the sacred geese of the invasion of the Gauls, and thus saved the citadel of Rome from capture.

MANTUA. A city in the Po Valley, near the birthplace of Vergil. The "three bloodlines" of the city's origin are given by Servius, an ancient commentator, as Thebans, Tuscans, and Gauls; each bloodline was further divided into "four peoples."

MARCELLUS. (1) In VI. 855–859, a hero of the second Punic War; he also defeated the Gauls in 222 B.C.; (2) in VI. 860–886, a nephew of the emperor Augustus, intended as his heir and successor. He died at the age of twenty in 23 B.C.

MARS. The Latin name for Ares, god of war.

MEDON. A Trojan, mentioned in the *Iliad* XVII as an associate of Hector.

MEGARA. A city at the southeastern corner of Sicily, not far from Syracuse.

MELIBOEA. A town in Thessaly. Apparently it was associated with the trade in purple dye.

MEMNON. An Ethiopian warrior who fought as an ally of the Trojans and was killed by Achilles. He was the son of the goddess Aurora and is represented as having a dark complexion (hence, "Memnon the Moor").

MENELAUS. Brother of Agamemnon (*q.v.*) and king of Sparta. Helen was his wife, and it was from his palace that she was abducted by Paris.

MERCURY. The Latin name for Hermes. In the *Aeneid* he functions almost exclusively as the messenger of the gods.

METTUS. Mettus (or Mettius) Fufetius, king of the Albans, was judged guilty of breaking his oath and treaty of loyalty to the Romans; for this he was torn apart by two chariots at the order of Tullus Hostilius, king of the Romans. Livy tells the story (I. 28).

MINCIUS. A river in the Po Valley of northern Italy. It runs past Mantua and near the birthplace of Vergil.

MINERVA. The Latin name for Pallas Athena, goddess of war,

wisdom, learning, and the household arts. In the *Aeneid,* her warlike aspect is of primary importance.

MINOS. A legendary king of Crete. In ancient thought he is most prominently associated with the labyrinth (*see* CNOSSUS) and with the Underworld, where he sits in judgment over the souls of the dead.

MISENUS. The "bugler" of the Trojan armies. In Italy he foolishly challenged the sea god Triton to a bugling match, only to be lured into the surf and drowned. The place where he died was called Cape Misenum; it is located at the northern end of the Bay of Naples.

MUSAEUS. A legendary poet of Greece. In the Underworld (Bk. VI), he appears as a chief of poets and musicians.

MYCENAE. A city in Argolis, the northeastern part of the Peloponnesus, directly south of Corinth; by tradition the home of Agamemnon.

MYCENEAN GENERAL. Agamemnon (*q.v.*).

MYRIMDONS. Homer's name for the soldiers of Achilles. They were from Thessaly, in northern Greece.

NARYX. A city in the extreme south of Italy. *See* LOCRIANS.

NAXOS. An island in the Aegean, center of a group commonly called the Cyclades. It was famous for its wines, and was an important center for the worship of Bacchus.

NEOPTOLEMUS. The son of Achilles; he is sometimes called Pyrrhus.

NEPTUNE. The god of the sea. In the story of Troy, he figures as an opponent of the Trojans, since their king, Laomedon, had refused to pay him the reward that had been promised him for his assistance in building the walls of Troy.

NEREIDS. Sea nymphs, daughters of Nereus.

NEREUS. One of the lesser sea gods, father of the Nereids.

NERITOS. An island near Ithaca (*q.v.*).

NISUS. The older of the two friends (the younger named Euryalus) who figure prominently in Bks. V and IX of the *Aeneid.*

NUMA. (1) Numa Pompilius, the second king of Rome, by tradition the founder of the state cult of the Romans; (2) the name of two different Latin warriors in Bks. IX and X.

NUMIDIANS. A nomadic people of North Africa. Vergil calls them *infreni,* which means either that they rode horses without bridles, or that they themselves were an "unbridled" lot. Perhaps a pun is intended.

NUMITOR. (1) An Alban king, father of Rhea Silvia, who was the mother of Romulus and Remus; (2) the Italian soldier of the same name, who, in the *Aeneid* X. 342ff., attacks Aeneas, is apparently no relation to the king.

NYSA. The name of a mountain in India, where by tradition the god Bacchus was born. It is from a city of the same name that he is supposed to have set out, driving a team of tigers, to conquer the world.

OECHALIA. A city on the island of Euboea (east of the Greek mainland). It was destroyed by Hercules because its king, Eurytus, first promised Hercules his daughter Iole and then reneged on the offer.

OENOTRI. A legendary people of early Italy, which is sometimes called Oenotria after them.

OLYMPUS. A mountain in Thessaly, in northeastern Greece, by tradition the home of the gods.

ORCUS. A name used (1) for Pluto, the god of the Underworld, and (2) for the Underworld itself.

ORESTES. The son of Agamemnon and Clytemnestra. Upon his return from Troy, Orestes killed his mother in vengeance for her murder of his father. In punishment for his act, he was driven mad by the Furies.

In the *Aeneid* III he appears as the murderer of Neoptolemus, son of Achilles.

ORION. The Huntsman, a constellation associated with the equinox, and thus with storms.

ORPHEUS. By legend, the first poet and musician. When his beloved Eurydice was killed by a snakebite, Orpheus with his singing persuaded Pluto to release her. However, Pluto imposed one condition: Orpheus must not look back to see if Eurydice was following him up from the Underworld. Overcome with anxiety, he did look behind him, whereupon Eurydice was snatched back into the Underworld.

ORTYGIA. The name is used twice in Bk. III: (1) in line 124, for the island of Delos (*q.v.*); and (2) in line 694 for an island off the Sicilian city of Syracuse.

OTHRYS. The name of a mountain in Thessaly.

PACHYNUS. A promontory at the extreme southeastern corner of Sicily.

PACTOLUS. The legendary river of gold. It flowed past Sardis, the capital of Lydia, in Asia Minor.

PALAMEDES. One of the Greeks who fought at Troy. He was put to death on a charge of treason trumped up by Ulysses.

PALICUS. A local Sicilian deity associated with a sulphurous spring or pond. Legend makes him the son of Jupiter by a nymph.

PALINURUS. The name of Aeneas' helmsman and pilot who fell asleep and was swept overboard on the passage from Sicily to Italy (V. 833ff.). According to legend, a promontory on the southwestern shore of Italy (the "arch" of the "boot") was named for him.

PALLANTEUM. The name of the city founded in Latium by Evander (*q.v.*).

PALLAS. A name used for three quite different individuals: (1) Minerva (Pallas Athena); (2) the father of King Evander (*q.v.*); (3) Evander's son, commissioned by his father to join the forces of Aeneas.

PALLAS THE LESS. A translation of *Palladium,* a Latinized form of the Greek diminutive for Pallas, one of the names of Athena. Presumably a small image, it stood in the citadel of Troy, and the safety of the city depended on its presence, unharmed, in the city. It was stolen by Ulysses and Diomede, who committed triple sacrilege by killing the guards in the temple, taking the statue from its place, and touching the statue with bloodstained hands.

PANDARUS. In the *Iliad,* and in the *Aeneid* V. 496, the Trojan soldier who violated the truce between the Trojans and the Greeks by shooting an arrow at Menelaus. Another Trojan of the same name figures prominently in the fighting in the *Aeneid* IX.

PANTAGIA. A river in eastern Sicily, near Syracuse.

PARCAE. A name for the Fates, the three old spinning women whose thread governed the lives of men.

PARIS. Son of Priam and abductor of Helen (*q.v.*).

PAROS. An island in the Aegean, just west of Naxos (*q.v.*).

PARTHENOPAEUS. A king of Argos, one of the "Seven against Thebes."

PARTHIANS. A powerful nation located about where modern Iran lies. The Parthians were one of Rome's deadliest and most dangerous enemies. They were expert archers who fought from horseback; their characteristic tactic was to charge full-tilt at the enemy, then suddenly wheel about as if in retreat; as the enemy broke ranks to follow them, they turned in their saddles and shot back across the rumps of their horses. In 53 B.C., they defeated the Romans at Carrhae in Mesopotamia, and even captured their standards. These were later recovered, by means of adroit diplomacy, by the emperor Augustus.

PASIPHAË. Wife of Minos, king of Crete; she fell in love with a beautiful bull, and by him became the mother of the Minotaur.

PELASGIANS. A name commonly given to the pre-Hellenic inhabitants of Greece.

PELORUS. A promontory at the extreme northeastern corner of Sicily. It marks the end of the passage between Scylla and Charybdis.

PENTHESILEA. Queen of the Amazons (q.v.).

PERGAMA. Another name for Troy; strictly speaking, it means the fort or citadel in the center of the city.

PETELIA. A fortified city in Lucania in southern Italy which Diomede (q.v.) founded after the fall of Troy.

PHAEACIA. The island of Corcyra (modern Corfu) off the coast of Epirus. In Homer's Odyssey, it is the home of King Alcinous.

PHAEDRA. The wife of King Theseus of Athens. She fell in love with her stepson, Hippolytus (q.v.).

PHAETHON. The son of Helios, the sun god. Phaethon was permitted by Helios to drive the chariot of the sun, but he was unable to control the team and veered too close to the earth. Jupiter, seeing the earth in danger of fire, hurled a thunderbolt at Phaethon, knocking him from the chariot. His sisters, overcome by grief at his death, were changed into poplar trees; their tears were, by legend, the source of amber.

PHILOCTETES. A Greek warrior who carried the bow and arrows of Hercules, without which Troy could not be taken and with which he killed Paris.

PHINEUS. A king of Thrace who blinded his sons and, in punishment, was himself blinded by Jupiter, who also sent the Harpies to trouble and befoul his table. The Harpies were finally driven off by Zetes and Calais, sons of the wind god Boreas.

PHLEGETHON. The river of fire in the Underworld.

PHLEGYAS. A king of the Lapiths (q.v.) in Thessaly. He showed his scorn for divine law by burning down Apollo's temple at Delphi; for this he was chained to a rock in the Underworld and there—according to Vergil—endlessly and hopelessly repeats a kind of pagan Summary of the Law.

PHOEBUS. Another name for Apollo, especially in his aspect as god of the sun.

PHORBAS. Name of a Trojan, whose likeness is taken by the

god of sleep in order to deceive the helmsman Palinurus.

PHORCUS. A minor sea god.

PHRYGIA. A district of Asia Minor, to the east of the Troad. The Trojans are sometimes called Phrygians, partly through identification of the one country with the other, partly as a derogatory epithet, implying weakness and effeminacy.

PHTHIA. An alternate name for Thessaly, in northern Greece, the birthplace of Achilles.

PICUS. The son of Saturn, father of Faunus (q.v.), grandfather of Latinus. According to legend, Circe changed him into a woodpecker.

PILLARS OF PROTEUS. A name for Egypt, where Proteus was at one time king.

PILUMNUS. The grandfather (or perhaps great-grandfather; the exact degree of relationship is unclear) of Turnus; related, through Saturn, to Jupiter.

PIRITHOUS. Son of Ixion (q.v.). He and Theseus, king of Athens, attempted to steal Proserpina, wife of Pluto, from her palace in the Underworld. For this offense, he was condemned to remain forever in chains.

PLEMYRIUM. A promontory on the southeastern coast of Sicily. It forms the southern end of the harbor of Syracuse.

PLUTO. God of the Underworld, brother of Jupiter. He is also called Orcus, Hades, and Dis.

POLLUX. Son of Jupiter by Leda (q.v.). He had a mortal half-brother, Castor, son of Tyndarus, whom he loved so dearly that after Castor's death he obtained Jupiter's leave to share immortality with him: Each of the brothers spends six months in the heavens and six in the Underworld.

POLYBOETES. A Trojan warrior, priest of Ceres.

POLYPHEMUS. One of the Cyclopes (q.v.). In Homer's Odyssey, he was attacked and blinded by Ulysses.

PORSENNA. King of Etruria, he tried to force the Romans to take back Tarquin, whom they had dethroned and banished.

PORTUNUS. A minor sea god. His name suggests that he was specifically a harbor god.

PRAENESTE. A city in the hills of eastern Latium, about 25 miles from Rome; the modern Palestrina.

PRIAM. King of Troy throughout the Trojan War. He was the son of Laomedon (q.v.) and sired 50 sons, among them Hector and Paris, and 50 daughters, among them Cassandra and Polyxena. He was killed by Neoptolemus.

PRIEST OF THRACE. Orpheus, who was a priest of Apollo, and

hence wears the long gown of the priest and musician.

PROCRIS. Thinking that her husband Cephalus was being unfaithful to her, she followed him into the forest where, mistaking her for an animal, he shot and killed her.

PROSERPINA. Queen of the Underworld, wife of Pluto (*q.v.*). She was the daughter of Ceres, the goddess of grain.

PROTEUS. A sea god, famous for his ability to change himself into many different forms. He also had prophetic powers.

PUNIC. A synonym for Carthaginian.

"PURSE." A translation of *Byrsa*, a name derived from the Greek word βύρσα, "bull's hide." As a name for Carthage, it is supposed to be a Greek corruption of the Punic *bosra,* the name of the citadel of Carthage.

PYRRHUS. Another name for Neoptolemus (*q.v.*).

QUEEN OF HEAVEN. Juno (*q.v.*).

QUEEN OF HELL. Proserpina (*q.v.*).

RAIN-STARS. The Hyades, a cluster of seven stars in the constellation of Taurus.

REMUS. (1) Twin brother of Romulus; they were the sons of Ilia (or Rhea Silvia) and the god Mars. As infants they were thrown into the Tiber by King Amulius, who saw in them potential rivals to his power, but they miraculously floated ashore and were suckled by a she-wolf. At maturity, they founded the city of Rome; to determine who should have priority, they took auspices, but these were inconclusive. Romulus began building a wall; Remus in mockery jumped over it, whereupon he was killed by Romulus, who went on to build his city, name it for himself, and become its first king. The story is told by Livy (I. 3. 10). (2) The name of an Italian warrior killed by Nisus in Bk. IX.

RHADAMANTHUS. A king of Crete; with Minos, he is a judge of souls in the Underworld.

RHOETEUM. A promontory near Troy; the name is sometimes used as a synonym for Troy itself.

ROMULUS. *See* REMUS.

RUTULI (RUTULANS). A people of Latium, near neighbors of the Latins. Turnus was prince of the Rutuli.

SABAEANS. An Arabian people; their capital, Saba, was located in the southwestern corner of the Arabian peninsula. They were associated with the caravan trade in silks and spices from the Orient.

SABINUS. Legendary king of the Sabines, a people dwelling in a hilly section of Italy to the north of Latium.

SALAMIS. Two sites bear this name: (1) The island just off Piraeus where, in 480 B.C., a famous battle between the Greeks and the Persians took place; (2) a city in Cyprus, where Teucer, one of the Greeks who fought at Troy, settled after the destruction of Troy.

SALENTINE. The Salentines occupied a stretch of the eastern shore of the Bay of Tarentum, on the inner side of the "heel" of the peninsula of Italy.

SALII. Dancing priests of Mars who carried shields and danced the *tripudium*, a three-beat dance, in his honor.

SAME. An island near Ithaca (*q.v.*).

SAMOS. An island off the coast of Asia Minor, near the city of Ephesus. It was the birthplace of the goddess Juno, and an important seat of her cult.

SARPEDON. King of Lycia and a son of Jupiter, he was one of the allies of the Trojans. After his death at the hand of Patroclus (*Iliad* XVI), his body was carried by Death and Sleep to his native land of Lycia and buried there.

SATURN. The Latin equivalent for the Greek Kronos, father of Jupiter. In the *Aeneid,* Saturn appears primarily as a god of peace and agriculture, a status no doubt derived from his legendary position as ruling deity of the mythical Golden Age.

SCAEAN. A gate that faced the sea on the western side of the city of Troy. It was from this gate that the Trojans rode out to fight the Greeks.

SCIPIO. Several famous Romans of the third and second centuries B.C. bore this name, along with the family name of Cornelius. They played important parts in the Punic Wars. The most distinguished of the group was the one commonly called Scipio the Elder (236–184 B.C.). He inflicted final defeat on Hannibal in the battle of Zama in 202 B.C. His adoptive grandson, called Scipio the Younger, finally destroyed the city of Carthage in 146 B.C.

SCYLAX. More accurately, Scylaceum, a promontory in Bruttium, southern Italy, on the "instep" of the Italian peninsula.

SCYLLA. A dangerous reef on the Italian side of the strait between Italy and Sicily (*see* CHARYBDIS). Legend describes it as a monster who lived in a cave, from which she stretched out her head to seize and devour ships.

SCYROS. An island in the Aegean, to the northeast of Euboea. It was the birthplace of Neoptolemus, whose men are therefore called Scyrians.

SEA OF THE CIRCLING ISLES. The Aegean Sea, where the Cyclades ("Circle Islands") are located.

SEA OF PEARLS. Called the "Red Sea" by the Romans and now known as the Arabian Gulf. In antiquity, it was famous as a source of pearls.

SELINUS. A city near the western tip of Sicily.

SERRANUS. M. Atilius Calatinus Serranus, more commonly known as Regulus. He was defeated and a large part of his army captured by the Carthaginians in 255 B.C. According to legend, he was sent back to Rome to arrange ransom for the captured Roman soldiers, but instead he convinced the Senate to reject the offer. Then he returned to Carthage to face his death. Horace tells the story in *Odes* III. 5.

SHEPHERD OF TROYLAND. Paris (*q.v.*).

SIBYL. The name given to a number of prophetic priestesses in various parts of the ancient world. The one mentioned in the *Aeneid* was the Sibyl of Cumae (*q.v.*).

SICANI. Early inhabitants of Italy and Sicily.

SIDON. A Phoenician city, the mother city of Tyre. Dido is sometimes called "Sidonian." Ancient Phoenicia extended from the borders of Palestine northward along the eastern shore of the Mediterranean; modern Lebanon occupies a portion of the same section.

SILVANUS. An ancient Italic farmer god. Horace calls him "guardian of boundaries" (Epode II. 22).

SIMOIS. A river that flows across the plain of Troy; it figures prominently in the action of the *Iliad*.

SIRENS. According to legend, a group of young women who by their beautiful singing enticed sailors to sail too close to their reefs. In order to hear their song safely, Ulysses put wax in his sailors' ears and had himself bound to the mast of his ship (see Homer, *Odyssey* XII).

SIRIUS. The Dog Star, whose rising in the late summer ushers in the hottest and most disease-ridden part of the year in the Mediterranean area.

SONS OF AENEAS. Latin *Aeneades,* a name for the Trojans who followed Aeneas after the fall of the city.

SPARTA. A city in the southeastern corner of the Peloponnesus. It was Menelaus' capital city.

STRYMON. A river in Thrace, in northern Greece. It is almost invariably mentioned in connection with cranes, who seem to have lived in large numbers along its banks.

STYX. The principal river in the Underworld.

SYCHAEUS. The husband of Dido. He was murdered by his brother Pygmalion.

SYMAETHUS. A river on the east-central coast of Sicily and a town nearby.

SYRTES. A large bay on the North African coast, extending from Tripolitania to Cyrenaica, with Carthage at its western end and Cyrenaica at its eastern. The bay is shallow, has many dangerous sand bars, and is subject to sudden and violent storms.

TARCHON. Commander of the Etruscans who joined Aeneas in the war against Turnus.

TARENTUM. A city on the southern coast of Italy, on a bay that forms the "instep" of the Italian peninsula; it is now called Taranto.

TARPEIA. A companion of Camilla (q.v.). She is not to be confused with the Tarpeia for whom the Tarpeian Rock (q.v.) was named.

TARPEIAN ROCK. Named after Tarpeia, who fell in love with Titus Tatius, king of the Sabines, and betrayed Rome to him. (See Livy, I. 11.) In historical times, convicted traitors were thrown to their death from this cliff. Sometimes the name is used for the whole of the citadel that stood on the Capitoline Hill.

TARQUIN. Two Etruscans, both of whom were kings of Rome, bore this name. The better known of the two was Tarquinius Superbus, "Tarquin the Proud," whose tyrannous rule led to his expulsion from Rome.

TATIUS. Titus Tatius, king of the Sabines. Originally an enemy of the Romans (see TARPEIAN ROCK), he later accepted an alliance with them.

TENEDOS. An island just off the coast of the Troad, southwest of Troy.

TEUCER. Two individuals bear this name: (1) the legendary founder of the Trojan nation. The Trojans are often called "Teucrians" or "Teucri" after him; (2) the archer, a son of Telamon, half brother and constant companion of Ajax in the *Iliad*. After the fall of Troy he migrated to Cyprus, where he founded the city of Salamis (q.v.) .

THAPSUS. An island or peninsula on the eastern coast of Sicily, not far from Syracuse.

THERSILOCHUS. A Trojan warrior.

THESEUS. Son of Aegeus, king of Athens. He entered the labyrinth of Minos in Crete, killed the Minotaur, and escaped by following the thread he had unwound as he went in. He abducted Ariadne, daughter of Minos; he also joined Pirithous (*q.v.*) in an attempt to abduct Proserpina.

THESSALY. A section of Greece north of Attica, south of Macedonia.

THETIS. A sea goddess, mother of Achilles. In the *Iliad* (XVIII. 428ff.), she asks Hephaestus (Vulcan) to make armor for her son.

THRACE. The northeastern section of Greece, running on past the Dardanelles and as far north as the Danube.

THYIAD. Another name for a Bacchante, a female devotee of the god Bacchus (*q.v.*).

TIBUR. A town in the foothills of the Apennines, some 15 miles east of Rome. In ancient times it was a favorite mountain resort of the Romans. It is now called Tivoli.

TIMAVUS. A small river in Istria, emptying into the northeastern Adriatic Sea.

TIRYNS. A city in the Peloponnesus, near Argos; the traditional birthplace of Hercules.

TISIPHONE. One of the Furies (*q.v.*); in the Underworld she punishes the souls of the damned.

TITHONUS. A young man with whom Aurora, goddess of the dawn, fell in love. She asked that he be granted the gift of immortality, but she forgot to ask for eternal youth; hence, he is represented as a tired, withered old man. Aurora is also represented (*Aeneid* I. 489, VIII. 384) as having asked Vulcan to provide armor for her son, Memnon.

TITYUS. A giant, the son of Jupiter. He attempted to rape Leto and for this was slain by her son, Apollo. As punishment, Tityus is chained on a field in the Underworld, and vultures forever tear at his liver.

TORQUATUS. L. Manlius Torquatus. In the Latin War of 340 B.C., he ordered his own son executed because he attacked the enemy without waiting for orders (Livy, VIII. 7).

"TORTOISE." The *testudo*, a military formation in which troops formed a solid square, the men in the inner ranks holding their shields above their heads, those on the sides holding theirs at their sides, those in the front holding theirs before them, those in the rear holding theirs behind. This tanklike formation was used primarily for getting up close to the walls of a city.

TRIONES. More commonly called Septentriones, a group of seven stars near the North Pole, commonly called the Wain (Boötes), the Little Bear (Ursa Minor), or the Little Dipper.

TRITON. A sea god, best known for blowing a horn made of a sea shell. Why the goddess Minerva is sometimes called Tritonia is not known.

TRITONIA. A name for Minerva. *See* TRITON.

TRIVIA. Another name for Hecate (*q.v.*). The name means "Lady of Crossroads."

TROILUS. A young—perhaps the youngest—son of Priam. He attempted to fight Achilles but was killed by him.

TROY. This famous city, the scene of the Trojan War, was located on the n orthwestern coast of Asia Minor, in a district known as the Troad, just at the southern entrance to the Hellespont (Dardanelles). The traditional date for the destruction of Troy is *ca.* 1180 B.C.

TULLUS. Tullus Hostilius, the 3rd king of Rome.

TURNUS. Prince of the Rutuli (Rutulans), he led the opposition to Aeneas and the Trojans.

TUSCANY. A district of Italy lying along the western coast to the north of Latium. It was the home of the Etruscans (*q.v.*).

TYDEUS. Father of Diomede (*q.v.*).

TYPHOEUS. One of the giants, the sons of Earth; they attacked and attempted to dethrone Jupiter, who defeated them and buried them under mountains. Typhoeus was imprisoned under the mountainous island Inarime, now known as Ischia.

TYRE. A city of Phoenicia. *See* SIDON.

UCALEGON. The name of a Trojan, drawn from the *Iliad* (III. 148), where he appears as one of the aged associates of Priam.

ULYSSES. The Latin name for Odysseus, "the man of many wiles," canny fighter, wise strategist and counselor, clever schemer—a prominent figure in the *Iliad,* and the hero of the *Odyssey.* His home was in Ithaca (*q.v.*).

VELIA. A bay, later the site of a city, in Lucania on the southwestern coast of Italy.

VENUS. The Latin name for Aphrodite, goddess of love and creative nature, mother of Aeneas by Anchises, prince of Troy. She was the tutelary deity of the house of the Caesars.

VESTA. Goddess of the hearth, much loved by the Romans. She was served at Rome by the Vestal Virgins, women sworn to eternal chastity.

VIRBIUS. According to *Aeneid* VII, this name was used (1) for the resurrected Hippolytus, and (2) for his son, who fought on the Italian side against Aeneas.

VOLSCIANS. A people living in the southern section of Latium.

VULCAN. The Latin name for Hephaestus, god of fire and metal-working. As his Greek counterpart in the *Iliad* (Bk. XVIII) makes new armor for Achilles, so Vulcan in the *Aeneid* makes a new outfit for Aeneas. Vulcan's home and smithy are located in the caverns of Vulcania, an island just off the northeastern corner of Sicily.

WAR (GODDESS). Bellona (*q.v.*).

WESTLAND. Hesperia (*q.v.*).

WIND MAID. Orithyia, daughter of Erechtheus, king of Athens; she was abducted by Boreas, god of the North Wind, and by him became the mother of Zetes and Calais, the "zephyr gods." Nothing is known of the story of her gift of horses to Pilumnus, to which Vergil seems to refer in *Aeneid* XII.

XANTHUS. A river on the plain of Troy. With its companion stream, Simois (*q.v.*), it figures largely in the story of the *Iliad*.

ZACYNTHUS. An island off the northwestern coast of Greece, near Ithaca.

The Library of Liberal Arts

Below is a representative selection from The Library of Liberal Arts. This partial listing—taken from the more than 200 scholarly editions of the world's finest literature and philosophy—indicates the scope, nature, and concept of this distinguished series.